Burning Faith

SOUTHERN DISSENT

UNIVERSITY PRESS OF FLORIDA

Florida A&M University, Tallahassee
Florida Atlantic University, Boca Raton
Florida Gulf Coast University, Ft. Myers
Florida International University, Miami
Florida State University, Tallahassee
New College of Florida, Sarasota
University of Central Florida, Orlando
University of Florida, Gainesville
University of North Florida, Jacksonville
University of South Florida, Tampa
University of West Florida, Pensacola

Christopher B. Strain

Foreword by Stanley Harrold and Randall M. Miller

University Press of Florida

Gainesville / Tallahassee / Tampa

Boca Raton / Pensacola / Orlando

Miami / Jacksonville / Ft. Myers / Sarasota

Burning Faith

Church Arson in the American South

First cloth printing, 2008
First paperback printing, 2020

25 24 23 22 21 20   6 5 4 3 2 1

Library of Congress Cataloging-in-Publication Data
Strain, Christopher B., 1970–
Burning faith: church arson in the American South/Christopher B. Strain; foreword by
Stanley Harrold and Randall M. Miller.
p. cm.—(Southern dissent)
Includes bibliographical references and index.
ISBN 978-0-8130-3239-9 (cloth)
ISBN 978-0-8130-6830-5 (pbk.)
1. Southern States—Race relations. 2. African American churches—Fires and fire
prevention—Southern States. 3. Hate crimes—Southern States. 4. African Americans—
Crimes against—Southern States. 5. Church buildings—Fires and fire prevention—
Southern States. 6. Arson—Southern States. I. Title.
E185.92.S82 2008
364.16'409759–dc22   2008002547

The University Press of Florida is the scholarly publishing agency for the State University
System of Florida, comprising Florida A&M University, Florida Atlantic University,
Florida Gulf Coast University, Florida International University, Florida State University,
New College of Florida, University of Central Florida, University of Florida, University of
North Florida, University of South Florida, and University of West Florida.

University Press of Florida
2046 NE Waldo Road
Suite 2100
Gainesville, FL 32609
http://upress.ufl.edu

Contents

Illustrations

Foreword

Politically and racially motivated use of fire as an instrument of hate has a long history in America. In 1636, as the Pequot Indian nation stood in the way of Puritan expansion from Massachusetts into the Connecticut River Valley, Puritan soldiers and their Narragansett allies burned the main Pequot town to the ground, killed the men who tried to escape, and sold Pequot women and children into West Indian slavery. In 1838 a white proslavery and anti-black mob burned Philadelphia's recently erected Pennsylvania Hall to keep it from being used as a racially integrated center for antislavery oratory. From the decades prior to the Civil War into the twentieth century, southern vigilantes publicly burned to death black men accused of crimes against white people. During Reconstruction, burning crosses became the symbol of the Ku Klux Klan and other terrorist organizations that brutalized African Americans and the minority of white southerners who challenged white supremacy. During the 1950s and 1960s the fiercest white opponents of the Civil Rights movement firebombed black churches, killing four young black girls in the worst instance.

But as Christopher B. Strain shows in *Burning Faith: Church Arson in the American South*, when during the 1990s black churches burned across (and beyond) the South, Americans had difficulty comprehending the forces at work. Although African Americans continued to lag behind other American groups in wealth and education, continued to face police brutality, and continued to struggle with a legal system that incarcerated growing numbers of young black men, there had been considerable progress in race relations. More African Americans graduated from high school and attended college, more held good jobs, more won elective office, and more gained prominence in the arts, mass media, and entertainment than had been the case a decade earlier. Black influence on American culture (always high) was expanding. Most Americans believed that the hatred that produced racially motivated arson had diminished.

Black progress, however, caused resentment among many white people, particularly those who felt left behind in an increasingly technological and global age. Many white people believed government-sponsored affirmative action programs unjustly favored members of minority groups. The establishment in 1983 of a national holiday honoring Martin Luther King Jr. angered those who resented the Civil Rights movement and its perceived successes. Others reacted negatively to the increasing prominence of African Americans in politics, the entertainment industry, and sports. Nevertheless, by the 1990s black and white southerners lived together in relative harmony, and the rash of black church burnings seemed inconsistent with signs of racial progress and understanding. Strain's identification of more complicated causative factors than resurgent race-based hatred in the church burnings helps solve this puzzle.

In many cases, the burnings were terrorist acts carried out by white racists against black congregations. They were acts of dissent from what their perpetrators regarded as a society that accorded too much to an undeserving race. But in other cases, the arsonists acted against religion rather than against African Americans, or their motives were unclear even to themselves. Behind all these vicious acts, Strain contends, was a breakdown in community, which other investigators have found to be characteristic of an increasingly depersonalized, disjointed, and fragmented American society. Strain also emphasizes the wide disagreement among American social groups and intellectuals concerning the nature, meaning, and significance of the church burnings. Dissent rather than harmony characterized responses to the burnings. Although most of the crimes occurred in the South, Strain shows how they fragmented opinion in all sections of the country. Yet, as he also shows, many black people and white people joined in condemning the arsons and in rebuilding the burned churches. In this manner, the burnings produced an interracial dissent from hate-based crimes and antisocial acts. From the churches' ashes, Strain suggests, might come the promise of a new America. One wonders yet when that day will come. *Burning Faith* is a welcome addition to the Southern Dissent series.

Stanley Harrold and Randall M. Miller
Series Editors

Preface

It is a fact that churches burn, accidentally and otherwise. Most often the cause is an untended candle, an errant space heater, or faulty wiring; like other old buildings, many churches have outdated and outmoded electrical systems, supporting the unprecedented needs of an increasingly electronic age. Sometimes it is a vagrant, homeless and cold, striking a small fire for warmth. Other times it is a pack of boys, unsupervised and bored, who skulk away from the watchful eyes of grown-ups: one of them produces a tattered matchbook, sparks a flame, and creates a blaze that quickly gets out of control. Sometimes there is dark intent—darker than simple vandalism or pyromania. It is possible, for example, to imagine a preacher or lay leader torching his or her own church to collect insurance monies, or an unscrupulous developer firing a building to chase someone away from a highly coveted piece of property. Sometimes the motivations are even more sinister.

Arson is the leading cause of fires in the United States and the number one cause of property damage. Each year, an estimated 267,000 fires are attributed to arson, resulting in $1.4 billion in property loss and over 2,000 injuries and 475 deaths. Churches, which account for well under 1 percent of reported structure fires, are not a major part of America's arson problem; however, arson is the leading cause of fires in churches, accounting for more than one of every four reported church fires and two-fifths of the reported property damage in those fires. Like other remote outbuildings, many houses of worship are particularly susceptible to arson. They are often unlit and un-inhabited, empty at night or during weekdays. They are sometimes isolated, located along lonely country highways or at the end of windy roads. Arsonists are drawn to easy targets, and churches often make easy targets.[1]

It is therefore not surprising that many, many churches burned in the United States during the mid- to late 1990s. What may be surprising is the fog of intrigue and controversy that continues to surround these fires, many of them unexplained and unsolved. Some skeptics have questioned whether or not many of these fires were arsons; in fact, some have questioned whether or not these fires occurred at all. In the course of investigating these fires, I have learned that these fires were quite real, quite widespread, and quite dev-astating for those involved.

Part history, part mystery, and part investigative journalism, this book is intended to rough out a general narrative of attacks on houses of worship in the last decade. It is selective and by no means comprehensive. It concentrates on church burning as hate crime, defined by the Hate Crime Statistics Act of 1990 as crime against a person or property motivated by bias toward race, religion, ethnicity, national origin, disability, or sexual orientation. The first chapter ("fire") describes the spate of church arsons during the mid-1990s, focusing on the summer of 1996, when a large number of predominantly Afri-can-American churches burned, dominating headlines for a number of weeks. The second chapter ("fear") discusses the terror caused by these crimes and the history of such arsons in the American South. The third chapter ("faith") examines the response of denominations and the efforts of local churches to aid their neighbors. The fourth chapter ("doubt") assesses the series of arsons as a racist conspiracy. The fifth chapter ("law") analyzes the government's re-sponse. The sixth chapter ("strength") deals with rebuilding efforts, and the fi-nal chapter ("hope") suggests that these incidents reveal much not only about the ongoing significance of race in American life but also about religion, poli-tics, economics, class, and civil strife in the Clinton era, as Americans moved with trepidation into a new millennium.

This book is not what I imagined it would be. At the height of the arsons, which occurred during a new nadir of American race relations, investigators exposed a number of the fires as malicious acts of hatred, but as I assembled what I thought would become a chronology of hate crimes against black peo-ple, I began to realize that telling this story accurately would require more than simply compiling a list of these crimes. My original theory was that the church burnings of the 1990s were connected to a broader racial ferment, illustrative of conflict in the United States. Because hate crime cannot be properly understood apart from the society in which it occurs, I realized it was necessary to contextualize the fires by juxtaposing them not only with other flashpoints of violence during this period but also with moments of social, cultural, political, and economic significance.

While my original theory certainly held true—that is, the fires did correspond with a downturn in race relations—I have had to reconcile the outlying fact that not all of the church arsons were racially motivated crimes of hate. Some of them, in fact, seem to have been *religiously* motivated crimes of hate, but many were irrational and senseless, devoid of any meaning at all. The more incidents I chronicled, the more I strayed from the central narrative of racial prejudice. As the story has taken shape, it has become clear that while it deals a great deal with black churches, this book is only partly about black churches; in fact, it is only partly about race relations and the deleterious effects of hate crime. Bluntly stated, race was only one factor in many of these crimes.

In the course of writing this book, I came to see how the church fires of the 1990s symbolize an absence of community in the United States in the late twentieth century. I use the word "absence" because to describe a "loss" or "disintegration" of community is to imply a more morally responsible civic past where stronger notions of community made hate crimes less common, and we know that this phase of American history never existed. The destruction of black churches (and black people) was much more common and openly tolerated in days gone by, and it is dangerous to court romantic notions of a more civil past in which notions of community flourished. Still, civic investment, for lack of a better phrase, has seemingly declined in recent years, and a number of social critics have noted fresh signs of social fragmentation, the disappearance of civility, and the breakdown of communal bonds. The church arsons represent one of the uglier sides of this fragmentation—even as efforts to rebuild burned churches and to combat hate crime represent new measures to establish community.[2]

If the word "community" once implied a number of people having common ties or interests and living in the same locality, then the meaning of community has itself changed in an ever-shrinking world of global telecommunications, digital commerce, cyberspaces, and e-life. Media and technology displace many of us from physical to virtual environs, where a certain degree of community is lost—even as new communities are formed. As Michael Bugeja notes in his book *Interpersonal Divide: The Search for Community in a Technological Age* (2005), "[t]he term community in the Internet age is as likely to mean 'network' as 'hometown.'" But the problem of defining community is only partly a problem of coping with new technologies. It is a problem of the erosion of public space and the disappearance of a sense of belonging. James Howard Kunstler has perhaps identified this trend best in his book *The Geography of Nowhere: The Rise and Decline of America's Man-Made Landscape* (1993), which illustrates just how much the anonymity of modern American cities and suburbs undercuts the common good.[3]

However one defines community, the word usually connotes connectedness, and it is this sense of connectedness that often seems lacking in contemporary American society. Community nurtures values such as civility and acceptance, developed through face-to-face interaction. People deprived of such contact tend to suspect rather than trust because their perception of reality has skewed, leading to misinterpretation, lack of empathy, fear, and an "us-against-them" (or, worse yet, "me-against-the-world") mentality. Interracial harmony suffers and hate crimes thrive in conditions where disconnectedness and enmity replace community. Arson, in particular, is an anonymous crime perpetrated against nameless, faceless victims: in virtually none of the incidents I have studied did the assailants know individuals at the churches they targeted. Accordingly, the best way to prevent such crime might be not only to teach tolerance but also, as Amitai Etzioni has observed, "to ensure that everybody has a well-paying job, is treated with dignity and not discriminated against, and is not alienated from society." While they may not snuff out the problem, efforts to ensure social justice and nourish the body politic can certainly lessen the likelihood of church arson.[4]

Therefore, in exploring these crimes, it pays also to explore the nuances of community—not only how it is destroyed but also how it is established, sustained, and nurtured. These fires were terrible, but it is worth noting that many of the congregants affected by these arsons experienced unity, goodwill, and faith—in both God and humanity—in ways heretofore unknown. In other words, much good came out of these tragedies. The fires prompted a rediscovery of community in many locales; in fact, they helped to create a new national dialogue on the meaning of community in the United States. It is my hope that reexamining these fires might somehow transmute into a deeper wisdom regarding diversity, tolerance, social justice, public welfare, nation building, and the ability of Americans—as Rodney King beseeched on the eve of the L.A. riots in 1992—to all just get along.

In its own way, each story of a burned church is remarkable and unique, even as it shares characteristics with similar events at other burned churches. Each congregation discussed in this book experienced a tremendous sense of loss, a terrible violation, a special trauma. Each victim cycled through a host of competing and often contradictory emotional responses. Each arson was violent and disruptive. Each building was irreplaceable, even if it was indeed rebuilt. Ripe with drama and pathos, every story of a burned church bears retelling, even if only a few of them can be retold here. While some readers might prefer more synthesis and less detail, I have attempted to catalog as many of these incidents as possible—in part because the sheer number of churches involved helps, I believe, to convey the scope of the matter. Even so, this book does not represent an exhaustive compilation of church arsons from this period.

The words of congregants themselves prove invaluable in conveying what happened, and I am grateful to those who have shared their stories with me, particularly Reverend Earl Howard, pastor of Amazing Grace Baptist Church in Crandall, Georgia; Earl Shoemaker, church clerk at Amazing Grace; Reverend Dr. Charles Hicks, pastor of Greater Mt. Zion Tabernacle Church of God in Christ in Portsmouth, Virginia; Reverend Glenn Harris, pastor of Spring Valley Baptist Church in Sumter County, Alabama; Barbara Edwards, Sunday-school director at Ashby Baptist Church in Bibb County, Alabama (as well as her son Jason and grandson Colby); J. L. Isaac, sheriff of Greene County, Alabama; Hollie Huey, a junior at the University of Alabama when I met her in 2006 and *the* reporter at the *Centreville (Ala.) Press*; and Rose Johnson-Mackey, research director of the National Coalition for Burned Churches.

Special thanks are due to Professor Jeffrey O. G. Ogbar at the University of Connecticut and Professor Devin Fergus at Vanderbilt University for reading the manuscript and making excellent comments; and to Stanley Harrold and Randall Miller, coeditors of the University Press of Florida's Southern Dissent series, of which this book is a part. I am indebted to the participants in the 2006 NEH Institute on African-American Civil Rights Struggles in the Twentieth Century at Harvard University, who inspired me and provided guidance as I researched the book; to the Avery Research

Center for African-American History and Culture, which granted access to its rich vertical file of newspaper clippings at the College of Charleston; to my colleagues and students at the Harriet L. Wilkes Honors College of Florida Atlantic University; to the hardworking staff of the University Press of Florida; and to my friends and family. Finally, I would like to thank my fiancée, Melanie Haskell, not only for her contributions to the cover design but also for her immeasurable support.

A few stylistic notes are in order. First, because few churches have completely white or black congregations, references to "white" or "black" churches identify the predominant race of their members. Second, while I have tried to be specific in my discussions of particular arsons, I sometimes use the phrases "church arson" or "church burning" in a general way to refer to fires not only at churches but also at synagogues, mosques, and other houses of worship. Third, and finally, the book is arranged both thematically and chronologically; that is, different chapters treat different topics, which generally proceed in order of their occurrence. Divisions between chapters are neither fast nor hard with regard to subject or periodization, but they do follow a general timeline. Any errors contained herein are my own.

1

fire

In the mid-1990s, a number of churches, many of them predominantly African-American, burned in a series of arsons across the nation. Initially treated as a chain of unrelated incidents, the fires signaled a resurgence in churches as targets of hate crime.

Mississippi Burning

On April 4, 1993, the twenty-fifth anniversary of the assassination of Dr. Martin Luther King Jr., three youths broke into and set fire to the Springhill Baptist Church in rural Amite County, Mississippi. A few hours later, they broke into and burned the Rocky Point Missionary Baptist Church in Pike County. Both churches, predominantly African-American, were completely destroyed. As the youths drove away from the burning churches, they shouted "burn, nigger, burn" and other racial slurs, as they later admitted in court. On October 1, the three young men—Charles W. McGeehee Jr., age eighteen; Jerome A. Bellelo, seventeen; and Roy J. McGovern, eighteen—pled guilty in U.S. District Court to conspiring to burn and burning the two churches in rural southern Mississippi; specifically, they pled guilty to violating Section 241 of Title 18, United States Code, by conspiring to injure, oppress, threaten, and intimidate the black church members in their constitutional right to hold and use religious property in the same manner as other citizens in the

United States. "There is no place in our society for racially motivated crimes like this one," said Attorney General Janet Reno. "The Justice Department and the United States Attorneys will prosecute these cases as a top priority." The boys were not the first white youths to attack black churches, nor were they the last, but they became the first individuals ever convicted in federal court of a church burning in Mississippi: at a time when state-level convictions for this kind of arson were still uncommon, each of the trio was sentenced to three to four years in federal prison. The incident received press coverage in local papers and in two black newspapers.[1]

The 1993 Springhill Baptist fire, with all of its racist symbolism, marked the beginning of a long series of fires at churches across the American South. In January 1994, a church burned in Fort Lauderdale, Florida. In February, three churches burned in Sumter County, Alabama: Bucks Chapel Church, Pine Top Baptist, and Oak Grove Missionary Church. That same month, two burned in Aiken County, South Carolina: Rock Hill Baptist Church and Old Rosemary Baptist Church. Five churches had burned in South Carolina in the previous two years; then, in June 1994, another church burned in Aiken County: Jerusalem Baptist Church. The following month, two churches burned in Georgia: Springfield Baptist Church in Madison and Elam Baptist Church in Jones County. In August, two houses of worship burned in Tennessee: Greater Missionary Baptist Church and Benevolent Lodge #210. The fires continued into the fall of 1994, when more churches burned in Tennessee, including New Wright's Chapel in Shelby County. Three more churches burned in South Carolina in September and October: Rice's Chapel in Buffalo, Shrub Branch Baptist Church in Blackville, and St. Paul AME Church in Cades. Winter snow flurries did not extinguish the fires as Salem Missionary Baptist Church burned in Fruitland, Tennessee, on December 30. Bluff Road United Methodist Church burned in Columbia, South Carolina, on New Year's Day. These fires were sometimes noted in local newspapers. They received little outside attention.[2]

The U.S. Bureau of Alcohol, Tobacco, and Firearms (ATF) documented a number of fires in the Deep South in the coming months. Two churches burned in Tennessee on January 13, 1995: Johnson Grove Baptist in Bells and Macedonia Baptist in Denmark. On January 31, Mt. Calvary Baptist burned in Hardeman County, Tennessee. On February 20, authorities charged two white men and a white teen with attacking three black churches with sledgehammers; prosecutors noted that nearby white churches were unharmed, suggesting the attacks were racially motivated.[3]

On May 15, someone broke into the Greater Mt. Zion Tabernacle Church of God in Christ in Portsmouth, Virginia, and set the burgundy velvet curtains near the pulpit on fire. Greater Mt. Zion had been founded in 1915 by a local woman, her daughter, and her granddaughter. For years after the church's founding, church members met in homes or on street corners. No one knows how old the building was when it burned, and no one seems to remember exactly when church members purchased the building, an old dance hall before it was converted. Former pastor D. Harvey Dunlap, a popular tent revivalist and radio minister, worked to remodel the church in 1951; more work was done in the 1980s. Anya Clarkson, a deaconess, described Greater Mt. Zion as a place where the pastor, Reverend Dr. Charles Hicks, called everyone by name and the fifty or sixty congregants packed the pews each Sunday. The church building was so small that the three different Sunday school classes split up and met in different areas of the sanctuary. The arson slipped into the crime report of the *Norfolk Virginian-Pilot* under the heading "Miscellaneous."[4]

The fire at Greater Mt. Zion devastated Reverend Hicks. He felt alone, a "little ol' poor preacher." He said, "You just feel like don't nobody care, nobody understands." Ten years after the arson, he still did not like to think or talk about the incident; doing so conjured up bad memories. Police had

Fig. 1.1. Sign at Greater Mt. Zion Tabernacle Church of God in Christ in Portsmouth, Va. 2005. Photo by author.

found a footprint in the middle of the church's backdoor, which someone kicked in before setting the fire. Hicks did not like to contemplate who might have set the fire or why. "It was a hurting thing," he said in 2005. Attending Greater Mt. Zion as a young boy, Hicks had grown up in the church he now pastored: he was baptized there, and he found God there. Seeing the church building in ruins was traumatic for him, and the fire precipitated a crisis of faith; he wondered how God could allow something like this to happen. Why did God not stop the assailant before he started the fire? Feeling that God had forsaken him, Reverend Hicks found it difficult to fill the pulpit in the months after the fire. "There's no need of preaching, there's no need to even stand there in the pulpit. . . . I just felt like I'd been let down."[5]

Other churches burned, too—and not just in the Deep South. In September 1994, officials said that the blaze that gutted St. John's African Union Methodist Protestant Church in Chester, Pennsylvania, appeared to have been arson. In October 1994, officials determined that a fire that destroyed the Bethel African Methodist Episcopal Church in Pittsburgh was deliberately set, and in February 1995, police looked at a possible link between the fire that gutted St. Paul United Methodist Church in Chambersburg and similar arsons in Pennsylvania. The incidents received coverage in local newspapers.[6]

Nor were such crimes limited to the United States. On June 3, 1995, a date that marked the one-thousand-year anniversary of the Norwegian Church, the *New York Times* reported the destruction of a church built in 1880 in Holen, twenty-five miles south of Oslo. The church was described as one of the most beautiful in Norway. Preparations for the anniversary had been marred by a series of deliberately set fires between 1992 and 1995 that had destroyed or damaged more than two dozen churches—including the legendary Fantoft Church, built in the twelfth century by early Christians. As in most of the other fires, satanic symbols were left in the churchyard of the Holen Church. What was meant to be a joyous celebration of the arrival of Christianity on Norway's west coast in the year 995 became a somber vigil as many churches across the country posted twenty-four-hour guards. At the historic Droebak Church outside Oslo, firefighters ringed the building with hoses to ensure a quick response if needed. Police officials noted that hundreds of people in Oslo, Bergen, and Stavinger were involved in satanic worship; Bjoern Soknes, chief public prosecutor, said most of them were young men infatuated with a Norwegian strain of heavy metal music known as black metal. At the time of the Holen fire, twelve Norwegians had been convicted of various charges

related to the church fires. "There must be something wrong in the community as a whole when young people resort to this kind of expression," said
Egil Laastad, who helped to rebuild the Fantoft Church in Bergen by day and
guarded the same site by night.[7]

Hate Nation

As the fires quietly bloomed across the United States, Timothy McVeigh and
Terry Nichols blew up the Alfred P. Murrah Federal Building in Oklahoma
City. The attack—which occurred two years to the day after the Branch Davidian compound went up in flames in Waco, Texas—killed 169 and wounded
hundreds more. McVeigh had been impressed by Linda Thompson's 1993 vid-
eotape *Waco: The Big Lie*, which faults the federal government in mishan-
dling its standoff with cult leader David Koresh and his followers; McVeigh
shared her belief that the government had conspired to cover up the Waco
incident, which culminated in the deaths of Koresh and his followers.[8]

In *American Militias: Rebellion, Racism, and Religion* (1996), Richard
Abanes traces the rise of right-wing militia movements in the United States
and explains McVeigh's association of Waco with virulent hatred of the federal government:

> Until the early 1990s, racists had neither the strength nor the funds
> to seriously destabilize the federal administration. As racist Michael
> Hanson stated in 1982, "we are both outnumbered and outgunned."
> Suddenly, however, a number of issues had arisen that could be used to
> swell anti-government ranks and bring about Armageddon. The plan
> was simple: Use millions of discontented non-racists to form a unified
> revolt. . . . To implement this plan, white supremacists joined and/or
> formed "patriot" groups, stirred up anti-government sentiments with
> hate rhetoric, spread conspiracy theories, and committed terrorist acts,
> which have in turn been blamed on the government (e.g., the Okla-
> homa bombing). By perpetuating an ever-maddening circle of obses-
> sive distrust of the government, the only thing left to do was patiently
> wait for America to crumble from within. The strategy has only been
> helped by the Weaver and Waco tragedies.[9]

In detonating a bomb at a federal government building, McVeigh and his
accomplice struck a blow against what they saw as a tyrannical regime. The
American public, slow to recognize the growth of hate as a homegrown

phenomenon, searched for culpability elsewhere. For example, on April 19, the day of the bombing, many American television stations speculated that Islamic fundamentalists were the prime suspects in destroying the Murrah Building. In the following three days, an anti-defamation group recorded 222 attacks against Muslims, ranging from spitting on women wearing *hijabs* (the head scarves of devout Muslims) to a fake bomb thrown at a Muslim day care center. Some mosques reported shots fired and death threats against members; a suspicious fire destroyed an Islamic center in High Point, North Carolina, on April 26. According to the *New York Times*, more anti-Muslim attacks occurred in the days after the Oklahoma bombing than during all of 1991, the year of the Persian Gulf War. It was hard to imagine that self-described "patriots" would have committed such an atrocity.[10]

In the early 1990s, journalists had noted with alarm the growth of the patriot movement, a far-right alliance of gun-rights advocates, fundamentalist Christians, anti-tax protesters, survivalists, libertarians, anti-abortion activists, states'-rights (and local-rights) advocates, white supremacists, and anti-environmentalists. United by negative attitudes toward the federal government and deep-seated anger, the patriots began to organize hundreds of armed militias throughout the nation in the days following the August 1992 shootings at Ruby Ridge involving Randy Weaver. The botched 1993 ATF raid of the Branch Davidian compound in Waco, Texas, further accelerated the growth of militias; but, it was Congress's passage in 1994 of two gun-control laws—the Brady Bill, which placed a five-day waiting period on all handgun purchases and required buyers to undergo a background check, and the Crime Bill, which outlawed nineteen kinds of semi-automatic assault rifles and related accessories—that really swelled the militias' ranks. New groups formed weekly. One such group was the Freemen, a Montana-based militia group that withdrew from society, created its own laws and courts, and issued bounties on local law-enforcement personnel. Educated guesses throughout 1995 placed militia membership at first ten, then twenty, then forty, then fifty thousand. A *Gannet News Service* article estimated in May 1995 that militias in thirty states had as many as one hundred thousand followers; in June 1995, the ATF noted militia activity in at least forty states, with membership rapidly climbing. At issue was nothing less than what the members understood to be the American way of life. Declining economic conditions, unwanted social change, the imposition of federal authority over states' rights, and environmental legislation that imposed strict regulations on what landowners could do with their property all fed a growing (and often conspiratorial) perception that the tyranny of the federal government necessitated violent resistance. Ostensibly nonracist, some patriots forged an unholy alliance with racists and anti-Semites over apocalyptic millennialism, the belief that the end of the world was nigh. The militias armed for a war with the federal government, but they were ready for a race war, too, should it ever come to pass; some of the more strident patriots began to refer to what they called "Ra-HoWa," or racial holy war. Whether bigoted or not, these individuals took themselves very seriously, and soon the rest of the nation would, too: the bombing of the Alfred P. Murrah Federal Building on April 19, 1995, silenced any doubt regarding the zealous commitment of patriots such as Timothy McVeigh and Terry Nichols.[11]

The Oklahoma City tragedy and the church fires represented two kinds of hate-related terrorist acts in the mid-1990s that coincided, perhaps feeding one another. For example, on June 20–21, 1995—just eight weeks after the Oklahoma City bombing—Timothy Welch and Christopher Cox burned two black churches near Manning, South Carolina. The two young men, recent converts to the Ku Klux Klan, kicked in the doors of Macedonia Baptist Church and Mt. Zion AME Church, poured accelerants over the pews and pulpits, and lit fires. "It was something that needed to be done, and I did it," Welch confessed. "It was such devastation, people were crying that night just like it was a funeral," said Reverend Jonathan Mouzon of Macedonia Baptist. "When you lose a church that's a major thing to black folk. To blacks the church is everything." The arsons recalled similar arsons years before in the same county. Fifty years earlier, the Reverend J. A. DeLaine had led twenty black families in Clarendon County in the fight for equal education in a lawsuit known as the Briggs Petition. Nineteen members of Reverend DeLaine's congregation were plaintiffs in the case of *Henry Briggs v. R. W. Elliott*, heard in U.S. District Court in 1952. Kenneth Clark, a black psychologist, provided evidence in the case: Clark's study, designed to prove that segregation harmed the self-esteem of black children, showed that the children in his experiment preferred playing with white dolls, which they regarded as more desirable than the black dolls offered them. The Briggs Petition, with other similar cases, would lead to the landmark U.S. Supreme Court decision *Brown v. Board of Education* that desegregated public schools in 1954. But the victory came at a cost: DeLaine's house and church were burned in response to the Clarendon County school desegregation case.[12]

The congruencies between white supremacist activity and church fires were often startling. In July 1995, for example, white supremacists from around the United States and Canada gathered for the Aryan World Congress at Hayden Lake, Idaho, an annual celebration of the white race. Participants paid forty-five dollars each to enter the gates of the Church of Jesus Christ Christian Aryan Nations for two days of speeches and ceremonies, highlighted by a cross-burning service. "We're growing, and we're starting to grow faster," said the seventy- eight-year-old pastor Richard G. Butler, a leading white supremacist and anti-Semite. Attendants were few—just over three hundred—but, following the Oklahoma City bombing, federal lawmakers watched with interest to learn more about white supremacists, "patriots," paramilitary organizations, and other right-wing fringe groups. Butler praised Pete Wilson, governor of California and 1996 Republican presidential candidate, for his support of the University of California's decision to end affirmative action policies in hiring, admissions, and contracting. Another participant credited Jesus Christ for having "the wisdom to empower the white race with the creativity of every material benefit you now enjoy."[13]

A month after the Aryan World Congress, St. John Baptist Church burned near Dixiana, South Carolina, in an isolated area of Lexington County only a couple of miles from a favorite gathering spot of the Ku Klux Klan. The following December, Mt. Zion Baptist burned in Boligee, Alabama, and Salem Baptist burned in Gibson County, Tennessee. As racial and ethnic tension increased, so too did the incidents of arson at black churches; however, the American public paid little attention to the fires smoldering in places like Boligee and Dixiana. Had someone noticed the increasing frequency of such arsons, the church fires in 1995 might have served as an accurate barometer for popular attitudes about race and politics across the rural South or, indeed, across the entire nation.[14]

O.J. and the Million Man March

The arsons flamed against the backdrop of what would become one of the most important trials of the century. As church fires sprang up across the nation, the 1995 murder trial of former football star O. J. Simpson—charged in the 1994 murder of his ex-wife Nicole Brown Simpson and her friend Ronald Goldman at her posh Beverly Hills home—riveted the nation. The ensuing nine-month televised trial transfixed the American public as defense attorneys argued that white police officer Mark Fuhrman and other white officers had intentionally sought to frame O.J. for the murders. From June 12, 1994, when Nicole Brown Simpson was found stabbed to death outside her West Los Angeles condominium, to October 3, 1995, when O.J. was acquitted of all charges, the story dominated the press. As Linda Deutsch and Michael Fleeman of the Associated Press have written, "the saga of O. J. Simpson would focus a searchlight on the soul of American justice and reveal a system stretched to its limits to cope with the power of celebrity, wealth, and an undercurrent of racism so virulent it would be blamed by some for the outcome of Simpson's murder trial."[15]

O. J. Simpson was the most famous American ever charged with murder. He was a sports legend, a movie actor, a commercial pitchman (most famous for hurdling luggage in Hertz ads), and a millionaire. He was also black. According to Simpson's attorney Johnnie Cochran, "Race plays a part of everything in America," and polls conducted a month after Simpson's arrest seemed to prove him right. While gender did not seem to be a factor in the American public's assessment of O.J.'s guilt or innocence, nearly twice as many whites thought Simpson was guilty, while African Americans surveyed were three times as likely to proclaim Simpson not guilty. The question of O.J.'s guilt weighed heavily on a nation recovering from the 1992 Los Angeles riots, instigated by the acquittal of four officers charged with police brutality in the videotaped 1991 beating of motorist Rodney King. Public attention was so rapt and emotional involvement so high that the LAPD feared widespread violence following a conviction. Many legal experts found the evidence against Simpson overwhelming, but the jury of nine African Americans, two whites, and one Hispanic disagreed, finding Simpson not guilty on all counts. (In 1997, a civil jury made up of nine whites, one Hispanic, one Asian American, and one juror of Asian and African heritage found Simpson guilty and ordered him to pay $8.5 million in damages.) The defense team's argument hinged on the fact that the bloody gloves found at the murder scene were too small for the accused's hands; "If it doesn't fit, you must acquit," said Cochran.

As Deutsch and Fleeman have explained, O. J. Simpson's acquittal marked the end of one saga and the beginning of another, "for the trial that had once unified the country, that had drawn us to our television sets and had us talking to friends, neighbors, co-workers, and strangers, suddenly started tearing us apart, exposing a racial gulf the size of which surprised many." Blacks cheered; whites shook their heads in stunned silence:

To some people, that just didn't seem right; it seemed to them like a murderer buying an acquittal the way he bought his Ferrari, aided and abetted by a high-paid team of con men that duped a jury with a high-stakes form of three-card monte. To others, it was sweet justice, a long-overdue nationally televised example of the system finally doing for a black man reared in the projects what it's done for decades for white men raised in the suburbs.[16]

The O. J. Simpson trial—a high-profile legal battle that in many ways mirrored its era—not only overshadowed the arsons in the press but also fore-shadowed the contentiousness of race in the closing half decade of twentieth-century America.

Nothing so neatly symbolized this contention as the Million Man March, an emotional gathering of approximately 1 million black men on the Mall in Washington, D.C., on October 16, less than two weeks after O.J.'s acquittal. Convened by the Nation of Islam minister Louis Farrakhan, this male-only event included efforts to register African Americans to vote, as well as efforts to increase black volunteerism and community activism. Organizers esti-mated the crowd size at between 1.5 and 2 million people; official estimates by the U.S. Park Service tallied fewer participants. Highly criticized, the event drew fire from critics who lambasted Farrakhan and his racist, sexist, and anti-Semitic messages; despite such criticism, it marked a high point of black empowerment and pride. Like similar convergences in the past, the gathering made white Americans nervous. It seemed to some as if the march organizers were capitalizing on a great miscarriage of justice. O.J.'s acquittal, the Million Man March, and white reactions to both helped to create a climate in which racialized hate crime might once again flourish. Black militancy, it appeared, was on the rise, and the forces of white supremacy silently mobilized to do battle.

The Devil's Job

It was not until early 1996, when hate flared in Knoxville, Tennessee, that the arsons attracted attention from those not immediately affected by the fires. On January 8, someone prepared and ignited a predawn fire at a house of wor-ship, the Inner City Community Church—a multiracial but predominantly African-American church with four hundred members. The church burned to the ground. According to one investigator, the arsonist put a great deal of time and effort into the crime. "We found accelerants," said Dick Garner of the ATF. "We found numerous Molotov cocktails. We found gunpowder. We found gasoline cans and numerous other items of evidence at the scene." The smell of kerosene—a telltale sign of arson—still hung over the site when investigators arrived. The perpetrators left graffiti on an outside wall that read, "DIE NIGGER AND DIE NIGGER LOVERS." No person or group claimed responsibility for the fire, but a few days after the incident, a couple of local businesses received leaflets reading, "1996 shall be the year of white triumph and justice for the master supreme race." One church member noted, "It's the devil's job."[17]

Reggie White, All-Pro defensive end for the Green Bay Packers, spoke out against the crime on Friday, January 12. "When is America going to stop tolerating these groups?" he asked.

> It is time for us to come together and to fight it. One of the problems is that the people financing and providing the resources for this type of activity are popular people with money who are hiding under the rug. Some of them may be policemen, doctors, lawyers, prominent people who speak out of both sides of their mouths. That makes it difficult to stop but not impossible. Not when we come together as one force against hate.[18]

The National Football League superstar was personally touched by the tragedy in Knoxville: White was not only a professional football player but also an associate pastor of the Inner City Community Church. While preparing for the biggest game of his eleven-year career in the NFL—Sunday's NFC championship against the Dallas Cowboys, with the winners earning a trip to Super Bowl XXX—White found his attention divided between football and hate crime.

White, who had preached in high school and become an ordained minister, worked hard not only to become the NFL's career sack leader but also to continue his ministries in Green Bay, Knoxville, and Philadelphia, where he often returned (as a former player for the Philadelphia Eagles) to lead weekday Bible studies, to volunteer his services at church councils, and to help at fund-raisers. In 1994, White had helped to organize the Community Development Bank in Knoxville for those who could not qualify for loans, putting up $1 million of his own money. "All of this hate, racism, and ill will, all it has done is made me more determined in my game and in my message," stated White, a native of Chattanooga and All-American at the University of Tennessee. "I feel like God has given me a message to get out, on and off the football field. And that's what I'm doing to do, regardless of the hate." The preaching Packer said he had a premonition that something might happen as early as the previous Friday evening at the team's hotel in San Francisco, where Green Bay was preparing for a playoff game against the San Francisco 49ers. "The team and hotel security told me on Friday night that they had received a message saying that something was going to happen," he claimed. "They said the caller told them he was tired of these interracial churches and marriages and schools and that he was going to do something about it. He said he was upset over the bank we opened in Knoxville to help people empower themselves, though it helps whites as well as blacks."[19]

Federal agents found no links between the fire and the four unsolved arsons at black churches in Tennessee in 1995. The Knoxville fire had "a modus operandi that was entirely different," said Richard Garner, special agent in charge of the ATF office in Nashville. Despite their finding racist graffiti and flyers, federal investigators hesitated to label the incident a hate crime. "This was an arson, without doubt," said FBI agent Scott Nowinski. "But to say that this is definitely a bias or hate crime, we cannot say that." Others saw the incident differently. "This is an unmistakable act of terrorism," said Brian Levin of the Southern Poverty Law Center, a nonprofit agency that not only provides legal aid to disadvantaged persons but also monitors white supremacist organizations. "The fact that a church would be targeted is . . . a symbolic act," he stated. "Even if it was done without a racial motive, the fact of the matter is, it still sends shock waves throughout a community."[20]

Rekindling Old Fears

Reggie White said he actually thanked God that it was his church that burned in Tennessee because his celebrity status finally brought national attention to the attacks. "I believe that out of every bad situation, something great will happen," he declared later that month. "When my church burned, it showed me that God is calling me to have an impact, to rally people from different ethnic backgrounds." White noted that other interracial and black churches in Tennessee had been burned in recent months, and that other churches had burned from the southern states to California. "At our site, some skinhead material was found there," he said. "They left the papers right in the parking lot." The leaflets claimed that integrated communities, schools, and churches would no longer be tolerated. He said that the life of another minister at his church, Reverend David Upton, had been threatened, but that he did not fear for himself or his family. "I know what God can do and I know now what He wants me to do. And they cannot tear that down with words, hate, or even fire."[21]

Reggie White's celebrity status and outspokenness drew attention not only to the plight of his own church but also to the plight of others. The fire at Inner City marked a troubling trend in the South as the national media began to notice that arsons appeared to be happening with greater frequency. Those who monitored the arsons began to wonder if racial hatred was on the rise as black churches again served as focal points for hate crime—just as they had done during the civil rights movement. The arsons prompted talk of a possible conspiracy. Klanwatch (the Southern Poverty Law Center's investigative arm, charged with surveillance of the KKK and other white supremacist organizations) noted the dramatic increase in such incidents in 1995; the group reported seventeen church burnings in the South over the preceding five years. "Compare that to the numbers in the last year, which have been nine," noted Joe Roy of Klanwatch; "it's a pretty good indicator that there may very well be some kind of orchestrated effort."[22]

As attention focused on Reggie White, the ATF began its investigations into a series of suspicious fires at four black churches in western Alabama that month to see if they were connected to the arsons in Tennessee the previous year. On January 11, Little Zion Baptist Church and Mt. Zoar Baptist Church, both within six miles of each other in the tiny town of Boligee in Greene County, burned to the ground on the same night. Two weeks before that, another black church in the area, Mt. Zion Baptist Church, burned to the ground, and neighboring Jerusalem Baptist Church was the target of an attempted arson in which the fire failed to ignite properly. "Given the locations of all of these fires, they could not have been started accidentally," said Barrown Langster, Greene County district attorney. "They may not be linked to any organized hate group, but we are concerned that it will continue if we don't have a thorough investigation." The Little Zion and Mt. Zoar fires followed the January 4 sentencing of two white men convicted of vandalizing three black churches in adjacent Sumter County in

February 1995. At the sentencing, one defendant called the action "stupid" and explained how he and his friends got drunk, went to the churches, and smashed pews, windows, and kitchen equipment with a sledgehammer. A third man convicted in the case died of self-inflicted gunshot wounds a few days before the sentencing. "I don't think any of this was accidental," said John Zippert, publisher of the weekly *Greene County Democrat*. "I think these particular churches were targeted. You have white churches in between all of them that were not touched." Morris Dees, head of the nonprofit Southern Poverty Law Center, attributed the vandalism to local rednecks. "This is deer hunting season and you have a lot of hunting clubs up there, and a lot of drunk white boys who might be angry at not getting a deer," he suggested. Dees noted that Greene and Sumter Counties are 80 percent and 75 percent African American, respectively, and that most of the elected officials were black; neither county fit the profile of areas where white supremacist activity would likely flourish. Meanwhile, in Zachary, Louisiana, three more churches burned on February 1.[23]

Fig. 1.2. Mt. Zion Baptist Church, rebuilt on a new site after being destroyed by fire in 1996 in Greene County, Ala. 2006. Photo by author.

Fig. 1.3. Mt. Zoar Baptist Church, rebuilt after being destroyed by fire in 1996 in Greene County, Ala. 2006. Photo by author.

Breaking the Story

Journalists working for *USA Today* were among the first to connect the dots and, in doing so, to identify a larger trend. "In scenes reminiscent of the 1960s' civil rights struggles, black churches in the South are being set afire at an alarming rate," wrote Gary Fields and Tom Watson on February 8, 1996. In an article entitled "Arson at Black Churches Echoes Bigotry of the Past," Fields and Watson laid out the facts. Arsonists had damaged at least seventeen churches in Alabama, Louisiana, South Carolina, Tennessee, and Texas since January 1995. Eleven fires were set in the previous two months. Fearful of attack, parishioners were patrolling their churches throughout the week. "I'm keeping an eye on my church," said the Reverend George Beck; his church, Ezekiel Baptist, held a fund-raiser for three neighboring churches that burned near Eutaw, Alabama. "One does not want to assume there is a connection but if there is, it obviously raises the specter of what we thought was a bygone era," said Wade Henderson, director of the National Association for the Advancement of Colored People (NAACP)'s Washington branch. The Reverend Joseph Lowery, president of the Southern Christian Leadership Conference (SCLC), declared, "We've marched too far, prayed too long, wept too bitterly, bled too much, and died too young to let anybody turn back the clock." The following day, the *New York Times* reported that the U.S. Department of Justice, at the instigation of the NAACP, had begun a civil rights investigation into the fires in Alabama and Tennessee. In a letter to Janet Reno dated January 29, the venerable civil rights organization said there appeared to be "a discernible pattern which links the fires, including the surprisingly large number." The letter mentioned at least eight fires.[24]

In a longer article the following week, Fields and Watson wrote, "A *USA Today* investigation found that black church fires have increased dramatically in recent years and are far more numerous than realized by the FBI and civil rights groups." All the church burnings have occurred in the South, the pair wrote, and most of the churches were destroyed. The article described the Justice Department's investigation into eight of the arsons to determine if the crimes were racially motivated; the article also pointed out that the investigation was expanded to include other church arsons after they were reported by *USA Today* in its earlier article. Fields and Watson reported that black churches were being burned at an even greater rate than noted in the previous week. Nineteen churches had been burned since January 1995, and seven of those fires occurred in the previous six weeks. The FBI found no evidence of a national conspiracy, but fires in Louisiana and Alabama appeared to be related, according to FBI deputy director Weldon Kennedy; in response, the FBI formed four task forces to investigate. Fifteen of the twenty-three arson investigations at black churches since 1993 remained unsolved. The article noted that black churches had been burned maliciously during the civil rights struggles of the 1960s, but that prior to recent events, that era had seemingly ended: an average of one or two fires were reported annually in the late 1980s and early 1990s. Mary Frances Berry, chairwoman of the U.S. Civil Rights Commission, said that most groups had stopped monitoring incidents like church fires. The recent spate of fires had, in her words, "caught everybody short." Meanwhile, another church, the Glorious Church of God and Christ, burned in Richmond, Virginia.[25]

Sweet Home Alabama

Ten days after *USA Today* posted its second major story on the events, lawyers in western Alabama offered a $10,000 reward for information leading to arrests in a shotgun attack on a judge's home. Two separate blasts shattered bedroom windows in the home of Sumter County Circuit Judge Eddie Hardaway, an African-American jurist who sent two white men to jail on January 4 for vandalizing the black churches in Tennessee. His wife, son, and nephew were sleeping in the house when the blasts were fired about 2:30 a.m. The couple's bed was covered with shards of glass from the blast that tore through a screen and window. No one was injured and no arrests were made in the attack. After finding a cut telephone line at the judge's home, and a light bulb near the front door removed, police moved Hardaway and his family to a secret location. "This wasn't done to intimidate me," the judge said. "This was done to murder me."[26]

Two months earlier, the judge had sentenced twenty-two-year-old Robert Michael Solliday and nineteen-year-old Albert Winston Short Jr. to six months in jail after they acknowledged vandalizing three black churches. Hardaway presided over cases in the tri-county region of Sumter, Green, and Marengo, where six black churches had been burned and vandalized in the past year. Police Chief Jeff Manuel said that race was one possible motive being explored; the district attorney, Barrow Lankster, was convinced that race was *the* motive: "I agree 100% with the judge in the belief that it was a hate crime." The Civil Rights Division of the U.S. Department of Justice and the White House were notified after the incident.[27]

On February 27, one day after the attack on Judge Hardaway's house, the U.S. Supreme Court let stand a Florida law making it a crime to burn a cross on someone else's property. The Court rejected the plea of a juvenile, Thomas Davis, who contended that the law violated the right to free speech. On February 28—the day after the Supreme Court ruling and two days after the attack on the judge's home—a white teenager named Christopher Allen Deer set fire to the New Liberty Baptist Church in Tyler, Alabama. The church was destroyed. In early March, authorities charged Deer with arson, and the nineteen-year-old confessed to the crime. ATF agent Jim Cavanaugh said that investigators ruled out the possibility of an organized effort linking the New Liberty fire with a string of fires that had destroyed four black churches in Alabama over the previous four months.[28]

Gary Fields, writing for *USA Today*, continued to spearhead the journalistic investigations into the crimes as other major new outlets began to pick up the stories. Fields reported in March that regional offices of the U.S. Civil Rights Commission were beginning to study race relations in areas of the nation where church arsons had occurred; that the arsons recalled the bombing of the Sixteenth Street Baptist Church in Birmingham in 1963; that federal investigators had identified suspects in arsons at six black churches but had not pinpointed a racial link; and that civil rights leaders and church officials were growing increasingly critical of federal investigations into the arsons. Some pastors felt that the investigations were unfairly focused on them rather than the perpetrators; others felt the investigations were lax. *USA Today* also noted that donations were being made to help churches rebuild. Noting the increase in church arsons and saying he wanted to "teach a lesson of public deterrence," Judge Thomas Higgins sentenced three men on March 12 to federal prison for three fires in Tennessee.[29]

As of March 19, fifteen arsons at black churches in the South remained under investigation. The ATF had identified—but not arrested—suspects in arsons at six of the churches and had determined that none of the fires appeared to be racially motivated. Civil rights groups met the ATF's investigations with skepticism; Wade Henderson of the NAACP said he strongly questioned the findings. "We are going to demand a more detailed investigation," he said. Some feared that the ATF focused too quickly on members of the churches as possible arsonists; however, Donnie Carter, who headed the ATF's investigation into the crimes, staunchly defended the bureau. As a black Baptist deacon and a native of McComb, Mississippi, where fourteen churches were burned in the 1960s, Carter was particularly attuned to any indications of hate crime. "You can bet your bottom dollar as the guy heading this investigation [that] I'm looking for evidence of [race as a motivating factor]," he noted. "It just hasn't happened yet."[30]

Rounding up Good Ol' Boys

The concerns of civil rights leaders and church officials regarding the seriousness of the investigations were not without warrant. On April 3, Gary Fields reported in *USA Today* that two of the federal agents investigating the church arsons also faced disciplinary action for attending an annual gathering in Tennessee known as the Good Ol' Boy Roundup. The agents first attended the Roundup in 1989, when participants performed racist skits, sold racist T-shirts and propaganda, and displayed racist signs and Confederate flags. The ATF agents, while not personally involved in any of these acts, did nothing to intervene and frequented more roundups in a government vehicle between 1989 and 1995. Wade Henderson, speaking on behalf of the NAACP, called the disclosure deeply troubling. The SCLC's Reverend Joseph Lowery worried, "I don't have any confidence that they would do the right thing if they find evidence that some good ol' boys are involved." On April 5, the two agents were taken off the case and reassigned pending further inquiry.[31]

A group of black ministers called for more aggressive federal investigations of the incidents. St. Paul's Primitive Baptist Church in Meridian, Mississippi, burned on Easter Sunday. On April 29, fire gutted Effingham Baptist, a 114-year-old predominantly black church in Florence County, South Carolina. Determining that an inflammable liquid was thrown through a window, authorities ruled the fire arson. Authorities searched for links between the arson and three other recent church fires in South Carolina as they considered the possibility that the blaze was racially motivated. A week after the incident, the prevailing mood in and around Effingham seemed to be one of incredulity. One man expressed anger. "Whoever did this needs punishment," declared David Johnson, a seventy-four-year-old retired farmer who said he would "put him behind a truck and drag him until his tongue hangs out." But most residents, black and white alike, shrugged and expressed bewilderment. Curtis Boswell, a principal, said he had seen no signs of racial tension at the local high school, where black and white students mixed easily on campus. "This surprised all of us," he said. "We just don't have trouble of that sort." Florence County prided itself on a progressive image that lured industries such as Hoffman-LaRoche, which was building a $500 million research and pharmaceuticals manufacturing facility in the area. Any suggestion of racial intolerance was painful for a community eager to shed any remaining vestiges of the Old South's stereotypical bigotry, and most residents seemed willing to interpret any hint of the possibility of racism as a lone anachronism. "It's just one of those things. . . . It don't mean nothing," said eighteen-year-old Christopher Allen at Effingham Feed and Seed, the local general store. "There's no need in getting mad," said sixty-five-year-old Willie McKever, a church deacon most concerned with getting an adjustment from the insurance company in order to begin the rebuilding process.[32]

May Day

Militia groups continued to provoke conflict with law-enforcement officials and vice versa. Problems with the Freemen climaxed on March 25, when FBI agents arrested two of them for a fraudulent money-order scheme and proceeded to surround the militia group's compound near Jordan, Montana. Two dozen heavily armed militiamen hunkered down inside, besieged.[33]

On May 1, as the Freemen drama played out in Montana, federal agents investigating the arson at Knoxville's Inner City Community Church released evidence that they hoped would lead to a breakthrough in the case. The evidence, a distinctive swatch of cloth from a child's T-shirt, came from unexploded Molotov cocktails found at the scene. Reggie White reported that church members had endured such harsh scrutiny that Reverend Upton would no longer talk to authorities without his lawyer present. That same day, officials in Alabama reported that Gary Henderson, a volunteer firefighter charged with burning a rural white church, may have been involved in a dozen suspicious blazes, none with an apparent racial motive.[34]

Leads were few and far between. On May 5, for example, the *New York Times* profiled a church burning that had occurred two weeks earlier in Kingston, New York. Tisa Washington-Taylor had witnessed two suspicious-looking white adolescents loitering in the street in front of the Riverview Missionary Baptist Church in her black neighborhood just before the church hall was engulfed in flames. The two-story hall, attached to the sanctuary by an enclosed walkway, housed the church library. It was used for large and small occasions: church banquets, Sunday school classes, fellowship programs, and meetings. Investigators said an accelerant had been used to set the fire. Reverend Willie Hardin said, "Kingston is not necessarily known for racial incidents," but quickly added, "I'm sure racism exists everywhere." He hoped that the fires in Virginia, Georgia, and Tennessee were not spreading northward. The *New York Times* reported, "Everyone is still hoping it was just two ignorant kids playing an ugly prank in an age of ugly pranks."[35]

On the eve of congressional hearings into the arsons, federal investigators continued to try to establish links between the crimes. Deval Patrick, assistant attorney general for civil rights, characterized the fires as "an epidemic of terror," even though the Justice Department disclosed no evidence of a regionwide conspiracy fomented by hate groups. Civil rights leaders began to blame what Reverend Jesse Jackson called "a cultural conspiracy"; that is, while there may have been no single organization plotting the arsons, and while few white Americans spoke in overtly racist terms anymore, an atmosphere of racial animosity was created by certain political and economic measures, namely: by the "Contract with America," the document written by Newt Gingrich, Tom DeLay, and other prominent Republican politicians during the 1994 congressional election that detailed campaign promises (including reducing "big government," lowering taxes, and reforming welfare) if Republicans became the majority party in the U.S. House of Representatives for the first time in forty years; by the 1994 North American Free Trade Agreement (NAFTA), which negated tariffs on many items traded between the United States, Canada, and Mexico and which, according to some critics, imperiled American workers forced to compete with cheap foreign labor; by political attacks on affirmative action; and by the neopopulist oratory of Republican politicians like Pat Buchanan. Jackson not only perceived forces aligning against black America but also saw connections between the church burnings and other signs of deteriorating race relations, including the murders of a black couple by white soldiers near Fort Bragg, North Carolina, earlier that year. "There's a clear pattern and practice now," he said, "and there's not the vigorous pursuit of these arsonist terrorists that we deserve." For him and others, the fires were unequivocal and unmistakable in their meaning. "They're not burning down black barbecue joints, they're not burning down black pool halls," said Randolph Scott-McLaughlin, vice president of the Center for Constitutional Rights, a New York–based civil liberties group. "They're burning down black churches. It's like they're burning a cross in my front yard. They're burning symbols of resistance and community and hope and refuge." Representative Henry J. Hyde (R-Illinois), who would preside over the congressional hearings, reserved judgment. "You know, burning churches can be a statement by people who are angry at God, not necessarily trying to send a message to the parishioners or the pastor," he said. "There are several reasons why these things occur, and then there's the question of conspiracy. We intend to listen tomorrow and develop some information about whether oversight is necessary."[36]

The U.S. House Judiciary Committee held hearings on May 22 to find facts about the church burnings. Federal agents told the committee that they had found no evidence linking the wave of arsons to any broad conspiracy or single hate group. "There has not been an identical modus operandi," Deval Patrick reported. Civil rights leaders and church officials expressed anger not only at the events themselves but also at the government's reluctance to respond. "It represents the 51st state, the state of denial," said Reverend Joseph Lowery, president of the Southern Christian Leadership Conference (SCLC). "While we have been shocked as a nation at the rise of hate groups and right-wing terrorists that have bombed federal buildings, and militia groups that pose serious threats to democracy, we have downsized the racist nature of these groups." Representative Donald Payne (D–New Jersey), the chairman of the Congressional Black Caucus, complained that it had taken too long for the House to pay attention, especially in light of the money spent investigating Whitewater, the real estate scandal involving President Clinton; the 1993 siege of the Branch Davidian compound in Waco, Texas; and the 1992 shootout at Ruby Ridge, Idaho, in which federal agents, trying to arrest survivalist Randy Weaver for illegal arms sales, shot and killed his wife and son in an eleven-day siege. "There is a disparity in the way justice is being dispensed in this country," said Payne. Similarly, Representative Sheila Jackson-Lee (D-Texas) noted that the federal government was currently fielding hundreds of agents at the Freemen standoff in Jordan, Montana, and should be doing as much to investigate the arsons. "I don't want to wake up and see a bloody mess at an African-American church because we allowed it," she said.[37]

On May 29, ATF agents began to investigate another fire, this time at the fellowship hall of Mt. Tabor Baptist Church in Cerro Gordo, North Carolina. The agents were following several leads in connection with threats phoned to the NAACP office in Durham. The caller, claiming he was "tired of you blacks," warned that three more black churches would burn by June. Special agent Mark Logan said, "We are aggressively pursuing the threats." Authorities continued to try to determine if the fires were either racially motivated or related or both.[38]

Conflicting Statistics

As investigative journalists and federal agents delved into the public record in an attempt to verify claims of arson, they met with difficulty. A lack of uniform reporting lent confusion to their efforts to establish patterns in the events. It was even unclear where, when, and how many churches had burned. There was no central repository of information on arsons. State insurance agencies kept accurate records of alleged arsons, but different newspapers posted different statistics on the events in question, and it was unclear which fires were accidental and which were set deliberately.

For example, in his second article with Tom Watson, Gary Fields reported that twenty-three black churches had been torched by arsonists since April 4, 1993, when white teenagers burned two Mississippi churches to celebrate the twenty-fifth anniversary of Martin Luther King Jr.'s assassination. Fields and

Richard Price reported in *USA Today* that thirty fires at black churches were being or had been investigated in the South between January 13, 1995 and June 4, 1996. CNN printed a record of fire investigations at black churches on June 8, 1996, that listed thirty-seven total fires since January 1995 (twenty-nine of them in the South); seven fires certified as accidental; five cases closed by arrest; and twenty-five investigations still open. The presiding bishop's office of Trinity Episcopal Church in Houston named *eighty* black churches that had burned between January 5, 1990, and June 17, 1996, in Alabama, Arkansas, Florida, Georgia, Kentucky, Louisiana, Mississippi, North Carolina, Oklahoma, South Carolina, Tennessee, Texas, and Virginia.[39]

Sifting for Clues

A black church burned near Greensboro in rural Hale County, Alabama, on June 3, 1996, but it was unclear if the fire was racially motivated or even if it was deliberately set. The Rising Star Baptist Church was engulfed in flames when firemen were summoned about 2:30 a.m. It was the fifth fire at a black church in west Alabama since late 1995. Church members waited for investigators, including federal agents aiding the state fire marshal's office, to determine the cause of the fire. "We did have investigators from the FBI and ATF on the scene as the fire was dying down, as the embers were still hot," said Assistant Attorney General for Civil Rights Deval Patrick. "They are literally sifting through the ashes for clues." Church members prayed that the fire was an accident. "My hope is that there isn't any wrongdoing," said Reverend Willie Coleman. "It'll feel worse if it's arson."[40]

While mainstream news outlets publicized the arsons, the black press decried the crimes. In his column for the *Philadelphia Inquirer*, Claude Lewis assured his readers that the fires would not intimidate black communities but would, in fact, bring them closer together. Bernice Powell Jackson expressed her shock at seeing the charred remains of St. Paul's Primitive Baptist Church, burned on Easter Sunday outside Meridian, Mississippi: "Gone were the pews. Gone was the pulpit. Gone was the cross. Only a few places of burned woods and ashes, a little bit of siding and the memories of the people were left." Local authorities visited the arson site, which met only twice a month, followed by officials from the Justice Department. After sifting through the ashes for two days, they left, and a second fire was started, destroying everything. Jackson bitterly complained that authorities investigated deacons and pastors first, accusing them of burning down their own churches. The official explanation was that the fire was accidentally started by a deacon who failed to extinguish a cigarette as he was locking up. "But when you see the building's remains and see that the church sat up two feet off the ground, you see how unlikely that was," she wrote. "When you know how reverent black folks are about their churches, you know no deacon would ever have been so careless. . . . And when you see the pattern of the firebombings in churches across the South, you realize how unlikely it is that these burnings are unconnected, random acts." Jackson called the fires "evil" and noted that arsons at black churches were nothing new. "Now is the time for all people of good will to speak out against these terrorist threats."[41]

Using dogs and special equipment, investigators from the ATF and state fire marshal's office continued their investigation at the Rising Star Baptist Church in Greensboro, Alabama, as government officials, church leaders, and community volunteers mobilized to help. Biding their time, investigators refused to show alarm, noting that arsons are notoriously difficult crimes to prove as many of the clues are consumed in the flames. They further noted that what seem to be arsons often turn out to be nothing more than accidents. However, as the fires continued around the South, it became easier for initial explanations to favor arson rather than accident. By early June 1996, it seemed clear—to many African Americans, at least—that something terrible was happening at black churches across the nation.[42]

2

fear

The fires recalled darker days in American history, harkening back to the days of Jim Crow segregation, when white southerners perfected the finer points of racial terror in keeping black folks "in their place" and hooded Klansmen destroyed property and lives at will. Like similar attacks in the civil rights era of the 1950s and 1960s, the fires of the 1990s created terror, as intended.

A Perfect Case of Race Hatred

Forrest Harris—director of the Kelly Miller Smith Institute, Vanderbilt University's African-American church studies program—saw in the arsons a residual imprint of the 1960s, a time when a number of white southerners refused to accept the world as it was and should have been. According to Harris, each burned church sends the message, "We don't like the way the world is now." Indeed, the fires of the 1990s paralleled the relentless attacks on houses of worship during the civil rights era.[1]

Even a partial list of attacks on houses of worship conveys the scope of such crimes in the 1950s and 1960s. For example, a bombing at the Temple, a synagogue in Atlanta, caused $200,000 worth of damage, tearing an eighteen-square-foot hole in the side of the building and shattering windows of two nearby buildings on October 12, 1958; this bombing paralleled similar attacks on synagogues in Miami, Jacksonville, and Birmingham. Teenagers vandalized synagogues in New York, Philadelphia, Chicago, Boston, and more than a dozen other cities in a two-day period in early January 1960. On June 25, 1964, a firebomb damaged a black church in Longdale, Mississippi; the following day, arsonists burned a black church in Clinton, Mississippi. On July 6, 1964, two black churches were burned to the ground in Raleigh, Mississippi. Someone bombed a black church in Oxford, Alabama, on May 13, 1965. On July 18, arsonists burned a black church in Elmwood, Alabama, and two more black churches in Greensboro, Alabama; the Imperial Wizard of the Ku Klux Klan, Sam Bowers, boasted that the Klan was responsible for more than sixteen arsons in Laurel, Mississippi. Arsonists burned a black church in Jones County, Mississippi, on September 26, 1965. On January 2, 1966, someone not only burned a black church in Newton, Georgia, but also threatened to kill the local sheriff if he investigated the incident. Bombs destroyed a black church in Ernul, North Carolina, on April 9, 1966. Arsonists destroyed a Catholic church in Carthage, Mississippi, on June 24, 1966, and someone bombed a black church in Richmond, Virginia, on October 5, 1966. When FBI agents pursued suspects in the September 18, 1967, bombing of Temple Beth Israel in Jackson, Mississippi, a carload of armed Klansmen rammed their vehicle from behind. Reverend A. D. King's church was bombed in Louisville, Kentucky, on August 14, 1968, and on November 27, four teenagers—all under the age of sixteen—were charged with torching the Yeshiva of Eastern Parkway in Brooklyn, New York. On January 19, 1970, fire damaged a synagogue in the Bronx that had been vandalized four times in the past year.[2]

In the twelve-week period surrounding the signing of the Civil Rights Act of 1964 by President Lyndon Baines Johnson, thirty-four black churches were burned in Mississippi, according to Michael and Judy Newton, authors of *The Ku Klux Klan: An Encyclopedia* (1990). Records kept by the Congress of Racial Equality (CORE) indicate that no fewer than two hundred black churches were burned and destroyed in the South during the civil rights era. The fires "signaled a strategy by anti-integrationist forces to destroy what they believed was the core ingredient in the lives of black Americans," according to Reginold Bundy of the *Tri-State Defender*. By doing so, the segregationists reasoned, they would weaken the collective activism of the civil rights movement. "The black church has always represented the bonding fiber of the African-American community," Bundy reported in 1996, "and its present role is no less important in rural communities around the South." CORE concluded in 1968 that the burning of African-American churches in the

South did more to raise the level of determination of African Americans than almost any other thing, including the stirring speeches of Dr. Martin Luther King Jr.[3]

Bundy aptly reported on the more recent arsons. The fires in 1996, while terrifying, did not surprise the members of Salem Baptist Church, one of the churches destroyed in Gibson County, Tennessee. "This is a perfect case of race hatred, aimed at the sanctuary of the African-American faith," said Avery Grooms, an eighty-seven-year-old deacon at the church. Grooms noted that racial intolerance in communities like his had been "fermenting" since the civil rights era, and that an unhealthy economy worsened the situation. Jobs in Gibson County were scarce and competition for employment stiff. "There's a growing feeling that with poverty rising in these rural communities, it's an us-against-them mentality," he said. "Whites tend to want to always blame blacks for their misfortunes."[4]

Bundy also speculated on the "code of silence" surrounding the ongoing investigations. While local, state, and federal authorities knew of white supremacist activity in certain areas, "getting someone to point the finger of guilt remains a near impossibility," he reported. Bundy interviewed Dr. Erlie Cummings, a professor at the University of Illinois at Chicago, who mused on the religious camaraderie among rural southern whites that sometimes excluded their black neighbors. "[O]pportunity is for whites because of historical biblical teaching," he explained, "and so is Christianity. There are many rural Christians who still believe Christ was in their image, and that blacks have no right to call him their God." This notion, once common among southern whites, still lingered, according to Professor Cummings. Following one incident in Birmingham in 1965, white supremacists allegedly distributed leaflets that claimed God had "retaliated" against African-American misconceptions that He was "the father of the Negroes." A year later in Biloxi, Mississippi, the burning of a black church was blamed on Jesus Christ's bitterness toward Negroes, according to an article in the *Atlanta Constitution*. No such proclamations were made in western Tennessee in 1996, and law-enforcement officials seemed less likely to believe that a blend of racism and religious zealotry had caused the burnings.

Good Ol' Rocky Top

The story of what had happened in Tennessee emerged in March 1996, when the men who burned Canaan African Methodist Episcopal Church and

Friendship Missionary Baptist Church were brought to trial, convicted, and sentenced. On Sunday, January 29, 1995—the day of Superbowl XXIX—Mark Jett, his cousin Michael Jett, and Robert Johnson reputedly drank a large quantity of beer while watching the game. Earlier, Michael Jett had gone to Knoxville in search of his runaway teenage daughter; all he found, he said, were "black pimps and white prostitutes." Frustrated and inebriated, he became enraged. The three decided to "teach the black race a lesson" and burn a church. Using tactics common in the 1960s, the men hurled Molotov cocktails and set crosses aflame at the churches. The churches were damaged, not destroyed: the 130-year-old Friendship Missionary was founded in February 1866, just two months after the Ku Klux Klan was created in nearby Pulaski, Tennessee (the church now stands not far from the General Motors Saturn automotive plant, the main industry in the area). The men were sentenced to three years each in federal prison and ordered to pay $20,000 in restitution. Police records indicated that two phone tips from the white community in Columbia helped lead to the arsonists' arrests. If the arrests and convictions exacted some sense of justice for the crimes, they did little to allay local concern. Reverend Dennis Lawson, pastor of Canaan AME, said, "It's amazing that thirty years later you are once again faced with the same scenarios. It seems like it's come full circle."[5]

Every Week for Sixty Weeks

To appreciate churches as targets, one must understand their central importance in black life. The historic role of churches in African-American communities cannot be overstated, nor can it be succinctly described. Churches are vital institutions in any community; in black communities, they have additionally served as places of refuge and focal points of community-based organizing and activism. More than houses of worship, black churches have provided retreat for those individuals and families seeking sanctuary in an often bigoted and intolerant society. Centers of black culture and solidarity, they are the places where black Americans have felt safest and strongest.

The social significance of black churches has been treated by some of the greatest scholars of the African-American experience. In his landmark study *The History of the Negro Church* (1921), the eminent historian Carter G. Woodson discussed not only slave meetinghouses but also the independent church movement that followed the American Revolution, when free blacks in the North began to assert themselves by breaking away from white churches; he also discussed the gravitation of early black pastors to politics. The sociologist E. Franklin Frazier similarly noted the centrality of black churches in African-American life. "In providing a structured social life in which the Negro could give expression to his deepest feeling and at the same time achieve status and find a meaningful existence, the Negro church provided a refuge in a hostile white world," wrote Frazier in 1963. "The Negro church with its own forms of religious worship was a world which the white man did not invade but only regarded with an attitude of condescending amusement," he wrote. "The Negro church could enjoy this freedom so long as it offered no threat to the white man's dominance in both economic and social relations."[6]

Their importance in the black community also made churches bull's-eyes for whites intent on subjugating their black countrymen. "There have been attacks on black churches ever since there have been black churches in this country," noted C. Eric Lincoln, professor emeritus of religion at Duke University and author of *Coming through the Fire: Surviving Race and Place in America* (1996). According to Lincoln, the first recorded torching of a black church occurred in South Carolina in 1822. In 1829, white mobs burned churches in Cincinnati's black district, and angry whites consistently attacked black churches in Philadelphia during the mid-1800s. In its campaign to "redeem" the South from black politicians, carpetbaggers, and scalawags

Fig. 2.1. Civil War reenactors in Gainesville, Ala. 2006. Photo by author.

following the Civil War, the Ku Klux Klan habitually targeted black churches during Reconstruction.[7]

As Reverend Lawson remembered, churches served as command centers for political activism and conduits of information in the civil rights movement. Holt Street Baptist Church was one of the headquarters for the Montgomery bus boycott in 1955. Volunteers for the SNCC and CORE worked, slept, ate, and held voter-registration drives in churches in Mississippi during Freedom Summer. During the five-day, fifty-four-mile walk from Selma to Montgomery in 1965, marchers stopped in churches along the way. "In those days, it didn't take a genius to figure out where the meetings were taking place," noted Benjamin Hooks, former executive director of the NAACP, in 1996. "And the anger, which was irrational to begin with, manifested itself there." As centers of activism, churches made likely targets for white supremacists.[8]

In August and September 1962, five black churches in Georgia were burned as nightriders conducted a campaign of terror, shooting into black homes. Vernon Jordan, a young civil rights worker who would become president of the National Urban League, later recalled how Mt. Olive Baptist Church, "with a picture of Jesus and the president of the United States on the wall," was burned to the ground in Terrell County several days after a civil rights meeting there. The FBI investigated and solved one of the church burnings in Terrell County on September 17, 1962, and charged two persons in conjunction with another church burning. January 1, 1963, marked the centennial of the Emancipation Proclamation; in September of that year, a bomb exploded at the Sixteenth Street Baptist Church in Birmingham, killing four young girls. This attack, one of the most infamous of the civil rights era, highlighted the tenacity of southern white supremacy at the same time as it elicited national sympathy for the cause of civil rights activists.[9]

The burning of what is now Mt. Zion United Methodist Church occurred in Philadelphia, Mississippi, on June 16, 1964—a few days before the slayings of civil rights workers James Chaney, Andrew Goodman, and Michael Schwerner. Mabel Steele remembered the night her church was burned. "We came to this church to have a business meeting, eight adults and two children," she recalled. "We came in and had the meeting, and after, a car came up out in the yard. The people in the car were white men. All the people from the church went to their cars and trucks. My son, ten years old, turned out the lights." The white men got out of their car and stopped her family and the others from leaving to ask them if they knew about the whereabouts of the

Fig. 2.2. Reverend H. C. McClain looking at the charred ruins of High Hope Baptist Church in Dawson, Ga. 1962. Library of Congress, Prints & Photographs Division, New York World-Telegram & Sun Newspaper Collection, LC-USZ62–125510.

"white boys": Andrew Goodman and Michael Schwerner. The next morning, Steele learned from neighbors that the church had burned. Four nights later, after viewing the burned-out church and visiting church members, the three activists disappeared. It turned out that local police in Neshoba County had arrested the three men on Sunday, June 21, and released them later that night only to inform Klan members where they were. A posse of Klansmen and sheriff's deputies tracked down the activists, abducted them, beat them, and shot them. In early August, federal agents found the remains of the three men buried in an earthen dam. The murders in Neshoba County made headlines across the nation.

After the burning, the tightly knit congregation rebuilt Mt. Zion; the church bell that sat in a pile of ashes in 1964 now stands outside the building, near a marker honoring the memory of Chaney, Goodman, and Schwerner. A group of church members gathered at the site in November 2001 to remember what had happened. The group recalled how common the burning of small black churches had been in 1964. "Every week for sixty consecutive weeks, a black church was burned in Mississippi," Reverend Ed King told the group. King had helped to officiate at the memorial service for Chaney. Mabel Steele, the oldest of the group, remembered those times with sadness. "That was the only place we came to worship," she said. "We hadn't done nothing. We were just trying to carry out the mission of the church and follow God's word." Now forty-seven, Arecia Steele, the ten-year-old boy who had turned out the lights that night in 1964, remembered holding worship services under the trees after the church burned and remembered hearing a white preacher on the radio say it was wrong to spill innocent blood.[10]

Forgotten Fires

Black churches remained citadels of strength in the 1990s as they had been in the 1960s; as such, they remained threatening to white supremacists. Michael Chandler, who discussed the context and aftermath of the Macedonia Baptist Church and Mt. Zion AME Church fires in his documentary film *Forgotten Fires* (1999), has noted that these two churches near Manning, South Carolina, burned in areas with a long tradition of white supremacy and arson-related terrorism. *Forgotten Fires* expertly explores the arsonists' motives, the losses sustained by the churches and local community, and the impact of the arsons on local citizens.[11]

Manning—"Matchless for Beauty and Hospitality," as its welcome sign proclaimed—harbored bigotry and racism, as do many small southern towns. The film describes how, in 1994, the Klan encamped in a field near Macedonia Baptist Church, whose members were forced to listen to the Klan's message of hate, amplified through loudspeakers during church services. Klansmen such as Horace King, the Grand Dragon of the Christian Knights of the KKK, decried how black people were unfairly advantaged in the United States, how black churches taught their congregations to manipulate the welfare system and procure government subsidies, and how the NAACP used the churches as fronts. If the Klan had forgotten that churches were erected as houses of worship, it astutely and rather enviously recognized that churches sustained black communities both economically and spiritually, providing a support network that poor whites sometimes lacked. The Klan found willing acolytes in Timothy Welch and Christopher Cox, who burned Macedonia Baptist Church and Mt. Zion AME Church after hearing the Klan's message.[12]

Chandler's portrayal of white supremacists in *Forgotten Fires* elicits pity, not contempt. The film dramatizes the limited opportunities of poor whites in rurally isolated communities like Manning. Poor, uneducated, and under-advantaged, white southerners such as Welch, who was physically and verbally abused as a child by his stepfather, remained locked out of the economic and cultural opportunities available to the white working class, the white middle class, and even the urban poor. Bored, angry, hopeless, and often drunk, young men like Welch were looking for purpose in the Ku Klux Klan, with its traditions, convictions, history, and excitement, all cloaked in Americanism and old-time religion. To hear Welch explain it, the Klan's insistence on racial hatred seemed, to him at least, almost incidental—not a primary motivator but a single plank in an otherwise reasonable platform of disenchantment with American society. "I don't have a chance out here in society anymore," said Lester Haley, former Exalted Cyclops of the KKK. "I'm a poor white man with very little education. . . . If a job comes available, they're gonna give it to a black man. . . . I hate to say that, but that's the way it is."[13]

But while the documentary does much to explain the actions of these racists, it certainly does not excuse them; indeed, if anything, the film dramatizes just how vicious such people can be. For example, after a day of fishing and drinking, Welch and his friends randomly assaulted Arthur Milligan on the side of the highway outside of Pineville—simply because he was black. The men hit, kicked, stomped, and stabbed Milligan, a mentally retarded clerk at a local grocery store. As Welch explained, he did it "for no reason . . . out of meanness . . . it seemed like something to do." As Horace King, explained, "I'm all heart, but I do have in me good and bad." The Haleys, a rather notorious lowcountry family, had a reputation for belligerence, racism, and being careless with fire around their enemies. A landowner who crossed a Haley seeking permission to hunt on his land might find his property burned, and a black person who failed to show proper deference to a Haley might find his car firebombed. Above all, the Klan engendered anger and hatred, and a proliferation of alcohol and firearms added volatility to the mix. "They're anti-drugs . . . they don't like black people, they're against homosexuals," Timothy Welch observed, after recanting in prison. "They're anti-people. They don't like anyone to be honest with you. And I'm not even sure they really like themselves."[14]

Welch, who later claimed he "never hated anybody," learned that one of the churches he torched was the church of a close family friend, his "Aunt Effie": Effie Cantey, an elderly black woman. "I could make exceptions," Welch said, meaning that he had black friends while espousing Klan beliefs. In 1998, Cox and Welch were found guilty of the burnings along with their two older accomplices, Arthur Haley and Hubert Rowell. In the strangest turn of events, the Haley family turned to the NAACP for help with Arthur, who claimed violation of his civil rights (though he recanted, he was still not allowed to change his guilty plea). Sentenced to fifteen to twenty-one years in prison for arson, Cox and Welch later had their sentences reduced to twelve years for testifying in a civil suit against the Klan. On July 24, 1998, in the largest judgment ever awarded against a hate group, a jury ordered the Christian Knights of the Ku Klux Klan, Grand Dragon Horace King, and four other Klansmen to pay $37.8 million for their roles in a conspiracy to burn Macedonia Baptist Church. The Klan appealed the ruling in September and asked for a new trial; the judge denied the request but reduced the size of the judgment to $21.5 million.[15]

Déjà vu

If the modern-day arsonists had intended to spread fear as their counterparts had done in the 1960s, their ploy worked. *Newsweek* profiled Reverend George Beck, who, as pastor of the Ezekiel Baptist Church in Eutaw, Alabama, typically spent four days each week at the church participating in choir rehearsals, Bible study, and of course, Sunday services. In the spring of 1996, however, the seventy-year-old Beck was spending practically every night at his church, where he would linger around the sanctuary or circle the parking lot "carrying a load of fear." Beck hoped that if Ezekiel Baptist looked busy, trouble would bypass his tiny church. "Folks don't be up all the time," he said, "and the devil moves when you think he ought to be asleep." The *Philadelphia Inquirer* reported that the church burnings had left black southerners "bewildered."[16]

In early June, another church—Matthews-Murkland Presbyterian Church in Charlotte, North Carolina—burned. Investigators said the crime did not appear to be racially motivated or linked to any other fires, but speculated that satanism, not racism, may have played a role. They were investigating whether markings and symbols painted on the church may have been connected to the fire. In the few days between the fire and the arrest, two more black churches burned, both in Greenville, Texas: the New Light House of Prayer and the Church of the Living God. "We cannot celebrate ours not being racially motivated when there are others that are," said Reverend Larry Hill, pastor of Matthews-Murkland. "A lot of people think it's real sick," said Martha Lewis, the white manager of a small grocery in Greenville. "They don't have the Lord in their heart. They don't have anything." Citing a lack of evidence, police questioned three men in the fire at the New Light church but released them on June 12 without being charged. "It's scary," confessed Skip Alton, acting president of the North Carolina NAACP chapter. "I have a better appreciation now for all the civil rights leaders who were active in the 1950s and 1960s. This is just a small fraction of what they had to go through, and it's still devastating to the African-American community." Whether caused by racists, devil worshippers, or troubled teens, the fires were traumatic and destructive. As the *New York Times* observed, "no matter how the sanctuary burned, it is still gone."[17]

As the ruins of Matthews-Murkland still smoldered, Morris Dees of the Southern Poverty Law Center filed a lawsuit on June 8 on behalf of the Macedonia Baptist Church against the Christian Knights of the Ku Klux Klan, based in North Carolina. The lawsuit represented one means of combating white supremacy that Dees had used with great effect: crippling white supremacist organizations financially with the damages wrought in civil suits. The Civil Rights Division of the Justice Department also prepared criminal charges against two members of the Klan, held in connection with the previous year's arson. "[T]he real point is that if Klansmen and Nazis find their property tied up in litigation they will be less likely to engage in these acts," said Randolph Scott-McLaughlin, vice president of the Center for Constitutional Rights. "The American way is that if you want people to change their conduct, then make them pay for it."[18]

On June 10, Myrlie Evers-Williams, national chairwoman of the NAACP, led a symbolic march to the charred remains of the former sanctuary of Matthews-Murkland in Charlotte, a 446,000–person city proud of its racial harmony and recent growth, including its two new professional sports teams. That same day, about thirty pastors from different burned churches met with Attorney General Janet Reno and other officials to voice dissatisfaction with ongoing federal investigations, which often seemed to target and even intimidate church members as possible suspects. Reverend Dr. Mac Charles Jones said that investigators had required lie-detector tests of church members, issued subpoenas for church records, and told congregations that each member was a suspect. Reno, while assuring that the federal government was committed to stopping the arsons, explained that investigators would take any and all steps they felt were necessary to complete the investigation. If some federal agents were insensitive to the trauma church members had experienced, others acted with speed and compassion. In Hale County, Alabama, investigators allegedly rushed so quickly into the glowing embers of one recent fire that their rubber-soled shoes melted. In neighboring Greene County, one thousand of the county's three thousand residents were interviewed by federal agents, some of whom even attended services at the churches to show care and support. The ATF opened a hotline, 1–888–ATF–FIRE, staffed twenty-four hours a day, seven days a week to receive tips. Working twelve- to fourteen-hour days, the one hundred ATF agents participating in the arson investigations comprised 6 percent of its force, and the agency was spending $180,000 a week on the investigation, the fifth-largest in its twenty-three-year history.[19]

By the second week of June, the national press had pounced on the issue of church arsons and reported them diligently. National newspapers, television networks, and magazines began to consolidate and disseminate reports of at least thirty churches burned across the nation in the preceding eighteen months; this media coverage raised national concern of a possible conspiracy. Government officials, including President Bill Clinton, spoke out against the crimes. On June 8, Clinton discussed the arsons in his weekly radio address, and on June 10, outside San Diego police headquarters, Clinton scrapped his planned anti-drug message and instead discussed the fires sweeping the nation. "We really fall into a dangerous trap when we start blaming our problems on other people just because they are different from us," he said. "To burn a church is a terrible thing."[20]

The fires continued unabated; in fact, they seemed to worsen, raising the specter of copycat crimes. Members of an arson task force in Florida had determined in late 1993 that thirty-nine fires unrelated to those admittedly set by a drifter named Pat Frank in 1990 had occurred at the same time; the task force said media coverage of the arsons resulted in a two-thirds increase in the number of copycat fires. In June 1996, civic and religious leaders in Dade County, Florida, discussed plans to deter copycat attempts in Miami. Later that month, reporters for *Newsweek* wrote that the sheer number of black church arsons, "which now equals the worst years of white racist terror in the 1950s and 1960s," suggested "a spreading virus of copycat malice." An article in *U.S. News & World Report* warned that publicity could be a two-edged sword. In the two weeks after President Clinton denounced the burnings in his weekly radio address, there were seven more arsons, the author observed, or about one every two days. Copycat crimes were a real danger, and "the pathological fringe has been incited, not deterred by the attention." The article listed the few suspects—brawlers, vandals, troubled teens, burglars, and pyros—who had been arrested, a mishmash of ne'er-do-wells who "don't think beyond the next six-pack," according to one U.S. attorney. The article praised the media's inclination toward greater public awareness and did not go so far as to suggest ignoring the story. "But there is such a thing as asking for too much," the article concluded. "Maybe it's time to stop giving them so many ideas in the interval."[21]

Don't Mess with Texas

In Greenville, Texas, authorities questioned three white men, ages eighteen to twenty-two, about the fires at the predominantly black churches near Dallas. Again, the cause of the fires had not been determined, and it was not known whether the blazes were racially motivated. One of the men, Bradley Blankenship, admitted that he and Mark David Gross were at the New Light House of Prayer in the hours before the fire but denied that he had anything to do with the arson. "We went back behind the church," he told the Associated Press. "We didn't even get out of the car. . . . We didn't do it." He said the two were smoking behind the church; after being stopped by police, Blankenship claimed to have spilled gasoline on himself while refueling his car on the way to pick up their friend, Juan Fernando Avila. The three men were released for lack of evidence as authorities promised to continue their investigation. Angered by the release, thirty shotgun-toting members of the New Black Panther Party drove to Greenville to denounce the arson. "We've come to Greenville to serve notice that we will not tolerate the burning of black churches," said Khalid Muhammad, former spokesman for the Nation of Islam. Later that month, police charged a black teenager—already in custody on charges of burning a vacant house—with burning the Church of the Living God and admitted that the fire was not racially motivated. Eighteen-year-old Mark Anthony Young confessed to the crime. In August, he was indicted on charges of torching the New Light House of Prayer, too, and remained a suspect in several other of the more than twenty suspicious fires reported in Greenville during June.[22]

On June 11, investigators charged a thirteen-year-old white girl in connection with the arson at Matthews-Murkland Presbyterian in Charlotte. Investigators refused to provide the identity or motive of the "very troubled" girl, who allegedly confessed to setting the fire with material she found in the ninety-three-year-old white clapboard structure; they did say that they believed she had acted alone and had not been involved in any other church fires. Despite the absence of racial motivation in either the Greenville fires or the Charlotte fires, the *New York Times* reported, "a wave of fear and frustration has fallen over many communities in the South after the thirty-two arsons at black churches in the last eighteen months"; the city of Greenville, about 20 percent African-American, had "a long history as a home to white supremacists"—and the Ku Klux Klan. "It's common knowledge that the KKK is active in Greenville," said Red Johnson, a thirty-six-year-old black man who lived near the New Light House of Prayer.[23]

The fires in Greenville burned away whatever racial harmony existed in the city of twenty-three thousand residents, who had only recently achieved a tenuous kind of coexistence. Local whites hoped that their black neighbors had forgotten the lynch mob that burned a black man to death on the town square in 1908, and the sign that spanned the city's main street from the 1920s to the 1960s, proclaiming, "Greenville. The Blackest Soil. The Whitest People." Local blacks, for their part, had interpreted integration as an indicator that whites accepted them as equals, and they were upset to have reason to suspect otherwise. "Neighbors are pointing at each other: blacks at blacks, blacks at whites, whites at blacks," said Bill Glenn, a NAACP official in Greenville. His wife, Barbara, expressed longing for the days of the Lee Street sign. "That town was better than this town. At least you knew what to expect," she told *Newsweek*, whose reporters concluded: "The fires have replaced those dreams [of equality] by a disappointment and distrust that have darkened this old cotton-mill town with an ashy film."[24]

Editorial Reactions

That same day, a *New York Times* editorialist asked his readers to imagine that the burned churches were white:

> Would it take the President a year to talk to the American people about it? Or Republican Presidential candidates? Would the public be satisfied when the federal law enforcement establishment—Attorney Gen-

eral, FBI, and federal attorneys—said they had not been able to break the case but had not run across any evidence of conspiracy? Would much of the press and TV wait until we got to the number 20 or so before deciding it was a big story? And how about ordinary, non-press, non-official Americans? When would they wake up to it? Would it take 30 and counting before supposedly alert and involved Americans would say, as a few did at a lunch this weekend—"Say, how long has this been going on? I just heard about it."[25]

The editorial raised an important point, apart from decrying the initial slug-gishness of political involvement, press attention, public concern, and re-lief efforts. Media reports seemed geared toward uncovering a racist plot, a conspiracy of white supremacists. If the initial lack of public outcry was any indicator, then the majority of Americans seemed relieved when the ATF dis-closed that the individual arsonists charged in the crimes had no developed ideologies or connections with one another. If there was no conspiracy, the public seemed to agree, then there was nothing to worry about: the fires were only the work of lone lunatics, acting individually. Such reasoning overlooked the fact that the arsonists had, indeed, acted, leaving a trail of ashes in their tracks. One can imagine that those persons directly affected by the arsons were uncomforted by the ATF's and Justice Department's findings; whether organized or not, the fires were disrupting and terrifying to those involved. Another editorial, in the June 12 *Miami Herald*, while reporting that federal officials had found no connection between the crimes, noted "an intercon-nection of another sort," the common denominator of "mindless hatred" between those responsible for the crimes. "It's so real as to be palpable, so deep as to be all but ineradicable, so long-lived as to corrode the concepts en-shrined in this nation's Declaration of Independence and Constitution."[26]

In another editorial for the *Miami Herald*, Leonard Pitts Jr. questioned the apparent lack of public concern about the arsons:

Hel-lo? Why isn't black America outraged? Why isn't America out-raged? Remember the Million Man March? We talked that one to death. Remember the O. J. Simpson trial? Couldn't go to the grocery store without hearing folks chewing that one over. But the churches are on fire and there is silence. The silence of the unconcerned, the un-engaged, the unenraged. . . . No story in Ebony magazine. No special edition of Oprah. No spate of angry essays from black columnists, this one included. Where is the outcry? Where is the urgency? Who will, as the rap group Public Enemy once phrased, "bring the noise"?[27]

Pitts suggested that it would take the torching of a famous church—such as Ebenezer Baptist in Atlanta, where Martin Luther King Sr. and Jr. both preached, or First Baptist in Selma, a key site in the 1965 voting rights campaign—to raise concern. Pitts realized that the struggle for black equality had changed since the civil rights era, that the church did not mean what it once did. "Our world is secularized and decentralized and it's almost quaint to think of a church house as the heart of a community," he wrote. "What the silence tells us is that the center of black political thought has moved on, become diffuse. Debates that were once confined to pulpits are now staged in the halls of academia, on talk television, in the corridors of cyberspace and the columns of daily newspapers. The idiots are burning what was, not what is." It was incumbent upon black America, Pitts concluded, to remember, honor, and embrace what was.[28]

Pitts was correct in noting general apathy with regard to the church burnings: an unwillingness, perhaps, to acknowledge that such a thing could be happening in 1996. "I don't think it's racial," said William Gary, presiding deacon of the Dexter Avenue Baptist Church in Montgomery, Alabama, where Martin Luther King Jr. had preached and led the bus boycott forty years earlier. "I think it's hate crimes. More hate than racial." An editorial in the *Philadelphia Inquirer* excoriated those who were setting the fires but noted positive effects, such as the outpouring of support from all races and religious groups.[29]

The *Baltimore Afro-American* bluntly called the perpetrators cowards. "Those church buildings, whether in the South or the North, are the ties that bind the black community to their history and without them many people lose their roots." Dorothy Gilliam, writing for the *Washington Post*, contemplated the arsons not only as a journalist but also as the daughter of a black minister at an AME church in the South. Condemning the crimes, she talked about the historic role of the church and how that role had changed, even noting how the civil rights movement had in some ways weakened black churches. "The church sustained our will to go on in the face of danger and racism. The church assured us that we were children of God when society told us we were second-class citizens. . . . I saw how the civil rights movement, with all the benefits it yielded, fragmented the black community and, in doing so, affected church membership." In the 1990s, young African Americans were

Fig. 2.3. Grave near Amazing Grace Baptist Church, destroyed by fire in 1998 in Murray County, Ga. 2005. Photo by author.

finding their way back to church "to fill the voids that they have found in their lives and to give back to less affluent black communities facing staggering social problems."[30]

The Fire This Time

On June 14, another predominantly African-American church went up in flames in Enid, Oklahoma. Officials suspected arson at First Missionary Baptist, consumed at 4:00 a.m. in forty-foot flames. Police found accelerant at the scene and a window smashed from the outside, indicating a break-in. It was the fourth suspicious church fire in ten days. The next day, police arrested a suspect, a thirty-five-year-old white man named Christopher Harper, whose mother claimed that her son was mentally handicapped and could not have committed such a crime alone. Mary Smith told reporters that her son had spent ten years in a state school for the developmentally disabled and could not assemble an incendiary device without assistance. Investigators indicated that the fire was not racially motivated. "I'm not upset, I'm not mad," said Reverend Ivy Haynes Jr., associate pastor of the church. "I want whoever did it to know that we still love them. That's not to say it's not stupid and silly."[31]

A stunning announcement by the National Trust for Historic Preservation acted as an eye-opening wake-up to anyone not paying attention to the angry editorials that had recently appeared in the national press. The extensive media coverage of the arsons prompted the National Trust to take the unprecedented action of placing black churches in the South on its "endangered list." In addition to labeling black southern churches as endangered, the National Trust made loans available to historical churches that have been damaged or destroyed, participated in a fund-raising campaign announced by the National Council of Churches, and provided technical assistance through its field offices in Charleston, South Carolina, and Fort Worth, Texas. The move was designed not only to condemn the recent flurry of arsons but also to mobilize support for the churches as historical monuments and community institutions. Richard Moe, the president of the National Trust, explained, "Over the past eight years, our list of endangered sites has alerted people to the threats from demolition, neglect, underfunding, the forces of nature, inappropriate development and sprawl, but never until now—the danger of arson." Calling arson "malicious and cowardly," Moe noted that the crime is "even more reprehensible and outrageous" when aimed at churches. "These institutions in many ways represent the best of America," he said. "These fires represent the worst."[32]

3

faith

Churches, synagogues, national denominations, and religious organizations reacted swiftly and proactively to denounce the violence. Uniformly, national denominations issued denunciations of the arsonists and pledged their support to victimized congregations. Local churches also united behind those affected. On the whole, churches were quick to treat the issue as a crisis.

Holy Smoke

Even before news of the arsons had become widespread, religious voices were speaking out against the crimes. For example, the General Board of Global Ministries (GBGM) sponsored a special meeting on hate crime in St. Louis in July 1995. Eighty-eight participants focused on creative responses to the problem by focusing on contextual Bible study as a primary strategy; break-out sessions stressed the role of Scripture in enabling Christians to reject hate and violence while working for redemption of those who committed hate crime. The GBGM looked for ways to celebrate diversity, express the whole-ness of the human family, and develop strong interfaith networks. "Hate violence is not just a sociological or psychological phenomenon," wrote Reverend Joseph E. Agne, a pastor at Memorial United Methodist Church in White Plains, New York, and a GBGM consultant. Penning a ten-point program for dealing with hate, Agne called hateful violence a violation of the rights that come from God in creation itself, a human attempt to deny that all of God's creation is good. "Concern for the healing of hate violence comes from the heart of the Gospel and is inherent in the second great commandment Christ prioritized: 'You shall love your neighbor as yourself' (Matthew 22:39)," he wrote in *New World Outlook*, the mission magazine of the United Methodist Church. The East Tennessee Chapter of the National Coalition Building Institute (NCBI) took an active role after the burning of the Inner City Community Church in Knoxville. Within twenty-four hours of the arson on January 8, 1996, a petition voicing the outrage of the community and pledging support of racial harmony was signed by several hundred residents of Knoxville and the east Tennessee area. More signatures were added to the petition and more than $1,000 in donations were forwarded to the Inner City Church for reconstruction.[1]

On April 22, 1996, a group of black ministers called for a more aggressive federal investigation into the arsons. The ministers, some of whose churches had been burned, appeared at a news conference sponsored by the Christian Coalition, a largely white organization associated with right-wing political causes. Ralph Reed, executive director of the Christian Coalition, announced a $25,000 reward for information in the arson cases. Because white evangelicals were quick to "look the other way" in violence directed toward black churches during the civil rights era, Reed said it was critical for contemporary Christians to show unity across racial lines. The National Council of Churches (NCC), a more liberal group, also offered support, announcing that it was trying to help congregations rebuild and recover. Two days later, on April 24, the South Carolina Coalition of Black Church Leaders launched a statewide "church watch" to curb arsons.[2]

A Serious and Frightening Assault

African-American leaders continued to complain bitterly of the lack of attention that the arsons were receiving. Reverend Joseph Lowery, president of the Southern Christian Leadership Conference, said the "feeble response" of the government and media represented a national "state of denial." Lowery said, "We are witnessing a serious and frightening assault on African Americans in this country. We must hold accountable the racist groups that fan the flames of intolerance." Expressing a fear of many African Americans, he recalled the days when law-enforcement agencies included personnel who were also members of white supremacist organizations. The National Council of Churches rejected the opportunity to present oral testimony at the U.S. House Judiciary Committee hearings, and instead submitted written testimony by NCC president Bishop Melvin G. Talbert and Reverend Joan Brown Campbell, NCC general secretary, that noted "striking similarities in these incidents." Talbert and Campbell also provided testimony from some of the affected pastors that racial epithets scrawled on the burned-out shells of their churches had been painted over by law-enforcement officials without the consent of the churches, and accused law-enforcement agencies of ignoring death threats received by pastors. Jesse Jackson suggested that "the story would have broken much earlier" if white churches or synagogues were ablaze.[3]

Methodists in South Carolina spoke out in late May against the arsons at the South Carolina Annual Conference, which urged people of all faiths to use worship services on the weekend of June 29–30 as a "Sabbath of Support" for congregations that had lost their houses of worship. The group, comprised of clergy and laypersons charged with electing bishops, passed a resolution and established a fund to distribute monies to arson victims. "We felt that the South Carolina Conference should send a message of love and healing to those congregations and to send a call to our own churches to reach out with gifts of time and money," said Rhett Jackson, a layman from Columbia. "We lament the fact that there still is so much tolerance for racism and bigotry in our state and we hope that this resolution will be a call to speak out on the evils of racism and intolerance, and for all of us, lay and clergy, to become a part of the healing and reconciling of all human beings." Through its Ethnic Local Church Concerns Committee, the United Methodist Church stood united with other groups in the Christian Action Council (CAC), including the Columbia Jewish Federation, the Church of God, the Church of the Nazarene, the Episcopal Dioceses of South Carolina and Upper South Carolina, the Evangelical Lutheran Church in America, the Greek Orthodox Diocese of Atlanta, the Presbyterian Church USA, the Reformed Episcopal Church, the Roman Catholic Church, Quakers, the Southern Baptist Convention, and Wesleyans.[4]

Overtones and Undertones

On June 10, black ministers met with federal officials to voice their concerns. "We come in great pain, frustration, anguish, and disappointment," said Spiver Gordon of the SCLC. About sixty clergymen met with Treasury Secretary

Robert Rubin who—as the person overseeing the Bureau of Alcohol, Tobacco, and Firearms (ATF)—pledged that federal investigators would work to win the trust of the black community. Reverend Dr. Mac Charles Jones of the National Council of Churches (NCC) reiterated his concern that pastors felt they were being interrogated rather than being assisted. Reggie White encouraged professional athletes and celebrities to "adopt" a congregation to help them rebuild. "We've got to come to our brothers' and sisters' rescue," he said. The following day, the Anti-Defamation League (ADL) commended President Clinton on his leadership and "unequivocal response to the rash of church arsons that literally and figuratively burn at the fabric of the country." Founded in 1913, the ADL represented the world's leading organization committed to fighting anti-Semitism through programs and services that counteract hatred, prejudice, and bigotry. The league had become involved in January 1996, when Abraham H. Foxman, ADL national director, contacted Attorney General Janet Reno, whom he urged to investigate the arsons across the South. Over the next few months, the league continued its involvement: urging investigations, assisting victims in local communities, reviewing existing hate crime laws with an eye toward revision, and offering use of its resources—including its extensive materials on hate groups—to law-enforcement officers and federal authorities. Also on June 11, a contingent of black pastors continued to press federal officials for solutions. President Clinton urged Congress to pass quickly a bipartisan bill sponsored by Representatives Henry J. Hyde and John Conyers Jr. that would make it easier to prosecute anyone who attacked a church.[5]

The United Methodist Church continued its involvement, describing its response as "intense and constructive." The head of the denomination's Commission on Religion and Race bemoaned the reluctance of some people to admit that "these acts of terrorism have racial overtones and undertones." Barbara Thompson, general secretary of the commission, likened combating racism to fighting the Hydra of Greek myth which would sprout two heads when one was cut off. "We challenge every local church pastor of every denomination to teach and preach that racism is more than just an issue of civil rights, but that it is a profoundly theological issue," she said. "It is a sin because it denies the creative genius of God." The United Methodist Church of Oklahoma offered money and a building in response to the predawn fire at First Missionary Baptist Church in Enid, Oklahoma: the bishop's office in Oklahoma offered Volunteers-in-Mission teams and money to rebuild while offering the temporary use of a vacant UMC facility.[6]

The Churches Are Burning!

Some fringe groups interpreted the fires as a sign of the Apocalypse. "The churches are burning!! The churches are burning!!" heralded one fundamentalist Web site. "The Plans of New World Order call for the burning of churches in the period immediately preceding the appearance of the New Age Christ!" The Web site anticipated what it called "the Kingdom of Antichrist."[7]

Other religious figures and civil rights leaders in the South questioned what they saw as the failures of white pastors to fight bigotry in their congregations, and interpreted the church burnings as a sign that much social change was still needed in the United States. Ralph Reed, executive director of the Christian Coalition, called on white evangelicals to seek repentance and reconciliation for their past unwillingness to embrace civil rights for African Americans. Reed acknowledged that "the white evangelical church was not only on the sidelines but on the wrong side" of the civil rights movement and announced that his organization would try to raise $1 million to help rebuild burned churches. Laced with quotations from liberal icons such as Martin

Fig. 3.1. Sign painted on shed near Amazing Grace Baptist Church, Murray County, Ga. 2005. Photo by author.

Luther King Jr. and Robert F. Kennedy, Reed's message was received warmly by some ministers. "What I'm hearing now is something I want to hear," said Reverend David Upton, minister of the Inner City Church in Knoxville. "I just pray it's not a one-shot statement." Others were more skeptical, saying that the conservative Christian Coalition had inflamed the racial tensions that caused the arsons. "If they're serious about reconciliation and getting on the right side of the struggle for racial justice, I would like to see them address the burning issues: the assault on affirmative action, on voting rights, on women's rights, on welfare," said Reverend Joseph Lowery of the SCLC. "I think he's trying to exploit and absolve himself and his group of their exploitation of fears in this country." Nelson B. Rivers III, southeast regional director of the NAACP, said after hearing Reed that African Americans must be watchful. "We have to be wary of any Trojan horse when the issue is used to get into our community to achieve other goals that may not be in our best interests," he warned.[8]

Flashpoint

The greatest press coverage of the arsons coincided with the announcement by the National Trust for Historic Preservation that it had placed black churches on its "endangered list" in June 1996 as the fires continued, seemingly unabated, on a daily basis. On June 17, a black church—Hills Chapel Baptist Church—burned in Rocky Point, North Carolina, the second suspicious fire in that state in less than two weeks; investigators quickly determined that faulty florescent lighting caused the fire. That same day, CNN reported that a fire heavily damaged a sanctuary at Pine Lake Baptist Church, a white church in suburban Atlanta. Neighbors said they heard a car blaring loud music just before the fire broke out at Pine Lake. In Mississippi, two black churches burned on June 18 in Kossuth, in the northeast corner of the state. The fires at Mt. Pleasant Missionary Baptist Church and Central Grove Church broke out within minutes of each other. Hundreds of onlookers, many in tears or saying prayers, watched the sanctuaries burn as volunteer firefighters waged a futile battle to extinguish the flames. "It hurts," said Janice Hand, Sunday school secretary at Hills Chapel. "It makes me feel as if I have lost a loved member of my family." Other church members expressed disbelief. A number of related developments made the news that same day. Police arrested and charged a seventeen-year-old white volunteer firefighter, Billy Shawn Baxley, in the May 25 burning of Pleasant Hill Baptist Church, a black church in

Robeson County, North Carolina. Ralph Reed of the Christian Coalition announced that he would ask the one hundred thousand churches on his group's mailing list to help raise $1 million to rebuild burned churches. In New York, another fund-raising drive began with speeches by rabbis who likened the fires to Nazi Germany's Kristallnacht attack on synagogues in 1938, and in Washington, D.C., the House of Representatives unanimously passed legislation that would broaden federal authority to prosecute crimes against religious property. The following day, authorities ruled yet another fire at a black church as accidental. A fire at St. John's Methodist Church, on Maryland's Eastern Shore, apparently started at an electrical socket in the kitchen. "It's quite evident it's accidental, said Rocco Gabriele, state fire marshal.[9]

Conversely, investigators reported that a fire at a black church the following day in Portland, Oregon, was deliberately set. A spokesman for the Portland Fire Bureau announced that physical evidence of arson at Immanuel Free Methodist Church was recovered and taken to a lab for analysis. "It's just toast," said Mark Strong, church pastor. "I'm trying not to think the worst until we find out from investigators what actually took place." Congregants held a prayer service on the church lawn later that evening. Also on June 20, police arrested two black men in connection with the

Fig. 3.2. Former site of Mt. Zion Baptist Church, destroyed by fire in 1996 in Greene County, Ala. 2006. Photo by author.

Fig. 3.3. Road to Little Zion Baptist Church, rebuilt after being destroyed by fire in 1996 in Boligee, Ala. 2006. Photo by author.

May 23 fire at Mt. Tabor Baptist Church in Cerro Gerdo, North Carolina. The two men, Curtis Gilbert and Rodney Bullock, had worked as contractors restoring a 132-year-old wooden building on the church grounds for use as a fellowship hall; already having been paid $40,000 for their work, they apparently burned the building when it became apparent they would not meet their construction deadline of June 1. In Boligee, Alabama, where arsons at three black churches within a five-mile radius were among the first to raise fears in December 1995, authorities indicated that they were no closer to solving the crimes. Six months later, there had been no arrests, and investigators acknowledged that the trail of the arsonist or arsonists had grown cold.[10]

A columnist for the *Washington Post* used the opportunity to decry the continuing existence of segregation in houses of worship. "The clash between this country's high ideals and low regard for African Americans will be on display at 11 a.m. tomorrow [Sunday morning]," wrote Colbert King. "Many Christian congregations still conduct themselves as if there are two heavens: one black and one white; as if some human souls are priceless and others are not; and as if Paul never taught that we 'are all one in Christ Jesus.'" King blasted both black and white clergymen for worshipping separately and for fumbling the church's activist heritage. "If these men and women of the cloth are embarrassed by their own failure to speak incessantly from the pulpit against separatism and the Christian challenge of brotherhood, if their steering clear of sticky racial and moral issues bothers their consciences, most manage not to show it," he wrote. "They take to their pulpits, hew to other-worldly matters and things 'theological,' and leave to others, such as government, the handling of the difficult issues related to segregation's nasty legacies." A letter to the editor of the *New York Times* shared King's concern regarding the segregation of American churches. "Why are there still any 'black' churches at all?" asked Robert Feldmesser of Lambertville, New Jersey. "[T]he continued existence of identifiable black churches seems to represent a failure of the Christian spirit of brotherhood." Another letter lambasted the president of the Boston City Council for "shelving" a resolution that condemned the burnings, deemed "too political and irrelevant to the business of Boston," according to the author, David Evans of Cambridge, Massachusetts. "How will we justify such indifference to our children when they examine computer disks, videotapes, and Internet archives with the details of our inaction?" A *New York Times* columnist decried those who committed the crimes and specified why the arsons were so onerous, writing, "In America, where people rank among the most religious in the industrialized world, to burn a church is to commit an act of singular profanity." Gustav Niebuhr continued, "Its violence lies in the attempt to disrupt a community of believers, desecrate their altars, and smash the spiritual rhythm of their lives. The arsonist attacks not just planks and shingles but the space where life's most important transitions are marked, where babies are baptized, marriages celebrated, and the dead eulogized."[11]

Southern Exposure

Other news stories focused on the church arsons as a peculiarly southern phenomenon. A grandiloquent piece in the *New York Times*, ignoring the fact that fires had occurred across the entire nation, effused, "The flames rise into the sky like malignant ghosts from the South's past, evoking some of the most racially charged images in the nation's history." In some ways, the article continued, "the incidents reflect dynamics peculiar to the South, from the multilayered choreography of race in small southern towns to the vulnerable nature of little country churches perched amid kudzu vines and old oaks at the end of lonely dirt roads, their gravel parking areas empty for days"; however, in other ways, "what is occurring at the southern churches reflects the agonies of race, religion, and ethnicity that go beyond that region." A second columnist for the *New York Times* offered, "If the racist firebugs in the South had any sense at all they would stop torching black churches": the fires only elicited sympathy for the people they despised. Writers for *Newsweek* offered a wider view as they contemplated Atlanta as both host of the Olympics and capital of the New South. "[R]ace still matters in the South," they acknowledged. "It matters everywhere else, too, of course, and for Southerners confronting the latest fires, that's the damnable thing." Southerners had come far since World War II; as the crucible of the civil rights movement and the "nation's churchiest region," the South had endured the wracking pains of civil rights reform and emerged better for them. The fires were therefore a huge embarrassment to conscientious white southerners. "These fires confirm the country's assumption that we're the worst of the lot," said John Egerton, a Nashville historian interviewed by *Newsweek*. "So even if people do burn down L.A. or trash the Bronx or comes to blows in Boston, they can still tell themselves they're better than the crackers down South." Hard-core racists, a dying breed in the region, were "far from making a successful second stand," read the article, which featured the story of George Selph, a sixty-seven-year-old white man near Fruitland, Tennessee, who saw a local TV report on the reconstruction of Salem Baptist Church. Selph loaded up his cooler with soft drinks early the following morning and lugged it out to the volunteers working at Salem. "I would love to be on the jury trying the folks who did this," he said. The article concluded, "For the South—Old or New—that's progress."[12]

One southerner actually wanted to see the church burnings as a local problem. In a letter to the editor of the *Charleston (S.C.) Post and Courier*, Robert Templin saw the burned churches as isolated targets of opportunity by "cowardly thugs"; but, "make no mistake," he cautioned, "these cowardly thugs will be emboldened and we will begin to see occupied buildings destroyed and a consequent loss of life." The solution lay in local officials attacking the problem at its root, "at the local scene and by the action of duly constituted local authority," up to and including the declaration of martial law, if necessary. "[A] clear demonstration of willingness on the part of our local leaders to solve our problems would serve the double purpose of improving the quality in our daily living and halting the constant encroachment of Big Government," he wrote.[13]

A Climate of Silence

Press releases in late June 1996 announced ongoing Methodist efforts to address the problem. The Southeastern Jurisdiction of Black Methodists for Church Renewal (BMCR) condemned the "racist, terrorist acts." The BMCR said it is "imperative that the Christian community be the catalyst in bringing about a change in the attitudes of those who seek to destroy church property as a means of venting their frustrations," and asked, "How can we as Christians sit back and see the destruction caused by racism and be comfortable in doing nothing?" Reverend Randolph Nugent, general secretary of the General Board of Global Ministries, stated: "In this instance, there have been suggestions that the church burnings are designed to interfere with voter registration efforts in the South. If that is so, then Global Ministries will also assist in organizing teams of volunteers for voter registration efforts in the affected communities." The Mississippi Religious Leadership Conference expressed sympathy for "those who have suffered through the destruction of that which is most sacred to the heart and life of the religious community—the very house of God," and said, "a climate of silence implies consent for those who would perpetuate such acts." Reverend Thom White Wolf Fassett, staff executive for the United Methodist Board of Church and Society, said the viciousness and hate represented by the fires "are a threat to every church, synagogue, and mosque in the United States."[14]

Voices of the Civil Rights Movement

The American Ethical Union (AEU) passed a resolution on June 22 denouncing the arsons. That same day, Andrew Young spoke out as a concerned Georgian trying to project an image of his region as a cosmopolitan place worthy of hosting the Olympics. The former mayor of Atlanta and cochairman of the Atlanta Committee for the Olympic Games told reporters:

> Martin Luther King always said that violence is the language of the unheard. And white leadership has turned its backs on the white poor. . . . The white poor have become so alienated that they have gotten into these militia groups, they've gotten into these racists cliques. . . . The people who are burning churches are, for the most part, people who ought to be in colleges, but whom society has left behind.[15]

Young, who worked with King in the civil rights movement in the 1960s, said that Georgia offered "incredible opportunities" and that southern states "have probably grown faster than any other part of the nation, and these people [poor whites] don't participate in that growth." Poor whites were "as alienated and isolated as the blacks in our big cities in the North who are left behind." Young, former U.S. ambassador to the United Nations, would be one of the torchbearers in Selma, Alabama, to carry the Olympic flame across the Edmund Pettus Bridge, site of one of the bloodiest demonstrations of the civil rights era; he would be joined by Joe Smitherman, the mayor of Selma, who was elected a few months before the demonstration and had been in office ever since. In March 1965, marchers had been beaten by police and state troopers when they tried to cross the bridge en route to Montgomery to demand voting rights for African Americans; the confrontation shocked President Johnson and the nation and led to the passage of the Voting Rights Act of 1965. Young said blacks and whites would cross the bridge together in 1996 so that the Olympic torch run "becomes not a celebration of the violence in Selma, but a demonstration that we have moved beyond that."[16]

In what was becoming a familiar refrain, the widow of Reverend Martin Luther King Jr. spoke out against the arsons and expressed her concern that many white pastors and religious leaders had been silent on the issue. Speaking to nine hundred people at the thirty-second annual luncheon of the Greater Columbia [S.C.] Community Relations Council, Coretta Scott King implored citizens to come together to build an emotional "infrastructure of compassion and concern." The founder of the Martin Luther King Jr. Center for Nonviolent Social Change also explained how her husband understood that civil rights can be legislated "but genuine sister- and brotherhood cannot because it comes from the heart." King also used the opportunity to encourage increased voter participation and to blast political leaders who worked to dismantle affirmative action policies.[17]

The Ultimate Treasure

At St. Patrick's Cathedral in New York, Cardinal John O'Connor denounced the burnings on June 30 before a congregation that included Reverend Al Sharpton and two other black ministers, Minister Deves Toon and Reverend Carl Redding. The Cardinal described the black church as "the ultimate treasure for black people," a refuge and beacon of hope. "To strike at that church is to strike at their pearl." Racism has no place in Christianity, which celebrates the shared humanity of all people, he said. It was the third Sunday in a row that Cardinal O'Connor had drawn attention to the fires from his pulpit; he had also sent letters to every parish in the Archdiocese of New York appealing for donations.[18]

The following day, two more churches burned. On July 1, a black church burned in a rural, wooded area about one hundred miles southeast of Raleigh, and investigators found evidence of arson. Authorities found what appeared to be traces of accelerant at St. James AME Zion Church near Maysville, North Carolina; one Raleigh television station reported that gasoline had been poured on the floor of the brick church, while another station reported that gasoline was poured along the outside walls and that Molotov cocktails were thrown through several windows. The heat from the fire melted upholstery to the church pews and scorched the floor, but the fire did not spread. That same day, arson severely damaged Sacred Heart Roman Catholic Church, a white church in the northeast Kansas town of Bonner Springs.[19]

Responses varied across the nation. In Washington, D.C., a group of ministers gathered at a ceremony at the United States Holocaust Museum to denounce the arsons. Greater New Bethel Baptist Church, one of the largest black churches in Dade County, Florida, had its grounds inspected for fire safety; inspectors recommended ways to safeguard the property and to establish emergency evacuation plans. In neighboring Broward County, religious leaders, led by Lauderdale Lakes councilman David Shomers, sought similar advice from law-enforcement officials. In Philadelphia, Quakers worked on several projects to aid victims of the fires.[20]

Coast to Coast, North to South

Amidst widespread concern over the arsons, the NAACP prepared to begin its eighty-seventh annual conference on July 6 in Charlotte. Leaders of the venerable civil rights organization—which had been troubled for years with financial and organizational problems—recognized that the church arsons had brought black Americans together in a way they had not experienced since the civil rights era; they also worried about how the organization could rebuild and attract not only middle-class members but also young members. During the conference, another black church burned—this time in the Pacific Northwest, in a rural area thirty-eight miles south of Seattle. The fire at

Pleasant Hills Missionary Baptist Church near Graham, Washington, was set late July 7 or early July 8 and caused about $80,000 worth of damage. There were signs of forced entry through a window; Reverend Forrest Hudson, the pastor, discovered the damage when he arrived to open the building for Sunday school.[21]

On July 12, police arrested a white man in connection with an arson fire that caused about $100,000 in damage to the church he attended in Garland, Texas, a suburb of Dallas. Investigators could determine no motive for the fire, which began in the Audubon Park Baptist Church's sanctuary. Four days later, flames engulfed a black Pentecostal church in Neptune, New Jersey. Officials believed that the fire at Greater Emmanuel Temple Pentecostal Church was probably started by lightning; however, such was the state of affairs in July 1996 that the New York Times felt obligated to report any church fire anywhere, intentional or not.[22]

On July 19, a repairman at the Evangelist Temple Church of God in Christ in Marianna, Florida, was arrested on arson charges. Two days later, a black teenager already jailed on a charge of setting fire to a vacant house in Greenville, Texas, admitted setting fire to a black church as well. Authorities charged eighteen-year-old Mark Anthony Young with arson at the Church of the Living God; the fire at the church caused $2,000 in damage just hours after an apparent arson caused $60,000 in damage at another black church in Greenville, the New Light House of Prayer. In Denton County, Texas, an arson fire caused an estimated $25,000 to $30,000 in damage at a white church, Bolivar Baptist.[23]

Shelling Peas, Talking Racism

Two days later, the New York Times broke news of what had happened in Dixiana, South Carolina, in the period preceding the arson at St. John Baptist in August 1995. Attacks on St. John, a former slave church established in 1765, had been going on "as long as anyone in this hamlet eight miles southeast of Columbia can remember." Young troublemakers, enticed by a local myth that the church was haunted, vandalized the site; older whites telephoned death threats to people associated with the church. In 1984, a group of whites shot out the church's windows during Sunday services, then returned later and scrawled "KKK" on the door, littered the pews with beer cans, chopped up the piano, smashed the crucifix, tore up all the Bibles, and took the sacrament cloth out of the sanctuary and defecated on it. In the church's small graveyard, they unearthed the coffin of a deacon who had recently died and ran over it with a truck. In 1985, Ammie Murray, the president of the county school board, formed a biracial organization, the Save St. John Committee, to address the attacks; someone smashed the skulls of her two dogs and tried to run her off the road. "I could see the hatred in their red faces when they tried to ram me off the road," said Murray, a white woman. She received threatening phone calls full of racial epithets; after moving from her rural home closer to Columbia, someone fired shots through the door of her new house. Some nights, especially on Halloween, sheriff's deputies staked out the church to protect it. One night in 1991, as Murray waited inside the church with local law-enforcement officers, a group of thirty whites smashed open the front door. As the leader of the group walked in, a deputy pulled out his pistol and held it to the man's head. "Ladies and gentlemen, come on in," Murray remembered the deputy saying. "Join us in prayer." In the dozen years before the arson, more than two hundred people had been arrested for vandalism at St. John, according to Sheriff James Metts of Lexington County.[24]

Only a few miles away, Klansmen often staged rallies at the home of the Grand Dragon of the South Carolina chapter of the Christian Knights of the Ku Klux Klan. Shelling peas on his front porch, Horace King told *New York Times* reporter Fox Butterfield: "I'm proud of standing up for the white race and I don't mind people knowing what I am. I never told anybody to burn a church. One day I will meet God and I don't want that on my head." Over the years, some members of St. John moved north and others were scared away; the membership shrank from one hundred to about twenty. But not all local whites were hostile. On Saturdays, about sixty people that Murray described as representative of the New South drove out to clean and restore the church. "They were people you'd never expect to see working together," she said, "half white and half black, Democrats and Republicans." One regular volunteer wore Confederate emblems on his hat. "Nobody said anything to him about them," Murray said, "but then one day I noticed they were gone." Sandra Johnson would later detail what happened at St. John in *Standing on Holy Ground: A Triumph over Hate Crime in the Deep South* (2002).[25]

The Demon at Its Core

An article in the magazine *In These Times* wondered if Americans grasped the implications of the church arsons. "[D]espite President Clinton's call for interracial solidarity and the belated appeals of white evangelical Christian leaders for racial reconciliation," wrote Salim Muwakkil, "many African Americans are left wondering whether white America grasps the meaning and significance of this reign of terror." The article quoted Morris Dees, of the Southern Poverty Law Center, who seemed to grasp the fires' significance after initially calling the fires the work of frustrated deer hunters. "This is the most serious thing that I think has happened in the South in years—far more serious than the dollar value of a church building that is burned," said Dees in July 1996. "Symbolically, the burning of black churches is more important than the [1993] World Trade Center bombing." The author seemed to agree with Ron Daniels, executive director of the New York–based Center for Constitutional Rights, who argued that the fires be labeled as acts of domestic terrorism; doing so would "mobilize the additional resources that critics argue are necessary to mount an effective probe." Daniels compared the church fire investigations to the investigation of the Oklahoma City bombing, which produced two suspects within weeks, and the World Trade Center bombing. "In New York City, when the World Trade Center was bombed, a piece of scrap metal was enough to indict ten men—that's how vigorous that investigation was," he noted. "Why haven't we seen those kinds of investigations with the church bombings?" he asked. Daniels echoed other critics who blamed a social climate rife with race-baiting for the upsurge in church arsons. "The black community—through the myths of welfare, affirmative action, and crime—has become the scapegoat for the pressures and dislocations that are being felt in the larger U.S. economy," he told Muwakkil. "We have a bunch of angry white males who are being told to look for answers in white supremacy and domestic terrorism. We must confront that." The author concluded, "Now that these burnings have awakened even the long-slumbering conscience of the white Christian right, a slender opportunity may be opening for more serious attempts at racial reconciliation"; until then, stopgap measures would have to suffice until the nation is ready "to confront the demon at its core."[26]

4

doubt

A number of people claimed that the story of churches burning across the na-
tion was not what it appeared to be. Some people saw in the fires a coordinated,
conspiratorial effort by white supremacists to terrorize black churches. Others
proclaimed that the spike in arsons did not represent a conspiracy, and some
believed that the arsons were in fact a "hoax."

Misguided Scrutiny, Unsettling Allegation

In mid-June 1996, at the height of the arson scare and just days before the
National Trust for Historic Preservation placed black churches on its endangered list, the *Miami Herald* reported the comments of some arson experts
and state fire marshals who said that church burnings were not new and that
black churches were not the sole target. The arson experts noted that about
six hundred churches serving all races are targeted by arsonists of all colors
each year; the article also reported that many black leaders disagreed with the
notion that the current wave of arsons was not notable.[1]

Calling the federal investigations of the fires "misguided scrutiny," *Time*
magazine highlighted several churches where members had been given the
third-degree after the fires. "They took me and the church treasurer to the
federal building, put us in two separate rooms and asked us all kinds of questions about our insurance policies, about whether we were behind in paying

off our mortgage or if any members of the congregation were angry," complained Reverend Sherron Eugene Brown, pastor of Macedonia Missionary Baptist Church in Fruitvale, Tennessee. "They were acting as if we had set our own church on fire." One member of Mt. Calvary Baptist Church in Bolivar, Tennessee—a seventeen-year-old girl—was reportedly taken out of her classroom by an FBI agent and questioned so roughly that she broke down in tears. "In most cases the lines of inquiry with regard to white supremacists are not being followed by any of the authorities," charged Reverend Dr. Mac Charles Jones, who, as associate general secretary for racial justice of the National Council of Churches, had visited dozens of arson sites over the previous three months. "The questioning has been about problems in the churches, about the pastors, about the churches' money or insurance. That was the first line of inquiry, and sometimes the only one." Jack White of *Time* found Reverend Jones's charge to be an "unsettling allegation" that could mean that hundreds of agents from the FBI, ATF, and state agencies had been chasing scapegoats rather than the real culprits. "Either the ministers are grossly exaggerating their mistreatment," White concluded, "or top Clinton-administration officials are not getting adequate information about

Fig. 4.1. Sign at Morning Star Baptist Church, destroyed by fire in 2006, Greene County, Ala. 2006. Photo by author.

their agents' conduct in the field." Black mistrust of federal law enforcement dated back at least to the days when J. Edgar Hoover's FBI zealously collected dirt on Martin Luther King Jr. instead of protecting civil rights workers, and many black southerners remained convinced that the fires had been set by organized hate groups—even if the Justice Department found no evidence of a widespread conspiracy. However, in a post–Ruby Ridge, post-Waco America, both of White's conclusions were equally plausible.[2]

The *Washington Post* reported on June 19 that those responsible for the church arsons were generally white, male, and young; usually economically marginalized or poorly educated; frequently drunk or high on drugs; and rarely affiliated with hate groups—but often deeply driven by racism. Few of the suspects were "hardcore hate-mongers" or belonged to organized groups, and much of what was happening appeared to be copycat crimes; only one alleged arsonist, Timothy Welsh, had direct ties to the Ku Klux Klan. "Little evidence has emerged to suggest a national or regional conspiracy, according to investigators," reported the *Post*. "But they point to a climate of underlying racism that encourages the arsonists to strike at African-American churches." The article acknowledged that while the ATF was investigating a roughly equal number of suspicious fires at white and black churches, "the burning of small, usually rural and isolated black churches in the South has a special historical resonance." Deval Patrick continued to insist that federal agents had yet to find a conspiracy and that little about the times, dates, and methods of the fires suggested a pattern; however, he quickly added, "The climate of racial division across the country is extreme." While black southerners understandably feared a conspiracy of terror by organized hate groups, Patrick noted that conspiracy was not the worst-case scenario. "The prospect of a conspiracy is a chilling thing," he said, "But the prospect that these are separate acts of racism is even worse." Not only would the legal cases against the arsonists "be harder to prove and more work," but also "an epidemic of individual terrorists . . . is tougher as a social problem," Patrick said. "Conspiracies are easier to crack because it's harder for two people than one to keep a secret," said one Treasury agent. "We spent eighteen years chasing the Unabomber and ended up charging a total loner." While black ministers and federal agents argued about the possibility of conspiracy, Noah Chandler of the Center for Democratic Renewal tried to reframe the issue, saying, "The conspiracy is racism itself."[3]

The story became more politically polarized on June 21, when the *Wall Street Journal* weighed in with an editorial that contended that President

Clinton had feigned recollections of church burnings in Arkansas in order to garner black support. In a June 8 radio address, Clinton had said that the wave of church arsons brought back "vivid and painful memories of black churches being burned in my own state when I was a child"; historians in Arkansas later pointed out that there had been no church burnings there during Clinton's childhood, or perhaps ever. The *Journal* interpreted this misremembrance as a deliberate attempt to gain political capital from an emotionally volatile issue. It seems more likely that Clinton was guilty of appropriating memory—that is, of tapping into a collective memory that extends beyond one's personal memory; one author has termed this personalized assimilation of secondhand experience "prosthetic memory." Churches *had* burned in neighboring southern states, and Clinton may have misremembered such incidents as having happened in Arkansas. For some, the president's words provided comfort; for others, they provided yet another example of his unscrupulous politicking.[4]

Conspiracy?

As investigative journalists and others probed deeper into the church arsons, the issue of conspiracy became a focal point. Indeed, the same day that the *Wall Street Journal* cast doubt on the president's memory, Lennell Bowden told a reporter that she did not believe investigators' conclusions that her church—Hills Chapel Missionary Baptist Church in Rocky Point, North Carolina—had burned down by accident. "Deep down, I feel like someone is doing this and they know what they are doing," she said. "Lord knows there's too many churches that's been burning." Like her, some felt that the arsons signaled a coordinated effort by hate groups to strike at the heart of black communities; however, a growing number of people began to view the media's reporting of the arsons as exaggerated and inaccurate. This latter group found the idea that white supremacists were conspiring to burn black churches less plausible than the idea that African Americans themselves—with the help of unquestioning and overly sympathetic media sources, many of them liberal and suffering a kind of white guilt for past injustices against blacks—were exploiting the issue to their own economic and political advantage. In this way, two very different conspiracy theories—one left-wing, the other right-wing—began to swirl around the issue of church arsons.[5]

Questions about whether or not the fires constituted an epidemic began in July 1996. A review of six years of federal, state, and local data by the Associated Press found that arsons were up at both black and white churches, but that the arsons had only random links to racism. "There is no evidence that most of the seventy-three black church fires recorded since 1995 can be blamed on a conspiracy or a general climate of racial hatred," quoted the AP. "In fewer than twenty cases racism is the clear motivation." The news bureau reported that insurance-industry officials said that the 1996 toll of church fires was within the range of what they would normally expect. A review of black church fires in eleven southern states indicated racially motivated arsons in from twelve to eighteen cases; unlikely racism in fifteen cases (including nine cases in which black suspects were named, and six cases involving sprees at both black and white churches); and unclear motivation in the remaining dozen or so cases.[6]

Doubt regarding the church fires centered on a July 8 article in the *Wall Street Journal* by Michael Fumento, who called the wave of arsons against black churches in the South "a myth, probably a hoax." Fumento, a freelance writer and contributor to the *Washington Times*, wrote: "There is no good evidence of any increase in black church burnings. There is, however, compelling evidence that a single activist group has taken the media and the nation on a wild ride." The article challenged the statistics compiled by *USA Today*, the newspaper that had first noted an increase in church arsons; Fumento claimed that *USA Today*'s own data belied the claim that a sharp rise in black church arsons had begun in 1994 and continued. "It [the *USA Today* data] shows that two of the states didn't start reporting data until 1993 and a third one didn't until 1995," he wrote. "Naturally, when they did, the numbers went up." According to the data, there were two more church arsons in 1994 than in 1990, and the same number in 1991 as in 1995; 1996 was unrepresentative because media publicity had generated copycat crimes, according to Fumento. He noted that federally collected data was "too scattered and sketchy to be useful," and claimed that data provided by the National Fire Protection Association actually showed a dramatic *drop* in the number of church arsons between 1980 and 1994. "While arson committed against a house of worship is a heinous crime," Fumento wrote, "it should be reassuring to know there have been far fewer recently than in years past." The author blamed the Center for Democratic Renewal, a group created to combat bigotry, for creating a story where none existed. "The CDR, it turns out, regularly ignored fires set by blacks and those that occurred in the early part of the decade," he wrote, "and labeled fires as arsons that were not—all in an apparent effort to make black church torchings appear to be escalating." The article questioned the

CDR's statistics for South Carolina, Georgia, Alabama, and Mississippi and blamed media hype for ballooning the issue. "Herein lies the ultimate irony," the article concluded. "By claiming there has been an epidemic of black church burnings, it appears that the CDR and the media may have actually sparked one. They have also fomented tremendous racial division and caused great fear among southern black churchgoers. What the Ku Klux Klan can no longer do, a group established to fight the Klan is doing instead."[7]

Citing *USA Today,* Fumento pointed out that a higher percentage of black churches are in economically depressed areas where arson is most common; therefore, he reasoned, it is not remarkable that many black churches burn. Further, Fumento reasoned, "black churches tend to be smaller and therefore must be more numerous" than white ones; Catholic churches, by comparison, are typically constructed of brick or stone "and almost all are predominately white." Therefore, he concluded, "the claim that black churches have been singled out for arson is questionable." While Fumento correctly noted that arson was difficult to prove in many cases, that the numbers involved were variable, and that "we can't easily infer motives" in arson cases, the logic in his article was severely flawed. It stands to reason that rural, poor churches might burn more often than affluent ones in urban and suburban areas; however, because black churches are often smaller than other churches does not mean that they are more numerous—in fact, they were not, with African Americans comprising only 12 percent of the population. Like African Americans themselves, black churches were a minority in the United States, and Fumento failed to acknowledge that a *disproportionate* number of them were burning across the nation. Still, Fumento's article received much attention, and he filled the triple roles of skeptic, naysayer, and whistleblower.[8]

Claiming to speak for those Americans who "are becoming more and more incensed at the constant complaints [by African Americans]," one writer used a July 10 letter to the editor of the *Charleston (S.C.) Post and Courier* as an opportunity to rail against black people and to remind them of their good fortune. "The truth is blacks are immeasurably better off in this country than they would have been if they had remained in Africa," he wrote. "Some black preachers and other liberals who make their reputations and, in many cases, their living by promoting tension between the races say things ten times more critical of whites and American society and get away with it. . . . And a lot of white Americans, particularly the less well educated, less successful ones, who feel more threatened by blacks, are beginning to resent it." An online article by Steve Macko echoed Fumento's findings, concluding: "Bottom line—the

Fig. 4.2. Police tape at Morning Star Baptist Church, destroyed by fire in 2006, Greene County, Ala. 2006. Photo by author.

church fires are not anything new. Just as many, if not more, white churches are the victim of arson as black churches. The recent wave of media attention has contributed to the number of 'copycat' fires. It is our editorial belief that when the 'red-hot' media attention dies down, so should the number of fires."[9]

William L. Pierce, the author of *The Turner Diaries* (a 1978 novel that inspired Timothy McVeigh in the 1995 Oklahoma City bombing) and founder of the white-supremacist group National Alliance, wondered how liberals knew that organized white racism was responsible for the church arsons. "I wasn't sure at all that the burnings were an organized effort by white racists," wrote Pierce in *National Vanguard*, the National Alliance magazine. "It may yet turn out that way, but I strongly doubt it: I know lots of white racists, organized and otherwise, and this just isn't their style." He continued:

> A boozed-up Ku Kluxer might have torched a black church here or there, but the multi-state string of burnings just doesn't have the feel of the work of a white racist organization. Apparently the secret police figured that too. They learned in school that most cases of arson are associated with insurance fraud, and so they began questioning black parishioners and asking black preachers to take lie-detector tests, causing an outburst of liberal indignation in the controlled media. The racist cops are blaming the victims! Quit investigating blacks and start arresting white racists![10]

Pierce noted that John Robison, Alabama state fire marshal, had investigated thirty-eight cases of arson or suspected arson at churches in Alabama since 1991 and had found no racial motives in any of them; in one case, a black minister at Antioch AME Church in Fort Deposit was charged with burning her own church. "The pastor was upset with the congregation about money," Robison said, "she felt she didn't get paid enough."[11]

Editorial Reactions from the Black Press

A writer for the *Cincinnati Call and Post* viewed the fires as acts of racism, desecration, terrorism, "historical erasure," and opportunistic predation. For Chimbuko Tembo, the talk of conspiracy and copycat arsons camouflaged the underlying issue of racially motivated hate crime. "Certainly it would be easier for the dominant society to discover and then distance itself from a group of early-man types who, unable to adjust to modern moral life, continue to practice social savagery," Tembo wrote. "Then it could keep its self-congratulatory illusion of having developed beyond the social and personal pathology of racism. But even those early-man types grow in a definite culture, as does the copycat arsonist. Their ideas . . . do not drop from the sky." For him, the fires were a violation of holy ground, a plunder of sacred space "to demonstrate the ultimate disrespect for what a community holds in the highest respect." He remained skeptical of aid from conservative groups such as the Christian Coalition—"it is like another version of the old racist trick of quoting the Constitution and Bible in public and whistling Dixie in the dark"—and felt that even liberal groups could not cure what ailed American society. "It is a continuing weakness of liberalism and conservatism to imagine that the problem is one of attitudes rather than issues of wealth, power, and status," Tembo wrote. "They confuse racial prejudice, an attitude of hostility and hatred, with racism: a systemic imposition of ideology, an institutional arrangement which turns attitudes of hatred and hostility into public policy and practice."[12]

A piece in the *Michigan Citizen* similarly shunned the outstretched hand of the Christian Coalition:

> No group more than the Christian Coalition has been responsible for taking the shame out of racism by spearheading the assault on civil rights, affirmative action, welfare and social programs. No group more than the Christian Coalition has led the assault against women's rights,

labor, environmental and lesbian and gay rights. No group more than the Christian Coalition has advocated a return to the "good old days" of pro-corporate, pro-rich, laissez-faire capitalism and Euro-centric cultural domination.[13]

According to the article, black Americans should not see the Christian Coalition as a true ally of black people or black interests. "Their goal is to use the church burning issue to gain legitimacy in the black community as a means of forwarding their right-wing agenda that is diametrically opposed to the historic struggle of Africans in America for civil rights and democratic rights."[14]

Ellen Hyatt of the *Tri-State Defender* struggled to find truthful reporting in the shrill discussion of conspiracy. "I have dozens of reports and articles in front of me as I analyze the issue," she wrote. "But wait a minute—it is quite difficult to discern which articles are the result of responsible reporting and which are sensational fanning of fiery attitudes favoring racial prejudice as a cause for the fires." On the other, she wondered, "[A]re the media dispelling racial concerns by reporting that church fires have always been prevalent— that, in fact, reports of the 'recent spate' of church fires is misleading?" Hyatt found it difficult to form opinions about the fires, concluding only "racial tension is out there."[15]

A writer for the *Philadelphia Tribune* saw the fires as a function of a larger crisis of spirituality in the United States. "One can be Baptist, Catholic, Episcopalian, Sanctified, Coptic, Jewish, Amish, Mennonite, Lutheran, Calvinist, Christian Scientist, Buddhist, Jehovah's Witness, AME or CME, Methodist, Pentecostal, Greek Orthodox, Mormon, or whatever and still lack spirituality," wrote Dorothy Leavell. "It is from this lack of spirituality that the current church burning crisis has sprung." She also interpreted the arsons as crimes against the poor. The *Portland Skanner* saw the arrest of a black suspect in the June 19 arson at Immanuel Christian Fellowship in Portland as newsworthy but tangential, as did Lawrence Dark, president of the Urban League of Portland. "Just because a black man set fire to a black institution is no reason not to keep the focus on racism as a motive in many of the other black church fires that have taken place across the country," said Dark.[16]

Lowcountry Burn

As Americans debated whether they should be concerned about the fires, more black churches burned. Fire destroyed Springhill AME Church in Dillon, South Carolina, at 1:00 a.m. on August 1. C. W. Rowell, the Floydale fire chief, was the first person on the scene. He reported that the walls were collapsing as flames engulfed the church; it took several hours and fifteen thousand gallons of water to extinguish the fire. Reverend Lee Davis, the eighty-four-year-old pastor of Springhill AME, cried while investigators sifted through the ashes of his church. Governor David Beasley visited the church that afternoon and asked for donations to help the congregation re-build. "This church is in great need of repair and love and compassion and prayer," the governor said. Robert Stewart, chief of the State Law Enforce-ment Division (SLED), said, "It will be treated as an arson unless and until it can be proven differently." Keeping all possibilities open, another spokesman of SLED, Hugh Munn, also noted that a series of thunderstorms with light-ning had moved through the area during the night.[17]

Attention remained focused on the South Carolina lowcountry in the following weeks as news of what had happened at Mt. Zion AME Church in Greeleyville and the century-old Macedonia Baptist Church in nearby Bloomville came to light. Gary Cox and Timothy Welch pled guilty on Au-gust 15 to charges of civil rights violations and other charges in connection with the burning of the two churches on June 20, 1995; they also admitted attacking Arthur Milligan that same month in Berkeley County. The Klan insisted it had nothing to do with the men's actions and asked that the South-ern Poverty Law Center's lawsuit against the Christian Knights of the Ku Klux Klan for inciting Cox and Welch to act be dismissed as a violation of its members' freedom of religion and speech. Pleased by the guilty pleas, U.S. Attorney General Janet Reno responded to growing skepticism about the apparent epidemic of arsons. "I think it is important to recognize that in some of them there appears to be racial motivation; in others there is not," she said on August 16. "Since the beginning of 1995 there have clearly been more [arsons at churches of all kinds]. . . . And I don't think it's just a matter of [better] reporting." A twenty-count federal indictment accused two other men, Hubert Rowell and Arthur Haley, of helping to burn Macedonia Bap-tist Church as well as a migrant camp used by Hispanic farm workers.[18]

On August 4, a *New York Times* article tried to make sense of the Christian Coalition's protestation of the arsons, which some saw as genuine and others saw as insincere. "Whatever the ifs, ands, or buts, the new racial rhetoric is beginning to win the religious right some grudging admiration." Referring to the Promise Keepers, the men's revival ministry founded by University of

Colorado football coach Bill McCartney, the article asked, "Could Martin Luther King Jr. himself have pictured the day when white men across the South (and elsewhere) would march into stadiums and pay $60 each to get a stern lecture on the need for biracial, brotherly love?" The article marveled at the reversal of the religious right, whether it stemmed from enlightened self-interest or not: "[W]hat a long road from 'segregation now, segregation forever' to Ephesians 2:14, the verse highlighted in this year's Promise Keepers literature: 'For He Himself is our peace, who has made the two one and has destroyed the barrier, the dividing wall of hostility.'"[19]

An August 5 article in the *New Republic* specified how the fires represented something new—not racism as usual. "[I]t takes hard work not to see these fires as confirmation that, for black people, the world hasn't changed much," wrote Cinque Henderson. "Yet, no matter how familiar this all may seem, it's actually something new." The perpetrators were acting in isolation, "without the cultural or political sanction they could have taken for granted a generation ago." The fires and the public response to them demonstrated how the South had changed, but they also demonstrated the difficulty of African Americans in finding a proper balance of activism and acculturation in a post–civil rights era United States. "To admit the possibility of [the guilt of a black arsonist] would be to dispel the notion of blacks as perfect victims, to cease playing upon whatever sentiments this country still has toward the faithful, long-suffering darky," wrote Henderson. "It is the companion piece to blacks as violent marauders, though neither stereotype takes account of the human middle where most blacks reside." The author also noted how the fires afforded new capital to civil rights leaders bypassed in the post–civil rights era. "For all their errors in making this episode something it isn't . . . [t]he world of the civil right leaders is a better world than that of the Republicans or the nationalists, and if this episode helps us to return to it, it might be worth a spin."[20]

The Great Church-Burning Hoax

The *Wall Street Journal* reported on August 9 that the National Council of Churches, which had until recently been struggling to raise money, had raised $9 million in the wake of the church arsons, and money continued to pour in at a rate of $100,000 per day. According to the *Journal*, the donations confirmed the generosity of the American public, who were appalled at the apparently blatant racism of the attacks, but they also highlighted some troubling aspects of charity. The article suggested that the NCC was not being completely honest about how the raised funds were being spent, with much of the money going to NCC efforts to combat racism, rather than directly to burned churches. The churches needed $8.5 million to rebuild; the NCC and other charities had taken in $18.2 million. How they spent the surplus became the core of controversy.[21]

In an August 10 press release, Diane Knippers, president of the Washington-based Institute on Religion and Democracy (IRD), accused the National Council of Churches of creating the church arson story and manufacturing evidence that black churches burn more frequently than white churches "to raise money for its leftist political agenda." Knippers claimed that the NCC had "jawboned" the church-burning issue into a national crisis. Knippers charged that the NCC used church arson "to justify its thesis that America is on the verge of a race war" and "to smear . . . conservative Christians as racists." Responding to charges that they "should apologize for perpetuating the great church-fire hoax," the NCC shrugged off the IRD's accusations, replying "we have nothing for which to apologize." In a letter of reply to Knippers's accusations, an NCC staff executive wrote that the council was not perpetuating a hoax. The NCC had "played an important part in bringing to the nation's attention the suffering of pastors and their congregations, isolated from one another and largely ignored before June," wrote Reverend Joan Brown Campbell, who said the NCC had a long tradition of standing against racism. "Anything less would betray our commitment to a gospel of justice and love."[22]

Knippers and Campbell interpreted the statistics available to them differently. The IRD spokeswoman cited three major media outlets that showed that arsons at black churches represented a fraction of the six hundred churches torched every year in the United States, and noted that church arson had declined dramatically from a figure of over 1,400 in 1980. Campbell maintained that fires at black churches had "increased dramatically and persistently over the past eighteen to thirty months"—a trend "all the more startling" because church burnings overall had declined in recent years. She noted that the rate of arson at white churches had remained constant in the past eighteen months, while the rate of arson at black churches "is more than double" the rate in previous years. She noted that more than sixty churches had burned between January 1, 1995, and June 30, 1996—"more than in the previous five years combined." Most significantly, Campbell noted that while the same approximate number of black and white churches had burned since 1995, black churches were burning in proportion to their number at four times the rate of white churches; she estimated a total of 63,000 African-American churches in the United States compared to approximately 235,000 white churches. In her reply, Campbell finished by noting that when words are uttered by people to scapegoat and demonize people of color, "they grant permission for evil to flourish. Good religion is always on the side of all that unites and makes us whole, all that integrates and heals."[23]

Despite such controversy, the general public continued to respond with empathy. National denominations continued to aid arson victims. Stan Hankins, associate for U.S. disaster response in the Worldwide Ministries Division of the Presbyterian Church (PCUSA), said that Presbyterians were expected to have contributed more than $232,000 by the end of the summer to an account set up the Presbyterian World Service to help rebuild the churches. The PCUSA set up different accounts to help both burned Presbyterian churches, specifically, and other burned churches too.[24]

Writers for the television show *New York Undercover*, a Fox Network police drama, decided to write an episode that would deal with the church-arson epidemic. Reggie Bythewood, a supervising producer and writer, worked with six other writers to create a story line about a cluster of church burnings in Harlem. Initially intended as a single episode, the story evolved into a complex exploration of racial motives in two parts, with the first episode kicking off the series' new season on August 29. Natalie Chaidez, another writer and coproducer, suggested that people involved in the show raise money to donate toward the rebuilding of burned churches; actors Malik Yoba and Michael DeLorenzo, along with other cast members, not only raised money but also held a ceremony on the show's gritty set, a mock-up of a lower Manhattan police precinct. Recognizing an opportunity for good charity and valuable publicity, executives at Fox and Universal Television followed the lead of *New York Undercover* and donated $10,000 to the NCC rebuilding fund. Another TV show, the WB Network's *7th Heaven*, explored the personal toll of a church burning on two families in a special episode on October 14.[25]

In New York, in the aftermath of an explosion at a Queens synagogue, Mayor Rudolph Giuliani signed into law a city council bill that strengthened penalties against desecration of houses of worship and religious property. Bill 174-A, passed 48–0 by the New York City Council, allowed for individuals convicted of defacing or damaging houses of worship, or the destruction of religious artifacts, to be punished by a fine of at least $500 and up to $2,000 or up to one year in prison or both; it also subjected violators to a civil penalty of up to $10,000. Responding to a blaze at the New Home Missionary Baptist Church in Sacramento, Governor Pete Wilson signed similar legislation in California. Reverend Troy Diggs, pastor of the First Baptist Tabernacle Church in Sacramento, said, "New Home Baptist was one of the oldest black churches in Sacramento. . . . We've got to remember that we are responsible for one another. . . . It's not necessarily a blow against me or the New Home church. It's a blow against the nation and what it stands for with freedom of religion."[26]

Writing on the weekend of Father's Day, one writer encouraged African Americans to unite in their vocal opposition to the arsons. "There can be no fires if we are vigilant, outspoken, and united," wrote G. Quinton Brathwaite. "[T]he powers that control such things want to believe that if they don't talk about this issue it will go away . . . [but] when you keep things in the dark they grow just as mushrooms do." The newspaper *Workers World* continued the American Communist Party's ongoing battle against the Ku Klux Klan

Fig. 4.3. Baptistry at Morning Star Baptist Church, destroyed by fire in 2006, Greene County, Ala. 2006. Photo by author.

in an August 29 article that noted a conspiracy between the blue suits (politicians), black robes (judges), and white sheets (Klansmen). "An independent anti-racist movement of working and oppressed people who despise the aims of white supremacy can truly beat back the Klan," the paper asserted.[27]

National Hysteria?

The crash of TWA Flight 800 and a pipe-bomb explosion at Atlanta's Olympic Park displaced the church arsons from the nation's headlines in late August; right-wing commentators took the opportunity to continue their offensive, which had begun in mid-June. "The reaction to recent church fires is becoming a full-blown case of national hysteria," wrote Jared Taylor in *American Renaissance*. "Even in a country that manages to work itself into a frenzy over virtually any rumor of white 'racism,' the whooping and roaring of the past two months have been a fantastic fuss over what may turn out to have been nothing at all." Taylor predicted: "Like all chest-thumping campaigns against 'racism,' this one will fade away. There will be no final accounting of how many millions of dollars it cost to catch each arsonist, or how much foundation money was spent on churches that turned out to have been burned by blacks. There will be a steady trickle of small, embarrassed new stories about how this massive manhunt collared a few pyromaniac nuts and drunk teenagers." Wesley Pruden of the *Washington Times* excoriated President Clinton for his "Burnt-Church Tour of '96"; the president, who "has been eloquent in his denunciation of those who would defile and destroy one of God's holy houses," could be more effective if he would "scorn the cheap politics, and tell it like it is." In public officials' rush to judgment and rush to get on the front page or the evening news in opposition to the crimes, "perspective is the first casualty"; anyone who "puts in a good word for the facts," like Pruden attempted to do, "risks being labeled racist, or worse, politically incorrect." Pruden's article was reprinted on the online Patriot Information Mailing List. Another writer, reminding her Internet readers of the conflagration at the Branch Davidian compound in 1993, said it was too early to know who was committing the arsons or why; however, she added: "What we do know is that President Clinton and Attorney General Janet Reno burned down a church . . . while the congregation was still inside. . . . That church, of course, was Mount Carmel, located just outside Waco, Texas. Members of that church were black, white, Asian, and Mexican-American." The author found Clinton's vocal opposition to the church arsons "terribly ironic" and "breathtakingly hypocritical." Heightened criticism of right-wing conspiracists led some members of the militia movement to consider volunteering to watch over churches to deter arsonists.[28]

Media scrutiny began anew in September and continued through the end of the year. Calling the arsons "a media-driven concoction," John Elvin of *Insight* faulted "the crisis-promotion specialists" for blowing the matter out of proportion. Because the burning of a church is such a vile and despicable act, it took a while for anyone to dare to suggest that the epidemic was non-existent, according to Elvin. "The only real conspiracy I found," Michael Fumento told *Insight*, "is on the part of the media to fabricate this thing." Citing new data compiled by the FBI and ATF, the *Washington Post* reported that more than one-third of the suspects charged in recent months were African-American. "The new figures show a far different picture than that created by television images of smoldering black churches this summer, which to many rekindled memories of the violent racism that accompanied the civil rights movement," said Pierre Thomas and Michael Fletcher of the *Post*. "It had all the makings of a great story: mystery, race, religion, and an eerie echo of the past," wrote Kelly Heyboer in the *American Journalism Review*. "Churches were burning in the South and, for a few weeks this summer, it seemed like 1963 all over again. . . . But was there an epidemic, or were the media manipulated into hyping a problem and giving a distorted picture of what lay behind it?" Michael Fumento, in an article for the October issue of *Commentary* magazine, tersely stated, "the 'epidemic of terror' was a sham."[29]

Characterizing the arsons as "firebombings," activists in Chattanooga, Tennessee, planned a march and rally "to beat back this violent white supremacy." The following day, a federal district court sentenced a black man in Portland, Oregon, to five years in prison for setting a June 20 fire that gutted the Immanuel Christian Fellowship Church. An inmate who had served time with Antoine Jamar Dean apparently offered him $10,000 to burn the church. The inmate planned to double-cross Dean and collect reward money, or perhaps to use the information as leverage for a prison transfer.[30]

On October 9, the U.S. Commission on Civil Rights released the findings of its six-state study of church arsons across the South. Mary Frances Berry, chairwoman of the bipartisan commission, said people who want to debunk the notion of church arsons as a racist plot are ignoring real, growing, racial friction. "Racial tensions are awful in many of these places," Berry said of Louisiana, Mississippi, Alabama, North and South Carolina, and Tennessee.

"Anybody who doesn't think there's a race relations problem has eyes that see not and ears that hear not." While investigators had linked racism to only 20 percent of the arsons solved so far, Berry said, the commission's field hearings across the South produced enough evidence to indicate a sharp rise in racial tensions. The commission noted ongoing segregation in many communities in schools and other public facilities reminiscent of the Jim Crow era. From Berry's perspective, the absence of conspiracy made the fires even more frightening. "The perpetrators could be anybody," she said. "They could be anywhere." She noted that federal law-enforcement statistics showed a disproportionate number of black church fires since January 1995; of the 230 church arson investigations opened since that time, 41 percent involved black houses of worship, although there were many fewer black churches in the South than white ones. "White churches have burned, but not for racial reasons," Berry said. "People who try to pooh-pooh this issue and say it is not important don't realize the racial tension that is out there. . . . There clearly are underlying racial tensions, and they manifest themselves in church burnings."[31]

From a similar perspective, one journalist noted that if there was perhaps too great a rush to infer the existence of a nationwide racist conspiracy, then the great rush to discredit this theory was doubly disturbing. Indeed, the eagerness of some critics to treat the arsons with skepticism blinded them to a larger truth: *someone* was burning churches across the nation, and many of them—a disproportionate number of them, in fact—were African-American churches. As another journalist phrased it, "emotion and intuition can cloud analysis, but they can also rescue it from abstraction and sterility." At the end of 1996, skeptics attempted to encourage the American public to respond to the church fires with their heads as well as their hearts; in doing so, they politicized the issue, centering much of their criticism on the Clinton administration and the left-leaning operations of the National Council of Churches. The debate over the scope and significance of the rash of church arsons at this point seemed to reflect as much about the superheated political climate of the Clinton era as it did about the intensity and frequency of hate crime at mid-decade.[32]

5

law

The government responded vigorously to allegations of white racists burning black churches in the South. When publicity about the church burnings reached a peak in June 1996, President Clinton created the National Church Arson Task Force.

Epidemic of Terror

By virtue of their histories and specific duties, certain federal agencies were involved in the arson investigations from the beginning. For example, the United States Treasury Department's Bureau of Alcohol, Tobacco, and Firearms (ATF) took a leading role in the investigations. The ATF had grown out of the federal government's attempts to confiscate contraband and fight gangsterism; early variations of this unique law-enforcement agency hunted down rumrunners, moonshiners, bootleggers, and mobsters in the late nineteenth and early twentieth centuries. Gun regulation governed the bureau. Then, in the mid-1970s, ATF lab technicians discovered that certain accelerants used in arsons were explosives as defined by the 1970 Explosives Control Act (ECA); because explosives were a kind of controlled weapon, the bureau began to dabble in arson investigation. In 1982, Congress passed the Anti-Arson Act, which amended the ECA to redefine destruction of property by fire as a federal violation. This act clarified the role of the ATF in using federal law to investigate incendiary fires. In this way, the purview of the ATF came to include arson as well as organized crime.

The Federal Bureau of Investigation (FBI) also dealt with arson, particularly as it related to hate crime. The FBI's role in civil rights investigations dated back to the passage of the Civil Rights Act of 1964 under President Lyndon Baines Johnson. Prior to the bill's passage, the Eisenhower and Kennedy administrations had taken the position that the protection of civil rights workers was a local responsibility, not a federal one. The murders of three civil rights workers—James Chaney, Andrew Goodman, and Michael Schwerner—near Philadelphia, Mississippi, in June 1964 prompted a sustained federal involvement in black civil rights; seven suspects were convicted under federal law of violating the constitutional rights of the slain activists. After passage of the Hate Crime Statistics Act of 1990, hate crime investigations were often initially conducted by the FBI in cooperation with state and local law-enforcement agencies, which would prosecute suspects under state statutes such as murder or arson. Once state prosecution had begun, the FBI would monitor the proceedings and report the final results to the Department of Justice for review.

ATF and FBI agents investigated the 1995 fires in western Alabama and

Fig. 5.1. Church arson in Bibb County, Ala. 2006. Photo by Hollie Huey, "Centreville (Ala.) Press."

western Tennessee. "We want to make sure that we pursue the cases," said Attorney General Janet Reno, "to make sure that we do everything right with the evidence, to take us where the evidence leads us." The NAACP requested the increased involvement from the Justice Department in a letter dated January 29, 1996. A spokesman for the Civil Rights Division of the Justice Department said on February 9 that the department had begun its inquiry in late December, before receiving the letter, but black leaders pressed government officials to step up their efforts. "I used to say in the 1960s about Governor George Wallace, and I think it can be said today about certain politicians, that Governor Wallace never bombed a church, he never pulled a trigger," said Representative John Lewis (D-Georgia). "But some of the things he said helped create the environment for other people to do it." A group of black ministers, some of them from burned churches, called for a more aggressive federal investigation into the fires on April 23. Congress scheduled a hearing regarding the arsons for late May as federal agents continued their investigations. Some black leaders criticized the Clinton administration for not investigating the fires intensely enough; others, while pleased at congressional involvement, expressed concerns that Republicans would use the hearing to mount political attacks on the White House. "On the one hand, I think there are some folks in Washington that are generally concerned about the bombings of these churches," said Reverend Dr. Mac Charles Jones of the National Council of Churches. "But there are others who are concerned about the presidential campaign. I think there are some folks who want to be in line with an administration-bashing thing."[1]

On May 22, the House Judiciary Committee heard testimony from several church members whose churches had been torched. The victims recounted the pain of what they had experienced. "I can't comprehend why someone would burn a house of God," said Reverend Algie Jarrett, pastor of Mt. Calvary Baptist Church in Hardeman County, Tennessee. Federal law-enforcement officials spent most of the morning proclaiming progress in closing cases and in punishing arsonists; they also promised more arrests in the future. Deval Patrick, assistant attorney general for civil rights, told the committee that the Justice Department had investigated fifty-seven instances of fire and vandalism at houses of worship in the last five years—half of which had occurred in 1996, and most of which had occurred at black churches. Patrick said that the nation was facing an "epidemic of terror," precipitated in part by an extreme atmosphere of racial hostility. He also testified that there was no evidence at the time to link dozens of church arsons in the previous six years to a regional or nationwide campaign, or to a single hate group. At the hearing, some black lawmakers criticized the Clinton administration for responding slowly and for failing to take the fires seriously. "I'm concerned about the politeness of this hearing," said Representative Sheila Jackson Lee (D-Texas). "You've got burned churches and burned history. You have intimidated communities." In a strange political turn, some Republicans defended the president's approach and offered more money and agents. "There's too much emphasis on Washington to clear up this arson problem," said Representative Fred Heineman (R–North Carolina), a former New York City police officer. "You have to start at the local level, in schools and in homes. . . . It's a twenty-year job to cleanse the young people now of prejudice and racism." Robert Stewart, chief of the South Carolina State Law Enforcement Division (SLED), seemed to agree. "If we locked up every church arsonist in America today," Stewart stated, "it's not going to stop it." Calling the hearing both timely and necessary, a *New York Times* editorial speculated, "the proceedings offered little solace for the worshippers who have been burned out of their churches—or the thousands of others who fear that they will be next." Another piece in the *New York Times* said: "The hearing was too short and the lineup of witnesses left much to be desired. But it was helpful nonetheless. It gave a little more exposure to a terrible problem that has had a difficult time catching the media, and therefore the public."[2]

The day after the hearing, U.S. Representative John Conyers Jr. (D-Michigan) and House Judiciary Chairman Henry Hyde (R-Illinois) penned and cosponsored the Church Arson Prevention Act of 1996. The tragedy of the church burnings needs a national response," explained Conyers. "This legislation will increase the number of prosecutions and make the job easier for investigators so that terrorists involved can be brought to justice." He noted that Deval Patrick, assistant attorney general for civil rights, had explained to him that the current law was "nearly impossible to use" to prosecute those who destroy religious property. Conyers further noted that the rash of church burnings in the South "has clear and unmistakable meaning for African Americans," explaining:

> Its symbolism is that of Ku Klux Klan cross burnings and is the sort of vicious racial hatred that led to lynchings of African Americans just a few short generations ago. It is the ugliest part of our nation's

past. . . . Fire is a powerful image for African Americans. It reminds us not just of Birmingham and the other churches burned in the 1960s, but of the crosses burned in our front yards and our houses burned when we tried to move into white neighborhoods. Just like thirty years ago when the Ku Klux Klan burned black churches to the ground in defiance of the civil rights movement, hate mongers are again burning our houses of worship as a way of expressing hate.[3]

The legislation marked an unequivocal, bipartisan response to the arsons. The Reverend Joseph Lowery, president of the Southern Christian Leadership Conference praised the Justice Department and ATF for pressing forward. "I sympathize with [Deval] Patrick's situation and his explanation that when you burn something down and the intelligence with it, it becomes extremely difficult to identify the cause and the suspects," Lowery said. "But if we can identify terrorists all over the world, you'd think we'd at least be able to come up with something at a little ol' black church." Lowery concluded by linking the church arsons with the perceived unfairness of affirmative action and the problems caused by NAFTA:

A climate of hostility has been created that has convinced white folks that the economic problems they are facing are results of affirmative action and preferential treatment to blacks and Hispanics. The reality is that we are not responsible for the country's economic problems. The system is. They should join us in trying to change the system that thinks nothing of exporting jobs down under and putting people out of work.[4]

To Worship in Safety

The next day, as President Bill Clinton and Republican candidate Bob Dole intensified their televised advertising campaigns for the upcoming presidential election, fire consumed the ninety-three-year-old sanctuary of the Matthews-Murkland Presbyterian Church in Charlotte, North Carolina. Investigators said the fire had been set but they did not say how or by whom. That morning, President Clinton changed the text of his weekly radio address to discuss the arsons, which he called depraved. "We must rise up as a national community and safeguard the right of every citizen to worship in safety," he said. "As president, I am determined to do everything in my power to get to the bottom of these church burnings as quickly as possible.

And no matter how long it takes, no matter where the leads take us, we will devote whatever resources are necessary to solve these crimes." The president announced the creation of a task force consisting of, among others, Assistant Attorney General Deval Patrick, Assistant Secretary of the Treasury for Enforcement James Johnson, FBI Director Louis Freeh, and ATF Director John Magaw. He asked the task force to report directly to him, instructed the ATF to inform churches of steps they might take to protect their properties, announced his support of Conyers and Hyde's bill, and announced the creation of a toll-free, twenty-four-hour hotline to report information related to church arsons. "Every family has a right to expect that when they walk into a church or synagogue or mosque each week, they will find a house of worship, not the charred remains of a hateful act done by cowards in the night," said the president.[5]

The creation of the National Church Arson Task Force (NCATF) was a major step. Cochaired by Patrick and Johnson, the NCATF concentrated the resources of the FBI, ATF, HUD, the Federal Emergency Management Agency (FEMA), the Department of Justice's Civil Rights Division, and the U.S. Attorneys' Offices; it also coordinated the efforts of local prosecutors, local law-enforcement officers, victim and witness coordinators, and others to investigate fires, bombings, and attempted arsons on, at, or near houses of worship. The attorney general also directed all U.S. Attorneys to form local church arson task forces within their respective districts. The creation of the NCATF was a decisive and significant move that symbolized the federal government's full commitment to the plight of endangered churches. It would become the first government agency to collect information on church arsons systematically. In its utilization and coordination of multiple government agencies, the NCATF foreshadowed the multiagency Department of Homeland Security, created after September 11, 2001.

The following day, Sunday, June 9, Attorney General Janet Reno met with ministers and civil rights leaders in Washington to discuss the fires as services continued without interruption at Matthews-Murkland in Charlotte. The Clinton administration continued to get mixed reviews from African Americans for its handling of the church arsons. Reverend Jesse Jackson, civil rights activist and president of Operation PUSH/Rainbow Coalition, criticized the way Clinton addressed black people. When the president addressed Jewish leaders, he would speak on issues such as anti-Semitism, synagogue burning, and Israeli security, Jackson noted; however, when the president addressed African-American audiences, he would talk about curfews for young-sters. Jackson was referring to a speech Clinton delivered in New Orleans at the Women's International Convention of the Church of God in Christ in which he discussed curfews to keep young people off the street late at night. "The president should be discussing church burnings, summer jobs, summer school, red-lining, corporate lockout, banks and S & L's, and telecommunica-tions," said Jackson, who had apparently missed the president's most recent radio address. The *Philadelphia Tribune* praised Clinton. "It's one thing to talk about how horrible hate crimes are," the paper noted, "it's quite another to take action. . . . The president's statements and action are signs that the government is taking these crimes seriously." Tough governmental action "will show racist terrorists that they are the ones who will be 'put back in their place'—in jail." Reverend William Hunt, pastor of Sacramento's Bethel Church of God in Christ, said, "The tone of the times seems to give a green light to things like this because government is not backing the cause of mi-norities anymore"; however, Hunt was pleased by Clinton's authorization of federally backed private loans to rebuild burned-out churches and his en-dorsement of community block grants to restore churches. "The government can do more with tax dollars than we could do raising funds at the local level." That same day, another church burned in Greenville, Texas.[6]

Some grew impatient with the pace of federal investigations into the crimes while others clung to the idea of conspiracy. "We get 'we're working, we're working,' but they aren't finding much," said Reverend Daniel Donaldson of Salem Baptist Church in Tennessee. "There's no question in my mind that there's a conspiracy going on in these church burnings," said Spiver Gordon of the Southern Christian Leadership Conference. Still others looked to the federal government for more involvement. "If it means the National Guard, so be it," said Reverend Dr. Mac Charles Jones. "If it means declaring a state of emergency, so be it."[7]

A Political Event?

Officials in Florida, mindful of sixty-one arsons there in 1990 and 1991 and thankful that the Sunshine State had been spared in the latest rash of fires, offered to share the state's unique computerized arson file with other gov-ernments. Meanwhile, President Clinton visited Mt. Zion AME Church in Greeleyville, South Carolina, for the dedication of its new building. The president spoke of his native Arkansas and of a similar country church where his great-grandparents were buried; he also spoke of Jim Crow segregation and of lynchings. He encouraged "every citizen in America to say we are not going back, we are not slipping back to those dark days." Prior to the president's speech, Reverend Jesse Jackson delivered a spirited sermon with a very different message. Jackson said a "kind of anti-black mania, a kind of white riot" had swept the nation. He said it was not just Klansmen in white sheets who spread racial hatred but also legislators "in blue suits who use thinly coded, veiled race signals when they say 'welfare' and 'crime' and 'three strikes' and 'end affirmative action.'" Praising bipartisan efforts in Congress to address the issue, President Clinton encouraged Americans not to politicize the church burnings. "We must keep this out of politics," he implored. Nonetheless, Republicans criticized Clinton for his visit to Mt. Zion AME. Calling the appearance "a political event," South Carolina governor David Beasley said, "I only hope that the President is sincere." Haley Barbour, the Republican national chairman, said the visit was motivated by "transparent, shameless, politics."[8]

William Safire, on the other hand, admired the president's speech. "[A] pulpit in a black church brings out the best in Clinton," he reported. The editorial desk of the *New York Times* seemed pleased too, writing, "Congressional hearings on the wave of arson against African-American churches—together with strong steps by the Clinton administration—have finally brought the problem the attention it deserves. . . . President Clinton's personal intervention seems to have energized his bureaucracy." The black press also praised Clinton while continuing its vigilance. One black journalist noted with concern a renewed interest in southern heritage. "The *New York Times* reported recently that, whereas formerly it was not cool to be proud of the Confederacy, in the past five years hundreds of Confederate clubs have sprung up in the South to rehabilitate traditional southern culture," wrote Ron Walters in the *Washington Informer*. "One would have to be very naïve to believe that this is not associated with the attempted restoration of white supremacy in the South, through the traditional instrument of rural terrorism." Walters noted that the NAACP had launched "security programs" to protect a few churches, and that there was talk of contracting the Nation of Islam to provide security at black churches. "As a community, we must call or write President Clinton and Attorney General Janet Reno, demanding that until these church burnings stop they must remain at the top of law enforcement's agenda throughout America," wrote Rosa Reed in the *Miami Times*. "We cannot afford to allow the little racial stability that exists in America to be destroyed by the ultra-right-wing." Some editorialists continued to jab Clinton for "theatrical obfuscation and pandering." James Glassman wrote in the *Washington Post* that a fire "makes an excellent political smoke screen."[9]

Seven governors and one lieutenant governor joined President Clinton in the Cabinet Room of the White House on June 20 to discuss the problem. The meeting represented a bipartisan attempt to intensify efforts to prevent church burnings. The president ordered the Federal Emergency Management Agency (FEMA) to join the efforts of the Justice and Treasury Departments by helping communities to form church-watch programs to deter arson. He also said it was important to speak out against the church burnings despite the risk of copycat crimes. "I think this is a place where nearly 100 percent of

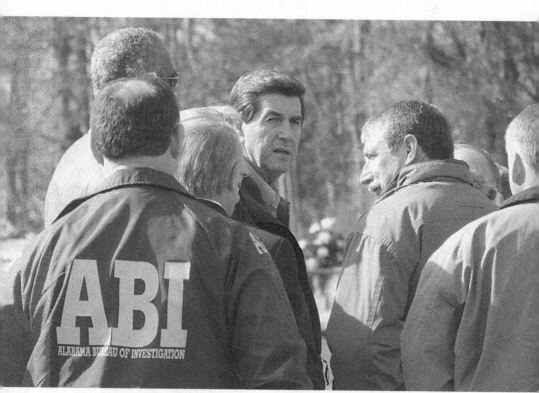

Fig. 5.2. Governor Bob Riley confers with investigators in Bibb County, Ala. 2006. Photo by Hollie Huey, "Centreville (Ala.) Press."

Americans are in accord," he said, "and I think we just need to make our voices heard and we need to do the right things." After the meeting, Vice President Al Gore said: "Part of the message coming out of today's meeting to anyone who would burn a church is, 'You will not win.' The houses of worship will be rebuilt. And in each case, the community will be stronger in the process." At the same time, the Department of Housing and Urban Development sought legislation, cosponsored by Senators Edward Kennedy (D-Massachusetts) and Lauch Faircloth (R-North Carolina), that would allow HUD to use existing money to guarantee up to $10 million in private loans for rebuilding churches damaged by arson or terrorism. The Senate measure would double to twenty years the maximum sentence for church arson; like the House bill introduced by Congressmen Conyers and Hyde, the Arson Prevention Act of 1996 would make it a federal crime to damage religious property because of racial hatred, ethnic hatred, or religious bias. Representative Jim Lightfoot (R-Iowa) also introduced legislation in the House providing $12 million to the ATF to be used specifically to investigate and stop church arsons. The *New York Times* praised the efforts of Democrats and Republicans who came together to address the church burnings, noting, "Such unanimity has become increasingly rare in an archly partisan Washington."[10]

Black ministers speculated as to why the church burnings were occurring. "It is significant that all of this began after the Million Man March was organized and occurred," said C. Nation Edwards, pastor of the Little Friendship Baptist Church in Mount Vernon, New York. "It is an attempt to hit back at black men in the center of their lives." Another minister said the O. J. Simpson verdict may have prompted the arsons, and yet another situated the arsons within a larger matrix of the Republican-controlled Congress's "Contract with America"; the controversial book *The Bell Curve: Intelligence and Class Structure in American Life* (1994) by R. J. Herrnstein and C. Murray; and the increase in prison building, welfare cuts, health care changes, education cuts, and gerrymandering. Reverend Al Sharpton called an Emergency Ministers' Summit for June 26 at Mother AME Zion Church in Harlem. A deacon at Dexter Avenue Baptist Church—the former pastorate of Martin Luther King Jr. and a key church in the civil rights movement—faulted Republicans in Congress. "These far-right groups don't really help the situation," said Richard Jordan in Montgomery, Alabama. "The Newt Gingrich tone of voice never helped, the Bob Dole tone of voice doesn't help. We need a more moderate tone."[11]

Senate Hearings

On June 27, the U.S. Senate Judiciary Committee held its own hearings on church burnings. The chairman, Senator Orrin Hatch (R-Utah) characterized the arsons as a First Amendment issue. "When one examines the founding documents of our great country, one will find that religious liberty is the first freedom protected in the Bill of Rights," he said in his opening statement. "[A]rson attacks on any house of worship, and especially those motivated by bigotry, are attacks on the very idea of America." Comparing the arsons to the persecution of Mormons in the nineteenth century, Hatch—as a Mormon—empathized with the victims of church arson. Paraphrasing the philosopher George Santayana, he concluded, "We must remember history because, as the saying goes, if we do not, we may be condemned to repeating it over and over again." Senator Joe Biden (D-Delaware) expressed surprise that such crimes could occur in 1996, but noted there is "almost an intuitive logic to [church] burning" because of the central role of churches in African-American communities; that is, if one wanted to strike at the heart of black communities, then attacking a church was effective in a coldly Machiavellian way. "Like all hate crimes, these fires send the message of exclusion," Biden said. "They say to those that congregate in those black churches, 'you are different,' 'you don't belong,' and 'we reject you.'" The senator from Delaware took little comfort in the apparent lack of conspiracy. "Somehow the idea of a tight-knit group of racist fanatics, though ugly and horrible, seems not quite as horrible as the picture that appears to be beginning to come into focus here, which is a substantial number of mean-spirited, ugly people, perhaps unconnected to each other or with other organized groups, who somehow think it is legitimate to burn to the ground African-American places of worship as an expression of their hatred." He continued:

> These fires stand as a stark reminder. America is not yet the national home that we all want it to be where all Americans can live together, free from fear, discrimination and hatred, and where all Americans can live with honor, dignity, and equality. We would all like to believe that we live in a color-blind society—I have heard that so many times lately—where tolerance always wins, where race doesn't matter. But we don't live in a color-blind society, tolerance does not always win, and race still matters in America. . . . If we pretend that we need not be vigilant and if we accept the myth that we have a color-blind society, and if we legislate and decide court cases based on these assumptions,

then hatred and intolerance will grow and spread like the fires that are being set.[12]

In addressing the church fires, Biden seemed to allude to efforts to dismantle affirmative action in the interest of creating a "color-blind" society.

Senator Patrick Leahy (D-Vermont) situated the arsons in a larger context. "From church burnings to the Unabomber to international and domestic terrorism, we have seen a terrible series of recent events. Our basic social fabric is being tested," he said. "Each of us, especially those of us in government, need to ask ourselves what more we can do to prevent these violent incidents and to make our democracy and our communities more inclusive rather than less." Leahy noted that if destructive acts could spread through imitation, then so too could positive ones. "Burning these churches is an assault on everyone's family and community," said Lauch Faircloth. Ted Kennedy, who coauthored legislation with Faircloth, was impressed by the outpouring of generosity from all sectors of the country. "[It] ought to be reassuring . . . that people do really care, that individuals do feel that pain and anguish of so many of those that have seen the destruction of their place of worship." He concluded, "Out of the ashes of the burned churches, let us build a new united spirit. Let us condemn bigotry in every form, wherever and whenever and however it appears."[13]

At the Senate hearing, the ATF and Justice Department presented evidence of incidents of violence at houses of worship in thirty-five states since 1990. The committee heard testimony from Deval Patrick and James Johnson, assistant secretary for enforcement at the Treasury Department, as well as Reverend Dr. Mac Charles Jones (who related that part of the initiation rite for "the Aryan factions" near Clarksville, Tennessee, was "to burn a church, burn down a home of a black family, or 'lynch a nigger'"), Ralph Reed, and Reverend Jonathan Mouzon, pastor of Macedonia Baptist Church in Manning, South Carolina. Senator Spencer Abraham (R-Michigan) sat on the committee because his own church in Livonia, Michigan, had accidentally burned to the ground a few months before the hearing.[14]

The following day, the House approved Congressmen Conyers and Hyde's legislation. President Clinton designated $6 million to fight church burnings on July 2. The president said he was ordering the Justice Department to provide the money to local police jurisdictions in areas considered at risk for arson. The money was to be used to hire more officers, to install security equipment, or to hire private security guards. The president urged Congress to approve the funding quickly, and also pledged to sign the House bill. On July 3, the Church Arson Prevention Act went into effect, amending Title 18, United States Code, Section 247, to strengthen criminal law against church burning and desecration. The law removed a cumbersome interstate commerce requirement, eliminated the minimum $20,000 damage criterion, and increased the sentence to twenty years for arson where an injury occurs.[15]

In a press release on July 9, Congressman Conyers, who also served as dean of the Congressional Black Caucus, said "racial hatred has clearly been the spark to ignite many of the fires." He praised the efforts of both the Justice Department and President Clinton. "We have to catch and punish the perpetrators, but we also need to look underneath the violence for the cultural motivations that have divided us," he said. "We need to use the tragedy of the church fires as an opportunity to take a long, careful look into the heart of this nation. It is time for a national dialogue on the state of race relations." Legislative efforts to address the fires continued in the following months. Representative Rob Filner (D-California) stated in August that legislation he cosponsored with Cynthia McKinney (D-Georgia) to prohibit insurers from refusing to cover churches due to threat of arson should come to a vote before Congress adjourned in October. The U.S. Commission on Civil Rights announced in October that its public forums revealed an alarming rise in racial tensions. "It was like turning over a rock and seeing what is beneath it," said chairwoman Mary Frances Berry. "It simply turned out that those fires were an indicator of problems in the community." The commission urged southern governors to meet with them on the issue.[16]

Still struggling to recover from the public-relations disaster of the 1993 Branch Davidian standoff in Waco, Texas, the ATF continued to draw fire for its handling of the church arsons. "The way the ATF treated African Americans in its own ranks leaves no doubt that the agency itself has been part of the problem," reported a July 11 editorial in the *Washington Post*, which reported the settlement of a $4.6 million class-action lawsuit that paid African-American ATF agents for discriminatory treatment in hiring, promotion, assignment, disciplinary procedures, and day-to-day workplace interactions, which included liberal use of the word "nigger." *Freedom*, the magazine of the Church of Scientology, credited ATF agents with not only participating in the "Good Ol' Boy Roundup" but also *creating* the annual event in Tennessee, where "bigotry was the order of the day and racism was in full bloom." *Freedom*, which reported that thirty-four white suspects and no black suspects had been arrested in connection with arsons at southern black churches since 1990, credited ATF agents with designing a "Pocket Nigger" T-shirt with artwork depicting a small black child peering out of a pocket for the 1992 roundup, and wondered why the ATF had not been dismantled, with its functions assigned to other agencies such as Customs and the FBI.[17]

Perfect Victims

As Cinque Henderson noted in the *New Republic* on August 5, the crimes were novel—not a continuation of civil rights–era terrorism. The South had progressed, and its people had progressed with it. The arsonists were committing these crimes "in isolation, without the cultural or political sanction they could have taken for granted a generation ago." The fires were proof of this change, as poor, white, uneducated men left behind by this regional progress "are finding the world they inherited fast shrinking around them"; accordingly, "the story here may be not the victims but the victimizers." Furthermore, Henderson believed that African Americans stood to gain much by maintaining the illusion of a racially regressive South:

> One crucial piece of information has been studiously avoided: one-third of those indicted in the burnings have been black. Jesse Jackson, sensing the damage this could inflict on the spin, flew to Tennessee to defend a black minister suspected by Bureau of Alcohol, Tobacco, and Firearms agents of torching his own church.[18]

In the author's view, the fires provided new capital for civil rights leaders bypassed in the post–civil rights era. "When did anyone last hear from Roger Wilkins," Henderson wondered. "When did anyone last see Andrew Young . . . ?" The author concluded by noting that the nation might benefit from the rediscovery of civil rights leaders who, on the one hand, now operated in older paradigms, but who, on the other hand, had provided much-needed moral guidance.[19]

Editorial perspectives continued to resound in the black press. *Third Force* praised the Clinton administration for its proactive involvement in stopping the crimes, but noted that at the local level, "where the investigation takes hold or disappears," nothing of substance had happened. "There still is not a single civil rights prosecution ongoing in any of the recent attacks," the paper noted, worrying that authorities had deflected their investigations from the key issue of race. "At times, even in the face of what appears to be overwhelming evidence that racism is at the core of the attack, other explanations are suggested. Even in cases where white perpetrators have traveled miles off major pathways to get to secluded black churches—passing white churches on the way—the attacks are attributed to youth vandals, drunken vagrants, or pyromaniacs." The *Washington Afro-American* regretted that the arsons "were permitted to continue far too long before they became a Clinton administration focus," but threw its support to President Clinton in the upcoming election nonetheless, stating, "While Mr. Clinton's disappointments cannot be ignored, such first-term foul-ups do not compare with what we fear would be the case should Bob Dole be elected as President with a conservative Republican majority in Congress." *Ebony* magazine agreed with the notion that the arsons constituted domestic terrorism. The *New Pittsburgh Courier* focused on South Carolina, where twenty-seven churches had burned since 1991—more than in any other state. South Carolina "is proud of the 'New South,' proud of its many black elected officials and historically black colleges and universities," the paper reported. "But the Ku Klux Klan feels free to have public rallies, the Confederate flag flies from the state house, and 'The Redneck Shop,' a store that sells white racist paraphernalia, has opened up for business in recent years." The *Courier* stated that blacks and whites alike in South Carolina denied the prevalence of church burnings in their midst because the arsons went to the core of a problem that people do not like to discuss: racism.[20]

Ecumenical and Secular Response

A wide variety of church denominations continued to respond to the attacks. Like Methodists, Presbyterians continued to aid burned churches nationwide. According to Stan Hawkins, associate for disaster response in the Worldwide Ministries Division of the Presbyterian Church of the United States of America (PCUSA), Presbyterians contributed an estimated $232,000 to an account set up by Presbyterian World Service for donations; thousands of dollars in additional contributions went directly to the Charlotte Presbytery and the Sheppards and Lapsley Presbytery in Alabama, where churches had burned. Westminster Presbyterian Church in Cedar Rapids, Iowa, developed a program it called "Adopt a Burned Church," in which it "adopted" Matthews-Murkland Presbyterian Church and raised $1,400 in goodwill offerings. According to Reverend Herbert Isenberg, pastor of Westminster Presbyterian, the church pioneered the adoption effort after the church session researched the church arsons on the Internet and realized that not everything being said about the church burnings was factual. Political candidates were "making hay" over the issue of church arsons while they had the opportunity; direct donations circumvented the politicization of the arsons.[21]

Financial contributions increased exponentially in late summer and early fall. With new grants, the Burned Churches Fund Grants Committee of the UMC allocated $2.3 million for thirteen more churches in October 1996. As of October 16, the fund had received $4.7 million in cash donations for the restoration of thirty-four churches.[22]

Assistant U.S. Attorney General Deval Patrick, who had been commuting to Boston on weekends for two years to be with his wife and two daughters, announced his resignation in November. Looking for a job in the Boston area, Patrick was pensive as he left his post. "The increase in the rate of attacks on black churches—particularly in the South—was significant and had to be faced. As we have continued this investigation, we have seen many instances of racial hostility or religious bigotry driving these fires," he said. "We are a deeply diverse American society. American democracy is going to depend on people coming together across all those differences and being united by common civic values. The way that happens . . . is by overcoming our suspicion and occasionally even the hatred that we bring to the table by virtue of those differences." It is the ability to see across racial and ethnic lines "that makes the difference in the ability to see and imagine each other as fellow citizens with a stake in each other's struggles," he said. "That issue will become even more significant as this country continues to become more diverse and more culturally complex."[23]

In the December issue of the *American Spectator*, Michael Fumento again criticized *USA Today* for overreporting the church arsons when he pointed out that the newspaper had enjoyed not one but two journalistic coups related to the fires: first when it broke news of racially inspired arsons across the nation, and then again when it debunked its own story. "The scoop brought overnight credibility to a newspaper long mocked by its rivals," said Fumento, reminding his readers that critics had long derided *USA Today* as a fluff rag with little journalistic credibility. From Fumento's perspective, the paper had been irresponsible in spreading hype about the fires. "The supposed hero of the story is also its goat," he wrote. He was particularly critical of the Center for Democratic Renewal, which furnished statistics related to the arsons: "The CDR had systematically ignored fires set by blacks and those that occurred in the early part of the decade; it had also labeled some fires as arson that clearly were not—all in an apparent effort to make black church torchings appear to be an escalating phenomenon." Again, Fumento provided lots of information to prove that white racists were not primarily responsible and that the numbers of fires had been exaggerated; again, his logic was slightly wonky. Fumento worried that *USA Today* had compared incomparable data sets consisting of both accidental and intentional fires, which in turn led to a reporting error. "Apparently, none of *USA Today*'s reporters or editors realized that crimes are always underreported," he wrote. "According to the Bureau of Justice Statistics, 'About 35 percent of all victimizations, 42 percent of violent victimizations, 27 percent of personal thefts, and 33 percent of all property crimes were reported to police.'" If accurate, these percentages would indicate that an even greater number of church arsons may have occurred than had been reported, and that the number of church arsons that made the news was likely *under*reported rather than overreported, as Fumento claimed. He finished the article by noting that *USA Today* had similarly hyped news of an alleged epidemic of missing children in the mid-1980s.[24]

New Year, New Fires

In January 1997, the National Church Arson Task Force issued a preliminary report to President Clinton. The report conveyed great progress in the battle against church arsons. According to its report, the NCATF had opened investigations in 328 church arsons occurring between January 1, 1995, and January 7, 1997 (not including acts of vandalism or other desecration). "As a result of the exceptional partnership among federal, state and local law enforcement," the report read, "many of the incidents investigated have been solved, mainly by a combination of federal and state arrests and prosecutions." Arrests of 143 suspects had been made in connection with 107 fires; this rate of arrest (33 percent) was double the arrest rate for arsons in general (16 percent). Three-quarters of the defendants arrested in this two-year period had been arrested in the seven months since the creation of the NCATF, the report noted. Forty-eight defendants had been convicted; the remaining cases were pending trial. Notably, three-quarters of the black church fires had occurred in the South. The report detailed prevention and rebuilding efforts, outreach programs of federal law-enforcement agencies, and legislative measures. "Burning a church, whether racially motivated or not, implicates federal anti-arson and civil rights laws and warrants swift and certain investigation and prosecution. . . . This is one of the largest series of arson investigations in history and the largest current civil rights investigative effort." The NCATF would release four more reports annually, each building on the last, each conveying progress in efforts to stop church arson between 1997 and 2000.[25]

The fires continued in 1997. St. John the Baptist Roman Catholic Church in Manhattan burned on January 10; investigators did not know what or who had caused the flames that flared out from the fire's starting point, a confessional booth. "What caused it?" Reverend Francis Gasparik wondered. "I almost don't want to know because every answer is so damned painful." The church, across the street from Penn Station and a central subway hub, serviced a number of New York City's homeless persons and transients, and had just completed years of renovation work. Father Francis expressed hope that the fire was one of those accidents that sometimes befall buildings due to age or bad luck.[26]

Had an arsonist been arrested for the fire at St. John, then he would have faced severe new penalties for his crime. Congressional efforts to deter the fires greatly changed how arsonists were punished. For example, four teenagers were charged in federal district court in Raleigh, North Carolina, on January 23 with conspiring to destroy the St. James AME Zion Church in Maysville by hurling Molotov cocktails at it on June 30, 1996. The fire melted upholstery on the pews and scorched the floor but did not destroy the church. One of the teenagers, an eighteen-year-old, was considered to be an adult; the rest were considered juveniles. Under the new laws, eighteen-year-old Matthew Neal Blackburn faced up to 105 years in prison and a $770,000 fine, plus the costs of repairing the damage, estimated at $55,000.[27]

The nation's largest association of black churches, the Congress of National Black Churches Inc., announced on January 27 that it had established a fund to prevent arson and rebuild burned churches. The Eli Lilly Foundation in Indianapolis would provide $6 million of the fund's $12 million; the rest would come from public- and private-sector "partners" through fund-raising efforts. Bishop John Hurst Adams, founder of the organization, had determined that when congregations attempted to rebuild, there was typically a gap of about $150,000 between what was paid by insurance companies and the cost of rebuilding. The fund was intended to fill the gap, and the Congress of National Black Churches hoped to help some fifty black churches to rebuild.[28]

Reverend Dr. Mac Charles Jones, former director of the National Council of Churches' Burned Churches Project, died in March at age forty-seven, just one week before the Justice Department's Community Relations Service provided supplementary testimony to the House Judiciary Committee on March 19. The NCC continued the work Jones had begun. The NCC announced on May 23 that another seventeen churches would receive a total of $464,200 in grants from its Burned Churches Fund, completing the first phase of its assistance to arson victims. In early June, the NCC also announced its decision to publish *The Fire This Time: Burning Churches and an Ecumenical Response*, a 128–page paperback volume dedicated to the late Reverend Jones, a Baptist minister. According to Norman Hjelm, editor of the book and former director of the NCC's Faith-and-Order Commission, the intent of the book was to reflect on the solidarity that churches had shown toward those directly affected by the fires. More than one thousand civic and religious leaders participated in a NCC conference June 8–10, 1997, in Washington, D.C., not only to discuss progress and plans but also to honor Reverend Jones. Returning to the nation's capital on the anniversary of its initial 1996 meeting on the arsons, the NCC—the nation's leading ecumenical organization—opened the convocation at Shiloh Baptist Church with a tribute to the witness of Reverend Jones. Convocation participants included Vice President Al Gore, Attorney General Janet Reno, Treasury Secretary Robert Rubin, HUD Secretary Andrew Cuomo, Reverend Jesse Jackson, and Representative Maxine Waters (D-California).[29]

Prosecutors reached an agreement with Mark Anthony Young on March 24 to avoid trial on two federal arson charges stemming from the fires in Greenville, Texas, the previous summer. The eighteen-year-old pled guilty to one count of arson; the second was dismissed. The federal district court judge sentenced the mildly retarded teenager to time served and placed him on supervised release for three years. A couple of days later, a Nevada man became the first person prosecuted under the 1996 Church Arson Prevention Act. Richard Morrison, a twenty-three-year-old resident of Henderson, admitted he set fire to the Church of Christ in Henderson because its congregation was mostly black. Morrison was sentenced to a prison term of sixty-three months, the maximum term allowed by law, plus payment of $1,600 in restitution for damages. The following month, ministers unveiled a ten-foot-high, white marble monument on the campus of Allen University, a historically black college affiliated with the African Methodist Episcopal (AME) Church in Columbia, South Carolina. Intended as a memorial to the 200-plus black churches that had burned since 1990, the monument bore the names of burned churches and the dates they were torched, inscribed in black, with an orange-and-black image of a burning church etched on its face. The monument also bore a simple inscription that conveyed frustration with investigation efforts: "We are not satisfied."[30]

On May 4, two white men became the first defendants in Texas to be convicted under the new federal laws designed to combat church arson. The two men, Robert Allen Stillman and Randall Elliot Moore, pled guilty to federal arson charges and other charges in conjunction with the destruction of the Macedonia Baptist Church in Ferris on March 22. When asked why he wanted to burn the church, Stillman replied, "'Cause it was a nigger church." Editorials in both the *New Pittsburgh Courier* and the *Michigan Chronicle* published after the Texas indictments called for more federal disclosure of similar cases. Later that week, an arsonist burned a black church outside of Atlanta in eastern Cobb County, Georgia. Fire investigators said the blaze was set in six different places inside the Galilee Baptist Church on Blackjack Mountain. A police officer on patrol discovered the blaze, which damaged part of the cinder-block church, before 4:00 a.m. on May 7. At the end of the month, arson gutted a small black church in New Jersey. Investigators said there was no evidence that the fire at First Baptist Church in Glassboro was racially motivated; however, the fire coincided with Governor Christine Todd Whitman's plan to sign a bill that imposed a mandatory fifteen-year prison term for setting fire to a church, mosque, synagogue, or other house of worship. It was the second arson at a black church in New Jersey that year.[31]

The National Church Arson Task Force released its first annual report to the president on June 8, when it stated that houses of worship remained under attack but that no national conspiracy in the arsons existed. Michael Fumento penned another article for the *Wall Street Journal* on June 16, when he again blamed the news media for fanning the flames of the "epidemic" of black church burnings that he called a hoax. Civil rights leaders and scholars expressed a different kind of skepticism when President Clinton announced his yearlong effort to create a national dialogue on race and to make the United States the world's first truly successful multiethnic nation; nevertheless, many of them praised Clinton for his attempt. Kweisi Mfume, president of the NAACP, called Clinton's gesture "a good first step on a long path toward racial reconciliation." Professor Lani Guinier, professor of law at the University of Pennsylvania, applauded the president for trying to start a national conversation but encouraged him to do more. "[W]e have to go farther than talking about individual racial attitudes. I don't think the problem is a question of prejudice," she said. "I think the problem is that race masks much more systematic disadvantages and it camouflages issues of class and privilege that affect not only people of color but working-class and poor whites and all Americans who are financially challenged."[32]

As Americans began this new racial dialogue, a news story broke in July that not only embarrassed the nation's largest black religious denomination but also provoked a large amount of public criticism. Deborah Lyons, wife of Reverend Henry Lyons—pastor of Bethel Metropolitan Baptist Church in St. Petersburg and president of the 8 million–member National Baptist Convention USA Inc.—confessed to destroying property and setting fires at a waterfront house Mr. Lyons owned with another woman, a reported business partner named Bernice Edwards, in Pinellas County, Florida. Inspired by jealousy, the incident drew attention to Lyons's personal finances and assets, including a 1987 Rolls Royce, two Mercedes-Benzes, a twenty-three-foot pleasure boat, and several properties. "[A]t this time in the life of African Americans, we need accountable leadership," said Reverend Calvin Butts, senior minister of Abyssinian Baptist Church in Harlem.[33]

Accountable leadership came in the form of the NCC's book, published by Thomas Nelson Publishers under the new title *Out of the Ashes: Burned Churches and the Community of Faith* (1997). The book was an ecumenical show of strength and solidarity, first, and a kind of justification of the NCC's massive fund-raising efforts, second. A collection of ten essays by ministers, scholars, journalists, and civil rights leaders, the book represented not only theological and social reflections on the fires and their meaning but also the story of the NCC's Burned Churches Project, which had raised $10 million since June 1996. The essays ranged from an excellent contribution by Jesse Jackson that explored the "cultural conspiracy" of the fires, "causally connected by the politics and policies that help perpetuate racial fear and prejudice in the minds of whites," to an unnecessarily complicated theological explanation of why white Christians should help black Christians by Phillip Turner, dean of the Berkeley Divinity School at Yale University. A portion of the proceeds of each book sale went to the NCC's Burned Churches Project.[34]

Attacks on houses of worship continued. Brenda Wilkinson of the United Methodist News Service reported in the summer of 1997 that twenty black churches—including the First United Methodist Church in Tampa, Florida—had been victimized by arson or attempted arson so far that year; this figure compared to forty-five attacks during the same period in 1996. On July 17, Mary Frances Berry, chairwoman of the United States Commission on Civil Rights, wrote an editorial response to the NCATF, whose June 8 message was clear to her: "It is time to rebuild and move on." Berry disagreed with that notion, writing: "But it would be wrong to ignore the racial polarization left in the wake of the attacks, in town after town across the Deep South.... Two-thirds of all the fires remain unsolved, and new ones have been set in the past year." During the previous year, Berry had traveled throughout the South, where she heard people talk about the fires at community forums held by the U.S. Civil Rights Commission. She said folks in rural Missis-

Fig. 5.3. Officials in Bibb County, Ala. 2006. Photo by Hollie Huey, "Centreville (Ala.) Press."

sippi, Alabama, and Louisiana were not reassured by the NCATF's reports of progress. "Even if all the arsonists are never arrested, and even if race is not the motivation in the still-unsolved cases, we cannot afford to be smug," she said. "We must not close our eyes to what these fires have exposed: the rot of southern rural poverty and persistent racism."[35]

As the attacks continued, skeptics continued to deny them. In the autumn 1997 issue of the *American Atheist*, Conrad Goeringer wrote "The Great and Late Church Arson Conspiracy Hoax," in which he reiterated that no conspiracy had been found. "Persuasive evidence that there was a 'wave' of arsons directed at black churches required a statistical legerdemain that was ultimately impossible to achieve," the author wrote. The article's title belied the fact that it was both circumspect and well written—much better, in fact, than Michael Fumento's earlier pieces in a similar vein. "[T]he 'church arson conspiracy' was a narrative with remarkable similarities to other forms of social hysteria," Goeringer wrote. "The fires took on the dimension of a subversion mythos, a situation wherein a group or community is perceived as under attack by unseen forces." From his perspective, the fires provided an unprecedented opportunity for legislative bias in favor of religious groups.[36]

As Goeringer noted, in the year since the church arson story first broke, news of church burnings had steadily moved off the front pages of newspapers and no longer led prime-time news broadcasts. The NCATF report elicited only passing commentary and, after a two- or three-day period of news coverage, vanished into the voluminous archives of government bureaucracy. Still the fires continued, this time in Pennsylvania, where a series of fires closed out 1997 and continued in 1998. Authorities suspected arson in a fire that gutted the interior of First Baptist Church in Essington on November 17, and identified arson as the cause of fire that devastated First Baptist Church in Tinicum on November 18. Officials concluded that a fire that heavily damaged Pilgrim Holiness Church of the Apostolic Faith in Philadelphia also on November 18 was probably not arson, but that a fire that destroyed Pike Run Church of the Brethren in Somerset on January 28, 1998, was deliberately set. A fire that destroyed Trinity Episcopal Church in Solebury Township was ruled arson; however, the ATF did not believe this arson was connected to the earlier ones. If the fires were no longer front-page news, they nonetheless showed no signs of abating.[37]

6

strength

Some of the churches were rebuilt quickly; others took longer. Friends, neighbors, and relatives pitched in to help victims rebuild as aid poured in from other parts of the nation and from other countries. Volunteers traveled thousands of miles to help victims rebuild. The help these congregations received was impressive and generous, but unforeseen difficulties hindered the rebuilding process for many churches.

Better Than It Used to Be

In early December 1993, some 150 volunteers from thirty-eight churches, black and white, began to build a new building in Smithdale, Mississippi, on the site of Springhill Baptist Church, burned on the twenty-fifth anniversary of the assassination of Martin Luther King Jr. The *New York Times* reported that "something remarkable has unfolded in this corner of southwest Mississippi, where racial violence was almost a daily fact of life in the civil rights era," continuing:

> It is not just that volunteers from white and black churches got together to rebuild the churches or that the culprits were brought to justice, something rarely, if ever done thirty years ago. More important is the way that lives, black and white, were touched by what has unfolded. . . . No one thinks all the reopened wounds have been healed.

And like most stories about race in America, it is dangerous to draw too simple a metaphor. But, at the least, it was a reminder that in a nation where race relations often seem to be regressing, the enduring imagery of Mississippi's violent past does not go far toward describing life there today.[1]

For some folks in southwest Mississippi, evidence of change resided in small details of the rebuilding efforts. Jack Honea, a white volunteer, remembered a surprise meal of catfish and fried chicken that women from Springhill Baptist prepared for the workers one day. Others saw little evidence of change. "The idea you hear is that Mississippi has moved away from much of the hatred of the past," said Frank Lee, a lay leader at nearby Rocky Point Missionary Baptist Church, also torched that same night. "But beneath the surface, the same hatred that was present then is present today." To several folks, however, the efforts under way at Springhill Baptist signaled something new. "I was here in the 1960s. All the bombing and church burning and what have you, I was here," said Bubba Mathis, a local black restaurant owner. "And this is different altogether, as different than daylight and dark. There's room for improvement, but it's 99 percent better than it used to be." Rex Cowart, a white mail carrier from the neighboring town of Summit, had a similar view. "God took a tragedy and made a miracle out of it," he said. "It bonded people together who had lived here all their lives without really getting to know each other."[2]

Southerners disagreed over the levels of improvement made since the civil rights era. Some felt that, as a crucible of racial strife, the South had undergone a catharsis, undergoing a change for the better that other regions had not. For example, the director of the University of Mississippi's Afro-American Studies Department, James Payne, believed that the United States would be a better place if one could magically replicate his adopted hometown, Oxford, throughout the rest of the country. When he took the job at Ole Miss in 1990, his friends cautioned that it was no place for a black, Harvard-educated history professor; however, he found a wonderful town, largely untouched by racial unrest. On the eve of the contentious Million Man March, Payne told a London newspaper: "What you have here is an intellectual, creative environment you don't have in any other town of 10,000 people in the United States. It creates circumstances where you can disagree without being disagreeable." While polite conversation, a relaxed pace, and the oppressive humidity still reigned in Payne's Oxford, racism did not. Perhaps in the shadow of Rowan

Oak, the picturesque white mansion where William Faulkner finished his days, it would be difficult for anyone not to feel as if the O. J. Simpson trial and the black-white rifts it had exposed were a million miles away, but Payne's colleague Charles Wilson agreed. "What's helped us to make the necessary accommodation is that despite the differences, and the terrible history, we have a tradition of living together, a familiarity."[3]

Others wondered how much the South had really changed. As burning black churches lit up the night in isolated corners of Alabama in early 1996, the similarities to an earlier episode of southern history could not be ignored. "None of us wants to go back in history," said Jim Cavanaugh of the ATF's Birmingham office. "Let's hope it's not that." The unsolved firebombing of the Sixteenth Street Baptist Church in Birmingham in 1963 remained one of the most horrifying and most enduring memories of the civil rights era and, as Reverend W. D. Lewis, the ninety-two-year-old pastor of Boligee's Little Zion Baptist Church, said, "the devil is still around." Buddy Lavender, the mayor (and one-man police and fire departments) of Boligee, wondered who lit the fires. Was it friends of the two men sentenced on January 11 for vandalizing three other local black churches in 1995? Was it out-of-state visitors, the same culprits responsible for the Tennessee fires? Lavender speculated whether it could have been local drug dealers, angered by pastors railing against them from their pulpits, or even black community activists, attempting to galvanize a community indifferent to social and political issues. "The only question is who did it," he said, "and why."[4]

92 Pennies

Initially churches received donations directly from other congregations and individuals. As of April 1996, $400,000 in donations had been received from around the nation by various churches for rebuilding efforts. "People have been kind and very supportive and a great majority of them have been from white congregations," said Reverend Daniel Donaldson, pastor of Salem Baptist Church in Fruitland, Tennessee. Spiver Gordon estimated it would cost an average of $80,000 each to rebuild the three churches torched in Boligee, Alabama. "They need everything," he said. "They've got little or no insurance to cover [building] content." As Julie Stewart, president of a nonprofit advocacy group in Washington, D.C., stated, "We can't easily solve the problem of racism but we can raise money to rebuild the churches."[5]

Fig. 6.1. Interior renovation of Spring Valley Baptist Church, damaged by fire in 2006 in Gainesville, Ala. 2006. Photo by author.

The Inner City Community Church in Knoxville received the most financial support as donors contributed more than $300,000 to the church where NFL star Reggie White preached. In March 1996, White accepted a $143,261 check from donations to rebuild Inner City . "You'll have to be patient with me for a minute," he said as tears of thanks welled up in his eyes. "You might see a big man cry right here." A Milwaukee bank presented him with a check for $94,782 on April 4, when the Green Bay Packer shed a few more tears but promised not to cry to avoid further ribbing from his teammates. By June, more than $250,000 had been donated to Inner City, no doubt due in part to White's visibility and tireless efforts. The generous outpouring inspired him to change his unannounced plan to retire after the 1996 NFL season. "One boy sent us 92 [White's jersey number] pennies taped to a piece of cardboard," he said. "Those people forgot about me being a football player and said Reggie White, the man, needs our help. They revived me, to be honest." Work crews scheduled to break ground for a new foundation in June. As one member of Inner City put it: "The devil's been mighty busy. But that don't mean he gets the last say." Neither it would seem did Reggie White, whose outspokenness sometimes drew criticism, as on March 25, 1998, when he spoke before the state assembly of Wisconsin. Invited by Republican leaders to discuss his New Hope project, which encouraged urban redevelopment and minority ownership of small businesses in Wisconsin and Tennessee, White instead delivered an impromptu address that ranged from his thoughts on race relations to his interpretations of Scripture. White stated that he was offended by gay and lesbian groups who compared their own trials to the civil rights struggles of African Americans. The speech also played on a number of racial stereotypes; for example, in explaining the different "gifts" of racial and ethnic groups, White observed that blacks "like to sing and dance," whites "know how to tap into money," Hispanics are "gifted at family structure," and American Indians avoided enslavement in the eighteenth and nineteenth centuries because they "knew how to sneak up on people." Despite such gaffes, White was generally recognized as a big-hearted celebrity who used his wealth to better the community. As Dewey Roberts, president of the Knoxville chapter of the NAACP, said, "I would think even a racist would have to like some of the things Reggie does."[6]

The experience of Inner City was not atypical insofar as many burned churches enjoyed an outpouring of sympathy, aid, and money in their rebuilding efforts. For example, sixty volunteers, led by Washington Quaker Workcamps, headed toward western Alabama to help rebuilding efforts there in May 1996. Efforts stepped up considerably in the following month as the national news media focused on the issue of church arson. Reverend Terrance Mackey and his congregation at Mt. Zion AME Church in Greeleyville, South Carolina, wasted little time raising money to rebuild after getting permission to use the town's community center for worship the first Sunday after the fire that destroyed their church. Of the $220,000 they needed, $110,000 came from insurance, $90,000 came from a loan from a local bank, $20,000 came from black and white churches across the nation, and a little over $1,000 came from local white churches and individuals. By early June, they were installing new pews and preparing for the dedication of their new building. Reverend Mackey also began to formulate ideas about ways to help other churches that found themselves in similar situations.[7]

Hoping to redeem the sometimes strained relations between African Americans and Jews, Jewish religious leaders joined with black civil rights leaders in New York City to announce the formation of a fund to rebuild southern churches. Kenneth Lipper, an investment banker and former deputy mayor, made one of the first donations to the fund—as a duty, he explained, not as a favor. Hugh Price, president of the National Urban League, saw great hope in the new fund. "If those who struck the matches think they're stoking racial tensions, they were wrong," Price said. "They have galvanized us. It sets the base for people really coming to their senses in realizing that intolerance in society affects us all." Reverend Larry Hill, pastor of Matthews-Murkland Presbyterian in Charlotte, arrived in New York on June 18 to receive $10,000 from the fund. Other charitable organizations created similar funds. For example, eight philanthropic foundations, including the Pew Charitable Trusts and the Annenberg Foundation, announced the creation of a $2.7 million rebuilding grant on June 21.[8]

Pure Hell

The process did not come without problems. Insurance, or the lack thereof, would become a key issue in rebuilding. Few black churches destroyed by arson in the South carried insurance with Church Mutual Insurance Company, the largest U.S. church insurer, with policies for sixty-seven thousand houses of worship. Motivated by both altruism and self-interest, insurers joined the fight against arson. A coalition comprised of the Insurance Information Institute, Insurance Committee for Arson Control, International Association of Fire Investigators, Congressional Fire Services Institute (founded by U.S. Representative Curt Weldon, a Republican congressman from Pennsylvania and former volunteer fire chief), and other organizations announced at a joint press conference a number of anti-arson initiatives, including a fund designed by Cigna and the Volunteer Fireman's Insurance Service to offer monetary rewards for information leading to the arrest and conviction of church arsonists. The coalition offered free arson-prevention seminars and free, on-site safety inspections.[9]

Those churches that burned before widespread press coverage of the arsons sometimes experienced the greatest difficulties in rebuilding. "From January 13 up to the present, we've been through pure hell," said Reverend Sherron Brown on June 20, 1996. The pastor of Macedonia Missionary Baptist in Fruitvale, Tennessee, told of his congregation's trials. "We had to pay for everything ourselves," said Brown, whose church had burned in January 1995. "It has been one hurdle after another." First government investigators suggested that the fire was not a hate crime but the act of a member of the congregation. Then the church's insurance company, which settled in March 1995, refused to reinsure it—which in turn made it difficult to obtain a bank loan to rebuild. It was difficult to keep the congregation—many of whom had moved to nearby towns away from the church—together during those trying times. "My heart goes out to the other churches that have burned," said Brown, who wished that authorities and reporters had taken the fires more seriously. "Only since I went to Washington have we gotten some of the attention we've been waiting on for a year and a half." By October, Macedonia Baptist had been rebuilt on its original site. The church adopted a new name—New Macedonia—as its members struggled to repay a $100,000 loan they finally received to add a steeple and to pave the muddy driveway to the church.[10]

Rebuilding efforts in Boligee, Alabama, were somewhat contentious as well-meaning local groups vied for control. Local prosecutor Barrown Lankster said that at one point the three churches involved were caught in a tug-of-war between whites in the biracial group Citizens for a Better Greene County and blacks in a group headed by Spiver Gordon of the Southern Christian Leadership Conference. Some in Gordon's camp apparently felt that the Citizens' plan was too paternalistic. "Both groups wanted to direct the fund raising and help administer the rebuilding funds that were beginning to pour into the community," said Lankster. "Eventually the three churches indicated that they wanted Spiver Gordon's group to oversee the effort. So in spite of what has happened, the county remains as politically riven as it's ever been." Reverend W. D. Lewis, pastor of Little Zion Baptist Church, acknowledged the problems, which he called political, but said they were outweighed by the small gestures and individual acts of kindness he experienced everyday as his congregation recovered. At ninety-two years old, Reverend Lewis took to the road to raise money to rebuild his church; he needed $100,000 to supplement the $150,000 provided by Little Zion's insurance policy. With help from Mennonite and Quaker volunteers, and workers from as far away as Canada, England, and Tanzania, the outer shell of Little Zion was reconstructed; the remaining monies would go toward finishing the interior.[11]

Fig. 6.2. Interior of Little Zion Baptist Church, rebuilt after being destroyed by fire in 1996 in Boligee, Ala. 2006. Photo by author.

Rebuilding Mt. Zion

Speaking to the congregation of Greater Mt. Zion Church of God in Christ, which had burned in Portsmouth, Virginia, in 1995, Reverend Dr. Charles Hicks said what would become a mantra for pastors whose churches had burned. "You can burn a building," he said, "but you can't burn a church." He told one of his church members: "They burned the building down, but I'm still here. I'm the church. . . . *We* are the church." Three days after the fire at Greater Mt. Zion, Dr. Hicks sat down to sketch out building plans for the new sanctuary.[12]

Greater Mt. Zion was rebuilt by volunteers from across the country through a $80,000 grant from the National Council of Churches. As of January 15, 1997, the church had a new foundation, a floor, framed walls, and roof supports; a new red-brick exterior would replace the old white-frame wooden building that had served as a dance hall before it was purchased by the church. The construction was done by a hodgepodge crew of volunteers, including a retired engineer from Pittsburgh who drove his camper from Pennsylvania to Virginia so he could stay for a month; two seniors from a Mennonite high school near Philadelphia; several senior citizens; and three students and an instructor from a small New York college. The all-white construction team, many of whom had never heard of Greater Mt. Zion Tabernacle Church—or even Portsmouth—had volunteered through two national organizations, Habitat for Humanity and Christmas in April, both of which specialize in building or renovating low-income housing.

Shirley Hines, coordinator of the Greater Mt. Zion rebuilding project, appealed to the National Council of Churches for help in October 1997. Although the church did not appear on the council's state-compiled list of arsons in Virginia, the report of the local fire department, which determined that someone had set fire to curtains near the pulpit, was persuasive. The NCC promised a loan, a grant, volunteer labor, and in-kind donations of materials and services. Volunteers began arriving in January 1997; over one hundred would eventually come from all over the world to help Greater Mt. Zion rebuild. Christmas in April mobilized college students from Haverford and Bryn Mawr to spend their spring break working at the site. "They sent kids down here on their spring break," Dr. Hicks recalled. "Ain't never built nothin,' came down here, some came from Hawaii, some came from Illinois, some came from Mexico. . . . I said 'Any of y'all ever eat any neckbones?' 'Neckbones,' they said, '"what is neckbones'?" The women of the church made sure the volunteers ate well in Portsmouth. While several of the older volunteers had formal construction experience, none of the students did, and many of them had been only vaguely aware of church arsons in the news when they agreed to volunteer. Hicks considered himself to be blessed. "These are some of the most beautiful people you would ever want to see," he said. "Just to see that there is so much spirit and joy in them, it makes my heart overwhelmed." Of the arson, he said, "The devil meant it for our bad, but God meant it for our good."[13]

"I'm really touched when I see folks coming together," said Sara Coppler, director of the NCC's Church Rebuilding Project. "Really, honestly, these folks would not be side by side if they hadn't come to rebuild. There's a genuine love. I mean, it's permanent." Dan Howell, a nineteen-year-old freshman at Haverford College, was surprised to learn how much his white

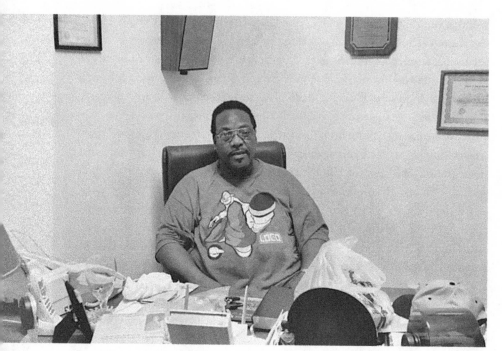

Fig. 6.3. Reverend Dr. Charles Hicks, pastor of Greater Mt. Zion Tabernacle Church of God in Christ, in his study. 2005. Photo by author.

Lutheran church in rural Maryland had with the black Pentecostal congregation at Greater Mt. Zion. Jeff Smith, another student at Haverford, helped out too, feeling that his own beliefs as an atheist applied to the situation in Portsmouth. "I think people should believe whatever they want," he said. "No one should try to stop them." Students from Pennsylvania and Colorado arrived in mid-March. Shirley Hines believed that the volunteers, all of whom were white, brought a symbolic message to Tidewater Virginia: "Every white person does not hate black people. Every white person is not a racist."[14]

In June 1997, Greater Mt. Zion became one of the first four churches in the nation approved for federal loan guarantees. Andrew Cuomo, secretary of the U.S. Department of Housing and Urban Development (HUD), announced $668,000 in federal loan guarantees at a national meeting in Washington of church representatives gathered to discuss federal programs to assist religious institutions damaged by arson or hate crimes; Greater Mt. Zion would receive a $180,000 guarantee. Another $4.3 million in loan guarantee applications were awaiting final approval by HUD. At the time it received the HUD loan, Greater Mt. Zion had received about $11,000 in donations, in addition to the grant from the NCC. The congregation continued to worship in borrowed spaces, including Coleman's—a local nursery—and a banquet room at the Holiday Inn.[15]

Aid poured into churches like Greater Mt. Zion from a number of sources. The Church Arson Prevention Act, signed into law by President Clinton in 1996, allowed HUD to make $10 million in loan guarantees to churches and other places of worship damaged by arson. As of June 1997, the National Council of Churches had raised more than $8 million in money, supplies, and services to rebuild. Habitat for Humanity lent its weight to rebuilding efforts. The Congress of National Black Churches launched a $12 million drive earlier that year to provide rebuilding assistance to fifty black churches over the next three years. The Ford Foundation, AFL-CIO, and the Anti-Defamation League were all involved in rebuilding efforts.[16]

Greater Mt. Zion began its third phase of rebuilding in July 1997. Through the HUD loan, NCC grant, private contributions (one woman gave Hicks $11,000), hours of donated labor, and piles of supplies, the congregation amassed $370,000 to rebuild. In October 1997, two years after the church had burned, the members of Greater Mt. Zion held a church dedication service for their new building, which could seat nearly three hundred people as compared to the old church, which had room for one hundred. "We have rebuilt God's temple," said Shirley Hines. "It's exciting what miracles God can work." The new building had a conference room, a fellowship hall, a kitchen, and a pastor's study as compared to the old one-room building. Three years after the arson, church members were able to look back on the incident with some sense of peace. Some thrilled at the new church, others missed the old one, and still others, soured by the arson, had stopped attending Greater Mt. Zion altogether. "It really put a hurt on everybody," said Dr. Hicks in 1998. "It was nightmarish, a hurting thing to see your church burn. We've had people leave. They couldn't handle what happened. But they're gradually coming back." Church members still planned to build a new parking lot, as well as a day-care/community center across the street. Hines, the rebuilding coordinator, said it was healing to witness the outpouring of support from other local churches and the hundreds of volunteers who helped to rebuild the church. The arson remained unsolved; no suspects were arrested.[17]

Brick, Not Wood

Like Greater Mt. Zion, other churches were often rebuilt stronger and bigger than before, and several took the opportunity to expand the seating capacity of their sanctuaries. More than a few of the new structures incorporated reminders of the arson. For example, Reverend Larry Hill, pastor of Matthews-Murkland Presbyterian Church in North Carolina, told NAACP chairwoman Myrlie Evers-Williams that Charlotte-area ministers planned to resurrect two of Matthews-Murkland's charred boards to make a symbolic cross. Notably, both Little Zion Baptist Church and Greater Mt. Zion, like many of the other burned churches, were rebuilt in brick.[18]

Congregation members, with much outside help, threw themselves into rebuilding efforts in late June 1996 at the height of the arson scare. Neighbors, friends, and total strangers volunteered money, time, labor, and building supplies as people in different localities were moved to act. In northeast Ohio, an interdenominational organization of black churches called United Pastors in Mission encouraged people to dig a little deeper in their pockets for Sunday offerings in an effort to raise cash. In Boston, groups such as the Jewish Community Relations Council of Greater Boston and the Combined Jewish Philanthropies of Greater Boston established funds for rebuilding efforts as the Northeast Council of the Union of American Hebrew Congregations made plans to send synagogue members to southern black churches to help them rebuild. In New York, a disaster- relief organization donated prefabricated structures to replace burned churches. Based in New Canaan, Connecticut, AmeriCares also provided the churches with new Steinway pianos. Actor James Earl Jones helped to provide a send-off for two new prefab churches, loaded aboard a cargo plane in Hangar 19 of John F. Kennedy Airport; the 3,000-square-foot aluminum structures were bound for Mississippi, where they would replace Central Grove Baptist Church and Mt. Pleasant Missionary Baptist Church. "When a church is gutted by hateful flames, we are challenged to act," boomed Jones inside the voluminous hangar. "By Sunday, a beautiful, simple structure, a cathedral of hope, will bloom in that rich soil." Resembling a space-age yurt, each freestanding structure, valued at more than $230,000 and capable of holding from seventy-five to one hundred people, could be erected in thirty-six hours. AmeriCares offered a new building and a new piano to thirty-eight black churches burned down by suspicious fires over the previous eighteen months. "For as long as these crimes occur, we will supply a church and a piano indefinitely."[19]

On June 27, Vice President Al Gore and his wife, Tipper, visited New Macedonia Missionary Baptist Church in Bells, Tennessee, to see the sanctuary that was rebuilt after being burned in January 1995. Located about ninety miles north of Memphis, New Macedonia was one of the first in the series of church arsons that swept the South. Shortly after the vice president's visit, a mysterious fire destroyed God's Gospel Tabernacle, a white church in Englewood, Tennessee. That same day, the African American Council of Christian Clergy Relief Fund unveiled a plan to raise $100,000 to rebuild black churches torched in arson attacks.[20]

Insurance Woes

Even as the insurance industry announced steps to reduce the likelihood of arson at houses of worship, word spread in the summer of 1996 that some insurance companies were canceling the policies of churches in the wake of the arsons. One of the other Tennessee churches burned in January 1995 reported insurance problems in early July 1996. Mt. Calvary Missionary Baptist Church's policy was not renewed in June; the insurer, Des Moines–based Preferred Risk Mutual Insurance, said it ended its coverage because of the large number of claims against the policy. Having little luck in finding another insurer to write a policy, Reverend Algie Jarrett said he felt "real edgy" about not having insurance. "When one drops you, it's hard to get another one to pick you up," he said. As with Mt. Calvary, Preferred Risk claimed that it dropped coverage of Salem Baptist Church in Humboldt, Tennessee, because of the frequency of claims by the church. Jack Kelly, senior vice president of Preferred Risk, said that both Mt. Calvary and Salem Baptist had each submitted claims for three additional losses in a short time. The churches' pastors said the claims were small. "Claims totaled $195,000 against our policy and $188,000 of that was against the burning of our church," said Reverend Daniel Donaldson of Salem Baptist. "The other three claims totaled $7,000. To me that is not fair, but yet it is legal in our system."[21]

The congregation of Glorious Church of God in Christ in Richmond, Virginia, found itself in a comparable predicament within a few weeks after Aetna/Travelers Insurance Company paid $450,000 for the arson that seriously damaged it on February 21, 1996. Told that their policy would not be renewed, church members purchased a temporary policy from another company; angry because the only other claim that year had been for $8,000 when lightning struck their chimney, they then complained to the state insurance commissioner, Alfred Gross. Gross told Glorious Church that the state had no authority to compel a company to underwrite a risk, but his office did contact Aetna/Travelers, which explained that its salespeople had mistakenly failed to offer a new policy for Glorious Church's new building. Aetna/Travelers later apologized and reinstated the policy it had canceled, along with a donation to the church. In a joint statement, insurance industry representatives reaffirmed, "Collectively, as an industry, we are deeply concerned about the rash of church fires and want to do our part as good corporate citizens of the affected communities to bring an end to these heinous crimes." The *New York Times* reported that, despite reports of insurance cancellations, there was no widespread pattern of loss of insurance coverage; the paper based this finding on interviews with state insurance commissioners, black ministers, and civil rights organizations such as the NAACP. As George Dale, Mississippi commissioner of insurance noted, failing to renew the policy of a burned church at a time when arsons were receiving such wide publicity would wind up "costing them [insurers] thousands in bad public relations."[22]

Spiritual Renewal or Bosnia?

"Evil people may be burning churches," said Lauren Levin, an attorney with the Anti-Defamation League, "but they are starting the fires of a spiritual renewal." The alternative to cohesive rebuilding efforts and spiritual rejuvenation was "Bosnia," according to Hugh Price, president of the National Urban League. "All the pressure pulls the country apart," he said, alluding to the civil strife in southeastern Europe's war-torn Balkan Peninsula. "The sense of dominating over someone else is prevalent in society, here and all over Europe. We manage it as a society with varying degrees of success."[23]

Evidence of the renewal Levin described was evident everywhere. Nineteen members of Operation Understanding, a Washington-based diversity program involving Jewish and black teenagers, enjoyed a kind of spiritual renewal as they participated in rebuilding efforts in Boligee on the Fourth of July. "Things in the 1990s are a lot like things in the 1960s—economic insecurity, advancement of African Americans and other minorities is seen as threatening," said Christian Dorsey, the group's leader. "Instead of using energy and resources they have, some people choose to lash out." Dorsey predicted that the church arsons would backfire, invigorating the silent majority to speak out against injustice. An *Atlanta Journal* article described how the volunteers—"young and powerless" but "driven by a refreshingly unsentimental optimism"—spent Independence Day rebuilding churches in Alabama while "leaving the speechmaking and sanctimony to politicians and self-servers."[24]

Responding to criticism, insurance company representatives and regulators pledged to help houses of worship find insurance in mid-July as gospel groups performed radio benefits in Boston to raise funds. The Burned Churches Fund disbursed $916,000 to nine black congregations in its first round of grants in July. The NCC had established a rebuilding fund at its New York City headquarters in March 1996. Its fund-raising campaign would collect over $9 million in gifts and loans from foundations, individuals, and other sources; however, the fund also drew controversy. Critics of the NCC campaign, most of whom represented politically conservative constituencies, argued that the NCC had misled people into thinking white racists had undertaken a massive offensive against black churches; they also questioned the NCC's plan to keep part of the funds for its own antiracism programs. Dianne Knippers of the Institute on Religion and Democracy asked the NCC to apologize for "the great church-fire hoax." Her organization issued a press release that said, "NCC spokespersons have jawboned church burnings into a national crisis."[25]

Others continued to give generously. The Korean Produce Association donated $1,000 on July 18 to Reverend Spencer Gibbs of the Presbytery of New York City. Following the presentation, the association donated fruits and vegetables to the Ella Baker/Cleveland Robinson Academy, a leadership-training program for youths. The association's efforts were part of a continuing effort to build bridges of understanding and appreciation in the wake of the 1992 Los Angeles riots, during which African Americans and Korean Americans battled in and around Korean-owned groceries in black neighborhoods. In September, the task of rebuilding got a significant boost when HUD, the NCC, and the Congress of National Black Churches announced a partnership to assist burned churches; the alliance revolved around grants, in-kind contributions, and professional and volunteer services.[26]

An October 31 article in *Third Force* described the relief efforts in the southern states, reporting, "A look across the South reveals an amazing array of church groups, civil rights activists, and individuals who have been moved to action by a wave of terrorist attacks aimed at black churches throughout the South. Indeed, an army of activists and volunteers, seasoned missionaries, and legal rights workers from Tanzania to Vancouver are showing up in obscure, tiny towns throughout the southern region to stand side by side with those under fire." A minister in Kossuth, Mississippi, called the outpouring "a genuine miracle." In western Alabama, Quakers moved quickly to rebuild Mt. Zion and Little Zion; one volunteer stated, "the roofs are on, much of the sheet rock is up, the electrical roughed in, and some windows and doors hung."[27]

Rebuilding efforts generated mountains of paperwork, and lawyers did plenty of pro bono work to assist churches in the process. "Helping churches with the rebuilding process, getting insurance problems resolved, working with accountants or architects, dealing with grant or loan matters—the work is transactional, almost corporate, legal work," said Thomas Henderson, deputy director for litigation of the Lawyers' Committee for Civil Rights Under Law. Forty firms from Chicago, San Francisco, Boston, New York, Miami, Birmingham, Atlanta, Washington, D.C., and other cities answered the call of the Lawyers' Committee for volunteers, but the lawyers faced different challenges than they had in the 1960s, when volunteers went south to provide legal help in the civil rights struggle. "Instead of racing into court to file a writ to get someone out of jail or to seek other relief for civil rights activists," explained Daniel Kohrman, supervising attorney for national litigation of the Lawyers' Committee, "we're asking lawyers to help with such things as insurance and contract matters, construction permits, and arson verification reports." Churches seemed reluctant to seek such help. "I was under the naïve impression that when you offered your services pro bono, you'd have people lining up at the door," said Laurel Bedig, a volunteer coordinator charged with matching lawyers with client churches. "What I've learned in helping to get this project off the ground is that we have to go out there and market ourselves just like we do in the private sector." Many of the churches had never employed legal counsel before, and the idea of lawyers helping with a contract, or helping with insurance, was almost as foreign as the idea that they were willing to do it for free. "Everyone kept asking, 'Free? Are these services really free?'" said Kohrman. "The idea of free lawyers was a concept that people just couldn't contemplate. . . . So we were very warmly received."[28]

The Devil Went Down to Norway

In August 1997, as lawyers fanned out across the American South, hundreds of worshipers and tourists made their way through the forest outside the coastal city of Bergen, Norway, for the consecration of the newly rebuilt Fantoft Church, a replica of the tiny, 850-year-old stave church burned in 1992. "There was a feeling of victory," said Arne Droi, a staff member and guide for the church. "It was a very happy day for everyone." Built by the same carpenters who built the great Viking ships, the stave churches blended Norse imagery—dragon heads, snakes, and vines—with traditional Christian symbols. Twenty-two of the stave churches, the country's most recognizable national treasures, had been torched in the mid-1990s by a small but committed group of Satanists who blended zealous Norwegian nationalism with a focus on ancient Norse gods and Viking practices. Investigators attributed the Fantoft fire to Varg Vikernes, a black metal musician and Satanist who in 1997 was serving twenty-one years for murdering a rival musician and setting four other church fires. Vikernes, the sole member of the band Burzum (Norwegian for "darkness"), was a hero among black metal fans, both in Norway and around the world. Dozens of fans devoted Web pages to him and to his band. After the Fantoft burning, he released an album called *Aske* (Ash). An image of a burning church glossed the cover of the album, each copy of which came packaged with a cigarette lighter. The night after his conviction, two more churches were torched. In September 1997, Vikernes released another album from prison.

The Fantoft stave church, a medieval structure built with post-and-beam construction, was rebuilt with donations by a private company, Norwegian Holding. Ole-Johan Minde and his partner, Huldor Skaatan, reconstructed most of the church by hand with wood from 400-year-old pine trees. The process was difficult given the lack of blueprints or plans for the building, originally constructed in 1150 and moved to its present site in 1883. "We measured and marked the few parts that survived the fire so that we could have an idea of how to start rebuilding," said Minde. "Then we put the parts in a shed down the hill. By the next morning, someone had burned down the shed." Only the original door frame survived. "People got very angry and very sad, but a lot were saying that we shouldn't be angry because then the Satanists would have won," said Arne Droi. "We wanted to show that they can destroy the church but not the message."[29]

This variation of what Americans viewed as "typical" racially motivated hate crimes ravaged churches in the United States, too. As the nation focused its attention on the plight of African-American church arson, white churches burned too, and white congregations suffered, particularly in the Midwest.

One man torched a historic Catholic church in Stuart, Iowa, on August 22, 1995, because of his admitted hatred of Catholicism. In 1998, the *South Bend Tribune* reported that arsonists had burned forty-one churches in Indiana since 1993, causing more than $12 million in damages, mostly at small, rural churches. The state's response was feeble, consisting mainly of handing out brochures of safety tips and providing local fire departments with free informational videos. Authorities made arrests in four of the fourteen church arsons in Indiana in 1997, and three in 1998; the three arrests in 1998 were all in connection with the same arson. No arrests were made in 1994, 1995, or 1996, and only one in 1993.[30]

Love, Hope, Happiness, and Sawdust

The fires recognized no color lines, as historically Native American congregations were affected, too. Destroyed in 1994 by arson, Davis Chapel United Methodist near Coweta, Oklahoma, received a $40,000 NCC grant in December 1997 to aid in its rebuilding efforts. The earliest members of Davis Chapel, which had a long history in the Coweta area, used to hold summer services at the turn of the twentieth century under a brush arbor, then in a log cabin east of its present site. The church got its name from Reverend Hilly Davis, a full-blood Creek Indian minister who opened the doors of his home in 1905 to hold winter services. Reverend Davis donated two acres of his homestead for the church, built in 1910 at his own expense. Davis, who preached for twenty-six years, conducted all of the church's services—sermons, songs, and prayers—in Creek. Descendants of those first church members worked to rebuild Davis Chapel with insurance money, the NCC grant, and additional funds they raised themselves.[31]

Other churches rebuilt with comparable aid. Founded in 1925, Gay's Hill Baptist Church had burned at 4:00 a.m. on March 26, 1996; investigators had determined that gasoline was used to accelerate the fire. "They watched it burn," said Barbara Campbell, a member of the Keysville AmeriCorps Vista Volunteers who specialized in arson. "The fire trucks were there, but they said it was 'too far gone.' They watched it burn to the ground." Reverend Harry Baldwin had reported several incidents of vandalism at Gay's Hill before the fire including a broken-down door and a piano smashed with a sledgehammer. Reverend Baldwin was one of several ministers who told his story to President Clinton at the NCC convention in Washington, D.C., in June 1996. Gay's Hill hosted thirty-seven volunteer construction teams—only about one-third of them from Georgia—who helped to complete the rebuilding of the church in July 1997. "Love, hope, happiness, and sawdust have come out of the ashes," said Reverend Baldwin. Construction efforts such as those at Gay's Hill relied on interdenominational cooperation. "When we get the call to work, we meet with the church and pastor and assess the situation," said Joe Hamilton, project coordinator for the Southeast Jurisdiction United Methodist Volunteers in Mission. "Then we bring in resources from wherever we can. We may have United Methodist teams working with a Presbyterian construction coordinator, using materials paid for by an NCC grant, the United Methodist Advance, and the American Jewish Committee, followed by a plan refined by the National Black Evangelical Association. Whatever it takes, that's what we do." Dennis Wolfe, a white contractor from the Causeway Corporation who spoke at the dedication service of the new Gay's Hill, said, "Whenever I pass by this church, I remember the sink we installed and the sheet rock we donated and I think: 'That's my church.'" Such a feeling of ownership by the wider community created a sense of solidarity between black church members and other community members outside the congregation; however, some churches on the NCC list refused the help of outsiders. In some cases, the congregation had enough resources to rebuild; in other cases, there was little basis for trust of outside aid.[32]

The National Coalition for Burned Churches

The National Coalition for Burned Churches and Community Empowerment (NCBC) was established in October 1997 as a faith-based response to the church-burning crisis. A multiracial, interdenominational coalition of clergy and laity whose places of worship had been burned or firebombed, the NCBC was led by Reverence Terrance Mackey and his wife, Rose Johnson-Mackey. Based in Charleston, South Carolina, the pair sought to aid victims by providing advocacy support and technical assistance to victims of church arson. A kind of research center and clearinghouse for information, the NCBC aimed—and continues to aim—to accomplish its mission through programs in research and analysis, in victim support, in church rebuilding, in volunteer coordination, in community leadership training, in youth organizing, and in public policy advocacy. The NCBC proved to be a powerful combatant in the fight against church arson—even as funding for the organization dried up in the early twenty-first century.

The NCBC kept pressure on the Clinton administration to pay attention to the church fires and prosecute them as hate crimes whenever applicable; however, it is unclear to what degree the new federal legislation impacted the crimes. For example, in the first case in which a jury considered the new federal charge, which imposed harsher penalties for racially motivated arson of a religious building, three white Alabaman youths were convicted of torching a rural black church just two days after a June 1997 rally of the Alabama Knights of the Ku Klux Klan. The jury convicted the three youths of arson and conspiracy to commit arson, rather than of committing a hate crime, which would have tacked an additional ten years on their sentences. The argument for hate crime in this case was strong: Brandy Boone, the nineteen-year-old young woman convicted of conspiracy to commit arson, had suggested to her two male friends that the trio "go burn the nigger church," according to one source, and one of the young men had attended the Klan rally.[33]

Extinguished Concern

As rebuilding efforts continued in 1998, so too did the fires. Officials investigated a series of blazes at churches in North Carolina in mid-February. As firefighters extinguished a blaze that gutted a newly renovated fellowship hall at Moore's Chapel United Methodist in Charlotte, a separate fire was reported about a mile away at the New Apostolic Church. Both of these churches were about a mile from Garden Memorial Presbyterian Church, damaged earlier that week, and near Sunset Forest Baptist Church, destroyed two days before Garden Memorial was damaged. First Baptist Church in Stanley was damaged earlier that same month. Investigators said all of the fires were set intentionally near doors or entranceways of the white churches. On March 8, the *New York Times* reported: "Four [Texas] teenagers claiming to be vampires went on a drug-crazed rampage on Thursday, vandalizing dozens of cars and homes, spray-painting racial slurs, and burning a church." The fire destroyed the office and fellowship hall of Bethany Lutheran Church in the white, middle-class suburb of Lake Highlands, outside Dallas. The outer walls of the church were scrawled with graffiti.[34]

Sandra Peters of the General Board of Global Ministries worried that the press and the public had lost interest in church fires even though arsonists had not. "The nation has been lulled back into quiet acceptance," she wrote.

Even though the June 1997 NCATF report said there was no evidence of conspiracy, the fires, which could be linked to "increased incidents of racially motivated violence," were continuing, wrote Peters. According to her, a church arson was reported in Tennessee within forty-eight hours of the October 1997 organizing meeting of the National Coalition for Burned Churches; two weeks later, a weekend youth conference for the children of burned churches sparked suspicious fires. Having reviewed several Internet "hate sites," Peters concluded that church fires were not only "the professed harbinger of a race war at the turn of the millennium" but also part of the initiation rites of some hate groups. "Many churches remain un-built, unable to get needed funds or bank loans," she reported. "Some have begun rebuilding without sufficient funds to complete construction—'stepping out on faith,' they call it. Many churches do not qualify for available grants, having been 'ruled' accidental by fire investigators."[35]

"During 1995–1996, a flurry of news reports detailed suspected arson at religious institutions," wrote Lynna Goch in a March 1998 article for *Best's Review*, an insurance industry publication. "But insurers are saying arson isn't the big issue." Goch reported that insurers were heeding the findings of the National Fire Protection Association, which found that the number of "church-related arson incidents" had decreased, though she admitted that church arson statistics were inconsistent and often contradictory. Robert Press, a *Christian Science Monitor* correspondent and Ph.D. candidate at the University of Florida, reported low public concern as fires continued through 1998 into 1999. Using statistics gathered by the NCATF, Press noted that church arsons continued in 1999 at the stunning rate of three to four per week, as compared to six per week in 1996. The number of burned black churches had declined from 40 percent in 1996 to 25 percent in 1997 and 1998; however, Press noted, even if only 25 percent of the churches burned during these years were black, that number still indicated a much larger percentage than African Americans represented in the general population. Yes, the National Church Arson Task Force had speeded up federal response to suspected arsons, and yes, there was better coordination among federal agencies investigating church burnings; at 34 percent, the arrest rate was more than double the 16 percent rate of arrests in arson cases nationwide. But Press worried that it was harder for groups to marshal funds and volunteers to help congregations rebuild because public attention had shifted elsewhere.[36]

Fig. 6.4. Former site of Rehobeth Baptist Church, destroyed by fire in 2006 in Bibb County, Ala. 2006. Photo by author.

Fig. 6.5. New prefabricated structure at Rehobeth Baptist Church, Bibb County, Ala. 2006. Photo by author.

Where There Is Smoke

In February 1999, authorities arrested and charged an Indiana man in connection with an Ohio church fire; on April 20, 1999, federal grand juries indicted the man, Jay Scott Ballinger, in ten church arsons in Indiana and Georgia. Ballinger told federal agents that he had burned between thirty and fifty churches between 1994 and 1998 in eleven different states. Police in Indiana said Ballinger, the most prolific arsonist snared in the National Church Arson Task Force's three-year crackdown, dabbled in satanic rituals. Ballinger's girlfriend, Angela Wood, pled guilty to conspiracy to burn churches in twenty states, and agreed to help prosecutors in their case against Ballinger. The Ballinger case underscored the fact that Satanism was oftentimes as common a motivation for church burnings as racism.[37]

One of the many churches adversely affected by Ballinger was Amazing Grace Baptist Church: a white church perched atop a hill overlooking three cemeteries (one of which contains the remains of a Confederate soldier) in Murray County, Georgia. Looking west toward the wooded, smoky-blue foothills of the Appalachians, the rear of the church faces that part of the Chattahoochee National Forest known as the Cohutta Wilderness: a beautiful, inhospitable chunk of nature untouched by roads and buildings. Ballinger and his girlfriend burned Amazing Grace on December 23, 1998. Responding quickly, the FBI and ATF cordoned off the charred building and did not allow church members inside. The day after the arson—Christmas Eve, when Ballinger burned another neighboring church—Amazing Grace members met in the fellowship hall and had services more or less as usual. "What you all must realize is that the *building* was burned. The *church* was not burned," Reverend Earl Howard told his congregation. "Once people realized that the church was still there, we got about the business of rebuilding the structure."[38]

The building, which was over 150 years old, was originally a Methodist church. It had been turned on its foundation in the 1950s by a tornado and left that way by the congregants, who felt the Lord wanted the church to face a new direction. The building was unoccupied for several years before being purchased by AGBC in 1986 for $25,000; church members worked for a decade to restore the church. "The carvings and woodwork inside were intricate," said Earl Shoemaker, the church clerk. "The ceiling was made of hand-hewn boards, straight from the forest." The building was more or less where the congregation wanted it to be when Ballinger burned it to the ground.[39]

The church carried $70,000 of insurance—not nearly enough to rebuild. The new building would cost over $250,000, but whenever Shoemaker received a bill, the money was there in the church account. Neighbors stuffed donations in jars at local convenience stores and grocery stores. A woman from Dalton, a nearby city and heart of the region's textile industry, gave Shoemaker a $10,000 check. A man pulled up in his car the morning after the fire as Howard and Shoemaker contemplated the smoking cinders, rolled down his car window, pressed a wad of bills into Howard's hand, and drove away. Volunteers showed up from all over the area to help the congregation rebuild. Most of the work was done by congregants themselves. For example, a carpetlayer from Dalton instructed men from the church how to lay the carpet, which they did late into the night (with over one hundred carpet mills within the city limits, Dalton is the self-proclaimed "Carpet Capital of the World"). A seventy-four-year-old man from Tennessee showed up at the church one day and said, "I'm a retired plumber and I'm here to do your plumbing." He did, completing the work in two long days. There were no architectural renderings of the new building; builders used a sketch penciled by Shoemaker, who erased his freehand sketches and made them a little bit bigger each time. The original building was 40' x 60'; the new building is probably half again that size.[40]

Congregants continued their work on the new building as Ballinger continued burning churches. Arson turned to murder when he started a fire at a church in Commerce, Georgia, in which a volunteer firefighter, twenty-seven-year-old Kennan Loy Williams, lost his life. Three months after the arson at Amazing Grace, Ballinger was caught in Ohio after severely burning himself in a botched arson attempt. Amazing Grace members learned bits and pieces of Ballinger's story through the news. "We were heartbroken," Reverend Howard said, remembering the days after the arson and after Ballinger's arrest. The pastor remembered that none of his congregants displayed any outward signs of anger—either after the crime or after Ballinger's arrest.[41]

Ballinger cried at his sentencing in Gainesville as family members of the firefighter slain in Commerce testified and called him "every name in the book" in court, according to Shoemaker, who attended Ballinger's trial. Williams's twin brother appeared in court wearing his brother's dress fireman's uniform, evoking memories of the slain firefighter. "I'm sorry, I'm sorry," Ballinger repeated. Shoemaker said that many congregation members wanted to write Ballinger and tell him that they "harbored no ill will towards him," but they did not know exactly where Ballinger was incarcerated. An FBI agent was going to help them locate Ballinger, but his whereabouts were still unknown: Shoemaker expected him to be held at the federal penitentiary in Atlanta but had jotted in his trial notes that Ballinger would be transferred after his sentencing to a minimum-security prison.[42]

Six months after the arson, the new building was completed and church members held a dedication ceremony and joyous celebration. The building had been burgled several times before the arson, and in the days after the church reopened in 1999, someone stole the three brand-new air-conditioning units that cooled the church; a team of several men apparently cut the lines and lifted the heavy units onto trucks. The larceny added insult to injury, and getting back to normal proved difficult; however, Reverend Howard maintains that much

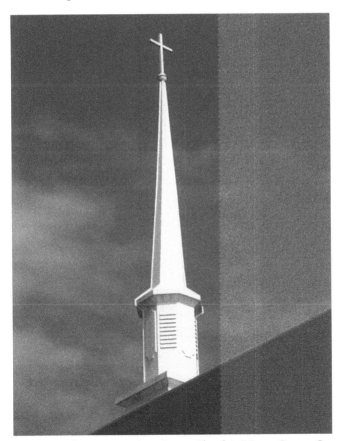

Fig. 6.6. Steeple at Amazing Grace Baptist Church in Murray County, Ga. 2005. Photo by author.

good came out of the arson for himself and for the other members of Amazing Grace. "The church is stronger," said Howard. "Our faith is stronger." The church members seemed ready to accept the terrible tragedy as the mysterious working of God's will.[43]

If media coverage of church fires had died down, the issue of church arson clearly had not gone away. As Reverend Terrance Mackey, executive director of the National Coalition for Burned Churches, said in April 1999, "We get fires every week that are reported to our office." No longer in the national spotlight, arsonists continued to burn and churches continued to rebuild. As congregations completed the arduous task of reconstruction, they rededicated their churches and celebrated faith and goodwill. In Dixiana, South Carolina, black and white members of St. John Baptist Church stood together at the dedication of their new church in August 1999. Grandmothers wore their finest hats, little girls fidgeted in new dresses, and deacons sported their best Sunday suits. Together they read a Bible verse, Matthew 16:18, which reads, "Upon this rock I will build my church; and the gates of Hell shall not prevail against it."[44]

7

hope

One of the most distinguishing characteristics of the 1990s was its violence. As particularly ugly examples of this violence, the church burnings of the mid- to late 1990s and the way the nation responded symbolized a search for community at the beginning of a new millennium. Americans were surprised to discover in both religious and secular efforts to aid the victims of church arson that community in the United States was stronger than they had believed—and stronger than the fires themselves would indicate.

All the Rage

Both 1998 and 1999 were signature years for hate crime in the United States. James Byrd Jr., an African-American man, was dragged behind a truck to his death in Jasper, Texas. Matthew Shepard, a gay college student, was beaten and left to die on a fence in Wyoming. Dr. Barnett Slepian, a pro-choice obstetrician, was gunned down by a sniper in his kitchen in New York. Congregation B'nai Israel and Knesset Israel Torah Center in Sacramento and Congregation Beth Shalom in Carmichael, California, were set ablaze, causing an estimated $3 million in damage; the following month, the same person who firebombed the three Sacramento-area synagogues shot a gay couple to death in their home outside Redding, California.

These incidents capped a season of hate, mirroring the violent rage of a nation in turmoil. The fabric of American society seemed to be tearing apart. Gang wars. Drive-by shootings. Road rage. Random, senseless violence. The shapeless rage churning beneath the surface of American life found its most disturbing and senseless expression in a series of school shootings that oc- curred in the late 1990s. They began in Pearl, Mississippi, on October 1, 1997, when a sixteen-year-old stabbed his mother to death and then fatally shot two girls and seven other high school students. Similar "wildings" by angry teenagers at West Paducah, Kentucky; Jonesboro, Arkansas; and Springfield, Oregon, in the 1997–98 school year left a trail of nine dead students, three adults killed, and many wounded. The killings culminated at Columbine High School in Littleton, Colorado, in April 1999, when Eric Harris and Dylan Klebold used a small arsenal of firearms to gun down twelve classmates and a teacher in the worst incident of school violence in American history. More school shootings have occurred since then.

The bombing of the Alfred P. Murrah Federal Building in 1995 symbol- ized the anger of the far-right patriot and militia movements, but violence ultimately knew no political allegiance. It was not the sole purview of the ul- traconservative; in fact, hatred of what America had become was as strong on the far left as it was on the far right. For example, between 1978 and 1995 an unknown assailant that the press labeled "the Unabomber" sent sixteen letter bombs to corporate executives and university professors; the packages killed three people and injured twenty-three others. In 1995, the *Washington Post* published the Unabomber's "manifesto," a 35,000-word, Luddite polemic against corporate America. Extolling individual freedom, the Unabomber claimed that the apparent blessings of computers, cell phones, and electric- ity actually destroyed the "power to control the circumstances of one's life." Nearly a year later, in April 1996, police identified the Unabomber as Theo- dore J. Kaczynski and arrested him at a remote cabin in Montana; Kaczynski, who had earned a doctorate in mathematics at Harvard University and held a tenure-track teaching position at the University of California at Berkeley, had withdrawn from modern life to live outside of what he saw as the madness of American civilization.[1]

Vying for headline space with these hate-inspired incidents, the church burnings of the mid- to late-1990s were part of a larger landscape of American rage. Reverend Monty Knight, pastor of First Christian Church, a Disciples of Christ church in South Carolina, believed the fires grew out of a deeper dysfunction eating away at the soul of America. "It's symptomatic of a certain violence in our culture that's pretty obvious," he said in June 1996. "There are so many expressions of violence and evil in the world that you hardly know where to start." Indeed, the church arsons were a symbol of the inchoate rage of the 1990s that Richard Cohen, writing for the *Washington Post*, identified in June 1996. Cohen, chastised by a black colleague for failing to discuss the arsons in his column, reflected on the historic role of black churches. "The black church of the South was the one institution not controlled by whites," he wrote. "Maybe that is why it was so detested." He continued:

> But that is no more. Today's burnings are disconnected from some movement, from some effort to give blacks the vote or the front seat on some oven of a city bus. They have nothing to do with who goes to what school or whether the breeze in the public parks is for whites or for blacks or for both. They are not about political power or civil rights, and they do not follow a threat—a telephone call, a note posted to the door, a buzz of a rumor making its way down the main street. No one can comply with any demand since, as far as we know, there are no demands.
>
> So these burnings, nearly forty of them at last count, are an anachronism. I imagine kids here or kids there, going out into the woods with courage taken from a six-pack. This, in fact, is the profile: kids. Drunk and dumb and dumb and drunk, destroying the churches and, if they get caught, their own lives. Pretty soon, the media get hold of the story, and then even more people get the idea, and soon the arsonists can see the fruits of their work on television. Churches make for great fires.[2]

Cohen recognized that what made the arson epidemic so frightening was its utter chaos. "If it were the Klan, the Militia, the White Citizen's Council, we would know their motivation and their names," he wrote. "But this is not organized racism, racism tied to political power and purpose; rather, it is racism that comes out of the ground itself." *Newsweek* agreed. "The recent outbreaks would make more sense if extremists were riled up over a clear cause, like preserving legalized segregation," a team of the magazine's writers noted. "But today's cutting racial issue—affirmative action—is a middle-class controversy seemingly far removed from the impoverished regions where the bombings are taking place. Which leaves us with honky-tonk terrorists careening around the countryside, mindlessly obsessed with race and evoking memories of genuinely divisive days." Reverend Joseph Lowery expressed a similar thought in different terms. "There is a hatred there, there is a lunacy there," he noted, "that thinks they can shake their fists at God without consequence."[3]

Of all of the violent episodes in the United States in the late twentieth century, the burning of churches did the most to make the violence of American hate crime stark and plain; in this way, they rendered visible an invisible phenomenon in American society. Many were left wondering how such things could happen in the United States in the 1990s. "There is no reason to ask 'why' since to ask 'why' is to enter some dark and crazy spot where one presumes there is 'reason,'" wrote the poet Nikki Giovanni, "and a reason that will make sense, which is not to say there is a craziness. I don't believe this is crazy, but rather mean, hateful, ugly." Giovanni continued, "This does not speak well of our society, because no people can be great who attack the old and the defenseless and I think it's a damned shame that no one in the age of the Internet wants to admit that this is a conspiracy to hurt the heart of an old and defenseless people."[4]

Fig. 7.1. Sign at Spring Valley Baptist Church, damaged by fire in 2006 in Gainesville, Ala. 2006. Photo by author.

Dedicating Resources

According to FBI statistics, 790 investigations were initiated under the National Church Arson initiative between 1996 and 1999. During this time, 343 individuals were arrested in connection with 259 church arsons; of those 343, there were 68 charged with federal violations and 275 charged with state violations. Of the church arsons investigated by the NCATF, 258 occurred at black churches.[5]

Some civil rights leaders and right-wing critics were—for different reasons—tough on President Clinton with regard to the church arsons. The former felt he was not doing enough; the latter thought he was doing too much. However, both sets of criticisms were largely unwarranted. Once news of the story broke, Clinton acted swiftly and proactively, channeling the efforts of multiple government agencies into the National Church Arson Task Force. Clinton generally received high marks for his handling of the church arsons. His identification with and admiration of African Americans may have led him to respond to the church fires in a way other public officials might not have; indeed, it is easy to imagine other white leaders, not sharing Clinton's interest in African-American issues, being completely unreceptive and nonreactive to an issue such as black church arson. As Toni Morrison observed in a 1998 essay in the *New Yorker*, "Clinton displays almost every trope of blackness: single-parent household, born poor, working-class, saxophone-playing, McDonald's-and-junk-food-loving boy from Arkansas." It was not only his background but also his demeanor and his commitment to improved race relations that gained him favor among African Americans. Indeed, on October 1, 2001, after Clinton opened his postpresidential headquarters in Harlem, the Congressional Black Caucus honored him as the nation's "first black president"—his whiteness notwithstanding—at its annual awards dinner in Washington, D.C.[6]

Clinton's personal concern regarding the fires was reflected in the response of his administration. Attorney General Janet Reno—who (according to the *Washington Afro-American*) called the federal government's church fire investigation "the largest criminal investigation to take place in American history"—led a vigorous but imperfect inquiry into the crimes. The ATF, for example, was accustomed to investigating "arson-for-profit" cases, in which a business owner firebombed his own establishment to collect insurance monies. When it investigated church arsons in a similar fashion, questioning pastors to determine if they might have burned their own churches, the agency seemed insensitive to the plight of potential hate crime victims. Still, the Clinton administration must be given credit for its commitment to the problem of church arson. As Franklin Delano Roosevelt responded to the Great Depression with the relief, recovery, and reform of the New Deal, so too did President Clinton respond to the church fires with the "triple *Rs*": immediate aid to arson victims, efforts to heal the nation's racial wounds, and measures to ensure that such arsons would not happen again.[7]

Hoping to sensitize Clinton's successor to the issue of "homegrown" terrorism as related to communities of color and to remind President Bush of the ongoing menace of church arson, the National Coalition for Burned Churches organized a National Church Burning Status Conference in Washington, D.C., in June 2001. "We are coming to the nation's capital to remind the president that the burning of churches is not a partisan issue. It is an issue that affects all of America across racial, ethnic, and denominational lines," said the NCBC's Reverend Terrance Mackey. "Therefore, dedicating resources to aggressively combat this ongoing problem must be a priority for this president and his administration." Pastors convened at different venues around Washington, including the Capitol, the Justice Department, the National Press Club, and the U.S. Holocaust Museum. Reverend Mackey noted that churches continue to burn across the nation at the astonishing rate of fifteen to twenty per month. Whether or not White House officials may have been swayed by the conference is unclear, but a few months later the Bush administration channeled nearly its entire energies toward fighting Islamic terrorism and avenging the September 11 attacks on the World Trade Center in New York. All federal agencies reprioritized in the fight against terrorism, and church arson slipped from concern. As a result, the NCATF has not made a public report to the president since 2000, during the Clinton administration. It is now defunct.[8]

A New Fraud?

Of course, church arson did not go away after September 11, 2001. As the embers died, as new churches rose from the ashes, and as it seemed that the frequency of such attacks was decreasing, hate crimes surged again—this time against a new target. Muslim Americans and Southeast Asian Americans were targeted in racially motivated assaults in the wake of the September 11 terrorist attacks on the World Trade Center and Pentagon. The Council on American-Islamic Relations received three hundred reports of harassment and abuse in the two days following the plane hijackings; in this two-day period, the council received half the number of reports it had received in the entire previous year. On September 12, three hundred men and women chanting "U.S.A., U.S.A." tried to storm a mosque in the Chicago suburb of Bridgeview, Illinois; more than one hundred police officers restrained the crowd. On September 15, Frank Roque, vowing vengeance for the September 11 terrorist attacks, murdered Balbir Singh Sodhi, a Sikh gas station owner in Mesa, Arizona. On September 30, two men stabbed Swaran Kaur Bhullar, a Sikh woman, twice in the head when she stopped her car at a red light in San Diego; never apprehended, the two attackers probably assumed she was a Muslim. A Hindu temple was firebombed in Matawan, New Jersey; two Muslim mosques in the Texas cities of Irving and Denton were attacked. A large firecracker detonated at the Islam Center of San Diego, and an armed man dumped gasoline on the parking lot of a Seattle mosque. The mosque attacks continued a trend begun in previous years. For example, as worshippers arrived at the Masjid Al-Nur (Mosque of Light) in Memphis, Tennessee, for predawn prayers on the morning of June 20, 2000, a neighbor shot one man and fired several bullets into the door of the mosque. In May 1999, a man was detained while loitering around a Denver mosque in the early morning hours; police found loaded weapons and bomb-making materials in his car.[9]

Notably, while these incidents *did* have the intended effect of terrorizing Muslims in America, just as black churchgoers had been traumatized, they also had the unintended effect of galvanizing communities, empowering congregations, and unifying Americans across racial lines—just as the attacks on black churches had done. To illustrate, Muslims in Seattle, afraid to visit their mosque during the week of September 11, 2001, found non-Muslims waiting there with flowers when they finally returned. On Sunday, September 14, the Islamic Society of Denton, Texas, held a prayer vigil, joined by the city mayor and fifteen other church groups. "It is a gathering of peace, prayer, and friendship. Baptist, Catholic, Presbyterian . . ." explained Irfan Ali, a member of the mosque. The day before, the Denton mosque received a gift from the student body of the University of North Texas: fifty posters with greetings, flowers, condolences, and prayers, all hand-delivered by the student body president. If the hate had morphed and mutated, finding a new outlet, so too had the compassion of fellow citizens, struggling to bring tolerance and harmony out of a powerful tradition of intolerance and discord.[10]

On September 20, 2001, the *National Review* cautioned its readers to distrust accounts of hate crimes against Muslims spread by the "anti-American Left," which will "suggest that hateful Americans are now engaged in a fit of anti-Muslim violence that is only one step removed from certified ethnic cleansing." The magazine noted that is was remarkable how little such violence occurred in the days following September 11. "Here is something to watch for: a new fraud perpetrated on the public along the lines of the church-burning phenomenon of several years ago." In comparing the earlier church arsons with the later wave of hate crimes directed against Arab Americans, the *National Review* not only assumed the "fraud" of the arsons but also seemed quick to disallow the suggestion of widespread acts of aggression against Arab Americans—just as Fumento and others had been quick to disallow the suggestion of widespread acts of aggression against black churchgoers. The *National Review* article did not acknowledge the similarities between Muslim Americans and black southerners, both of whom sought to worship in peace, but the parallels between the attacks on black churches and Islamic mosques in the United States could not have been clearer. Both were motivated by nativism, fear, and intolerance. The difference lay in whatever threat mosques posed as safe havens or potential training grounds for fundamentalist terrorists living within U.S. borders; but, in the days immediately following September 11, such threat was indeterminate.[11]

Was the American public suckered into believing news of an "epidemic" of church arsons? Some journalists felt so. "It seemed quite clear to me in the mid-1990s that certain activists on racial issues had seized on the church fires as a way of raising either consciousness about racism or money for their causes or both," wrote Ann Rodgers-Melnick, religion correspondent for the *Pittsburgh Post-Gazette*. "This story is a classic study in gullible reporters from even the most respected news organizations being taken in by 'spinners' and never bothering to check the facts."[12]

At first no one would touch the story—not even the black press. "We couldn't initially get anything in the black press—until the white press validated it," said Reverend Dr. Mac Charles Jones at a 1996 convention of the National Association of Black Journalists. "Now that's a telling statement. If you are getting your news from other media and institutions and never talk to the principals, it raises questions about the nature of that journalism." Things changed, according to Jones, when Gary Fields "lucked into" the assignment to investigate the fires. Fields's exposé of the church fires in *USA Today* ushered the lightweight newspaper into the world of serious journalism. Criticized as a "McPaper" for its full-color layout and insubstantial stories, *USA Today* had struggled in its first fifteen years to find a niche in the world of hard-hitting news reporting. After receiving editorial permission to pursue the story, Gary Fields and a dozen other reporters fanned out across the South, where they conducted more than five hundred interviews, examined fire records in every southern state, and visited the sites of forty-five church arsons. Fields's breaking of the church arson story in a four-page report—what Joe Holley called, in the September/October 1996 issue of the *Columbia Journalism Review*, "the longest and most comprehensive story *USA Today* has ever published"—catapulted the paper to another level. "*USA Today* pulled off the kind of once-in-a-lifetime journalistic coup that forges reputations and launches careers," wrote Michael Fumento; even the *New York Times* declared that *USA Today* had at last become "a real newspaper" with its coverage of the arsons. Also lauded, Fred Bayles of the Associated Press won an award for his exposé on the arsons. Such reporting not only generated accolades for the journalists but also swelled the coffers of the National Council of Churches, according to Fumento, who reported that there was enough money between insurance coverage and the NCC's Burned Churches Fund in October 1996 to rebuild each church three times over. *USA Today* later suggested that there was no evidence of conspiracy in the arsons; Fumento interpreted this angle of the story, coming as it did from *USA Today*, as a retreat from the paper's earlier position that the fires were an epidemic. "What *USA Today* did," Fumento wrote, "was the equivalent of an exterminator planting a cockroach nest in your house and later earning your undying gratitude for ridding your home of the horrid things."[13]

Gary Fields maintained that he was simply telling a story that needed to be told. "I didn't know it would grow legs and run like it did," he said. "Nobody was hyping it. Everyone was staying away from it, kind of in the same way we ignore homicides in black neighborhoods." He rejected the notion that he overplayed the story. "Who gets to decide what is the normal rate for churches to be burned?" he asked. "The one conspiracy there has been is a conspiracy of indifference." Explanations that pointed to youthful vandalism did not satisfy Fields. "What we found was yes, beyond everything, there was an undercurrent of racism . . . that was in every place I went. What we weren't going to say is, OK, this is a racist fire, this is a hate-related crime. The only thing we wanted to do is lay out the facts for readers and let them make up their mind." Employing the same metaphor used by Fumento, Fields said: "My grandmother used to have an expression: turn on the kitchen lights to see where the roaches are. Well, the kitchen lights are now on—it's time to find the roaches."[14]

Internet webloggers would later offer their two-cents' worth on Web sites such as www.FreeRepublic.com, the self-described "premier online gathering place for independent, grass-roots conservatism on the web." A blogger calling himself "Interesting Times" wrote in 2002, "Nearly six years later, the church fires disinformation campaign stands as an excellent example of leftist media tactics." He continued, "The truth of the matter appears to be that a very small number of black churches are burned each year by white racists, and that the rate has been relatively static." Comparing the racially motivated church arsons in the South—"less than ten per year"—to the "more than 620 buildings . . . burned during the 1992 Rodney King riots in Los Angeles alone," the writer seemed to suggest that urban blacks were far more destructive than southern white supremacists who occasionally burned a church or two. Responding to the first posting, another blogger wondered if anyone were bothered by the NCC's "bearing false witness for political and financial gain." A third blogger responded, "I really believe the 1990s will be remembered as the 'Decade of Frauds.'" These postings precipitated a rambling discussion thread on the conspiracy of the leftist-controlled media to spread lies and to benefit the "clintonites."[15]

As evidenced by such musings on the blogosphere, the known facts were few. Even if people had been able to agree what had burned and where and when—and they could not—different groups contemplating the same set of facts were seeing widely disparate scenarios. The media's problem in accurately reporting the number of church burnings reflected a larger problem in determining and recording the crime of arson. It would have been difficult for even the most diligent journalist to research and report definitive arson statistics before 1996, in the days before the federal government began to record the crimes in a systematic way; even after 1996, people could not agree on the figures involved. For example, in November 2002, the *Washington Post* reported that legal efforts did not halt the church arsons of the 1990s. The most recent NCATF report said that arsons, bombings, and attempts of both at houses of worship had decreased from 297 in 1996 to 140 in 1999—a drop from twenty-five per month to twelve. In 2001 and 2002, the number of incidents averaged about ten per month, according to Harold Scott Jr. of the Bureau of Alcohol, Tobacco, and Firearms. The National Coalition for Burned Churches, which kept its own national registry of incidents culled from government statistics and reports solicited from state fire marshals' offices, published very different findings. "The numbers have come down, but not too much," said Rose Johnson-Mackey, NCBC research director. The NCBC found that the incidents are occurring at a much higher rate of forty to eighty per month. Unlike those of the NCATF, the NCBC's figures include fires of undetermined cause, and attacks ranging from total to partial destruction of a building, as well as attacks causing no damage; however, Johnson-Mackey feels that the NCBC's own registry of incidents is incomplete due to underreporting by local fire departments. "The information . . . is based on available data reflecting less than 20 percent of all church burning and bombing activity nationwide," she said.[16]

Michael Fumento concluded, "one would think at least some journalists might have been led to wonder what this episode says about the way 'news' is manufactured, packaged, and shipped these days, or to reflect on their own role in plunging so many Americans into a paroxysm of utterly baseless recrimination." Fumento's skepticism and Mac Charles Jones's concerns about reporting in the black press pointed to a larger truth: the church burnings heralded the erosion of dependably accurate American journalism in the early twenty-first century. This erosion paradoxically stemmed from too much and too little information. The roles of social critics such as Rush Limbaugh and Molly Ivins, who served as healthy irritants for spirit and mind in the 1990s, were clearly defined; however, when some journalists began to mimic these same social critics in their reporting, it became harder to distinguish opinion from fact. Journalists chose sides in the culture wars of the 1990s, and editorializing often seemed to replace reporting; the American people, not knowing whom to trust, increasingly watched or read the news that suited them. As Fox News countermanded NBC (an editorial decision related to viewer-driven news reporting), newspapers increasingly ran stories secondhand (a cost-based decision related to news outsourcing), and opinion and rumor increasingly passed as fact. This trend—a product of not only twenty-four-hour news reporting but also the dissemination of information via the Internet—began to corrode the tenets of objective journalism: in a postmodern America of relative truths, people believed what they wanted to believe, picking and choosing their facts. With the church arsons, as with other newsworthy events, it was becoming increasingly difficult to say what had actually happened.[17]

If *USA Today* was guilty of overreporting the story of church arsons across the nation—and it is not clear that the paper did—then Michael Fumento and other critics may be accused of overzealously attacking the newspaper and politicizing the issue. Right-wing critics such as Fumento were not the only ones to politicize the arsons: while President Clinton's concern seems genuine enough, others on the left moved to capitalize on sentiment stirred by the atrocities. It should be noted that certain issues *need* to be politicized, requiring government attention and demanding state intervention. Certainly the civil rights movement was highly politicized, as was apartheid in South Africa, and while politicizing an issue is not inherently wrong, one must wonder if the occasion of Fumento's criticism was circumspect. Furthermore, one might argue that if extensive media coverage was what was needed to elicit an empathetic response to the horror of churches burned in the United States, then such coverage should be praised. That the collective American conscience needed such a barrage of news stories to be moved speaks more about compassion than it does the watchdog role of the media.

Fig. 7.2. Reporters covering the church arsons in Bibb County, Ala. 2006. Photo by Hollie Huey, "Centreville (Ala.) Press."

A Truer Reality

Religion exists in a unique space between the secular realm and the spiritual realm. Churches, marked off from the everyday world even as they are part of it, establish a concrete means of communion with the divine. Such structures transcend their utility. "I know it's just a building," explained Ken Pardue, pastor of Stony Hill Baptist Church in Purlear, North Carolina, "but it's the building we meet to worship in." As communal symbols, churches embody the values of a group of people, and to attack such symbols is to attack those values. Therefore, a church arson represents an attack on belief itself: an attack on faith as hope in the unknown. In African-American history, the known has often been trauma, persecution, and despair; the unknown has been the possibility of a better future. To attack that faith—that hope in the possibility of a better future—is the deepest of cuts.

Throughout the fires, an atheist Web site celebrated the burning of churches with the URL address www.churcharson.com, and some nativists lauded the persecution of Muslim Americans in the post–9/11 era. However, such searing hate could not burn brighter than the faith of those victimized by church arson. The most consistently high-minded responses—and often the most poignant ones—came from those ministers directly involved in the arsons, as exemplified by Reverend Terrance Mackey, among others. "God did not put a black soul or a white soul in Adam," he said from the pulpit of Mt. Zion AME Church in Greeleyville, South Carolina, in 1996. "The differences we have between the races, we created this mess."[18]

If arsonists intended to foment hatred and despair, then they grossly miscalculated the depth of faith of those affected. "Church members were renewed like a phoenix from the ashes of these fires," wrote Joseph Broadus in the *Atlanta Inquirer*. "[A] truer reality is now discovered in the link that exists between members of a larger faith community." Those affected "are now defined by the grace to undo these shameful acts and the joy of discovering that others care." For example, in 1998, as church members left their Sunday service, a loud explosion rocked the center of the Faith in Victory Church, leaving the sanctuary and the rest of the building in rubble. Faith in Victory serves the farmworker community at the tip of south Texas, five miles from the Mexican border. For the next two years, the congregation met "under trees outside, in little units," said Reverend Lucy Martinez. "People were calling us gypsies." With support from the National Coalition for Burned Churches, Martinez's congregation rebuilt in the same location.

"It's a blessing to get into the new building," she said in 2001. "We're literally living our name."[19]

A Kind of Forgotten America

Much like Hurricane Katrina, which left a trail of broken lives in its wake along the gulf coast in 2005, the church arsons spotlighted the dark-dwelling twins of race and class. "It's a hell of a thing that it took churches to burn down for the American media to take a look at the problems of poverty in rural America," said John Seigenthaler, chairman of the Freedom Forum's First Amendment Center in Nashville. Brian Levin, associate director of Klanwatch at the Southern Poverty Law Center and professor of criminal justice at Stockton College in New Jersey, told the *Los Angeles Times* that reports of

Fig. 7.3. Firefighter douses flames at church fire in Bibb County, Ala. 2006. Photo by Hollie Huey, "Centreville (Ala.) Press."

a greater number of white churches being burned than black were "a veiled attempt . . . to downplay the problem of racism."[20]

Accordingly, the story was as much about poor whites as it was poor blacks—though few people acknowledged it at the time. One of those who did was Paul Hemphill, author of *The Ballad of Little River: A Tale of Race and Restless Youth in the Rural South* (2001). Hemphill's book recalled, as one reviewer pointed out, James Agee's *Let Us Now Praise Famous Men* and Walker Evans's haunting photographs of rural poverty—what Hemphill himself called "a Faulknerian huddle of fairly exotic proportions." He wrote *The Ballad of Little River* with the intention of understanding this unremarkable community in southern Alabama where blacks and whites lived together, and where one day five local white youths burned down one tiny black church and vandalized another. The result of Hemphill's investigation was "a melancholy and savory story of a kind of forgotten America where people face dead-end jobs and despair with six-packs of beer, the occasional joint, and a kind of heedless self-justification," according to Richard Bernstein, a book reviewer for the *New York Times*. "Almost nobody has a happy story in Mr. Hemphill's instructive and finely tuned portrait, which serves as a reminder that the world of Agee, Evans, and Faulkner is not entirely behind us." To Bernstein, the phrase "hate crime" does not quite suffice to explain Hemphill's portrayal of Little River. "The church burning seemed more a consequence of a sort of moral disintegration—family violence, divorce, chronic feuding, infidelity, heavy drinking, and welfare cheating—that was a good deal more pronounced among Little River's whites than among its blacks." While both racial groups suffered equally in the poverty common to southern Alabama, it was a handful of shiftless yet pitiable youths who resorted to the time-honored practice of degrading someone whom they perceived as being on the next lowest rung.[21]

What Bernstein identified as a "moral disintegration" marked an erosion of community not only in individual locales such as Little River but also in American society as a whole. David Riesman partially identified this trend as early as 1950 in his book *The Lonely Crowd*, as did John Kenneth Galbraith in 1958 in *The Affluent Society*. Both books explored the atomized existence of individuals in modern American society. Robert Putnam has explored this phenomenon more recently in his book *Bowling Alone: The Collapse and Revival of American Community* (2000), in which he shows how Americans have become increasingly disconnected from one another and how social structures—be they bowling leagues, civic organizations, or political parties—have disintegrated. Many commentators interpreted the church fires as further evidence of this breakdown in community, which may be defined as the obligations people owe to one another and to the whole of which they are parts.[22]

A Story with Two Bookends

If the arsons signaled a breakdown in community, however, the response to them also revealed communal bonds that few Americans knew existed. The church fires of the 1990s cast a light that illuminated what a better society might be: one more deeply inclusive; one oriented to human wholeness rather than private acquisition; one less focused on competitive market calculation; one that serviced the poor, giving them the tools and education to succeed in American life; one of shared identity and cooperation; one in which people of different faiths, ethnic backgrounds, and political persuasions worked together toward achieving the ideals articulated by the Founding Fathers in the Declaration and Constitution—in short, one more sympathetic, compassionate, benevolent, and interdependent. Such a society would include a widening of democratic participation, an increase in general prosperity, and the accountability of governmental institutions. As Dennis McCann has phrased it, the common good is the pursuit of the good in common.[23]

On the edge of the twenty-first century, Americans from all walks of life faced a number of challenging and often frightening issues: corporate downsizing, outsourcing, globalization, economic uncertainty, and political divisiveness. Even as better and faster communication (and transportation) made possible a new kind of community at the national level, technological developments that pulled the nation together threatened to pull some towns and neighborhoods apart. American jobs shipped overseas. Housing costs skyrocketed. Well-paid jobs were replaced by those offered by Wal-Mart, the nation's largest employer, with jobs that pay seven or eight dollars an hour. American families cobbled together different jobs to make ends meet as the concept of the single breadwinner disappeared; many learned that a family needed at least two incomes—dual breadwinners—to pay the bills. As has often been the case, poor whites and poor blacks found themselves buffeted by large forces beyond their control that pushed them further from the mainstream of American life. Jobless with few prospects, some whites found familiar scapegoats in the form of their black neighbors.[24]

A familiar actor on the American stage, racism moved into the spotlight in the 1990s, as it tends to do in times of economic realignment and other major changes, but it was only one of many performers related to the church arson drama. The impact of the first generation of the twenty-four-hour news cycle, the media's recognition of the Christian right as major political and cultural mediators, the media's challenge to the civil rights establishment as legitimate racial brokers on behalf of black America, the hardening of political compromise and bipartisan cooperation, even the "great risk shift" of post-1990 America—when multinationals (like insurance companies) shifted financial liabilities and costs to smaller risk pools (like underinsured churches)—all played roles. In fact, many of the hot-button issues that have come to define the early years of post–Cold War America were illumined by the church fires.

Black churchmen and civil rights leaders were struck by the slowness of the national media and federal government to take notice and respond to the fires, but the response—when it came—was overwhelming. After news of the fires broke, the American people responded by dousing them with a coast-to-coast bucket brigade. Americans were so conscious of the fires as ugly reminders of their bigoted past—so conscious of revisiting the twisted days of naked racial intolerance—that they responded vigorously and swiftly to ostracize the perpetrators and aid the victims. If the fires themselves signaled something profoundly wrong with America, then the response of churches, governments, media outlets, and individual citizens signaled something profoundly right. The arsons served as tests of communal bonds in an age of seemingly diminishing community. They were blows against community by a minority in which the majority discovered how resilient its communities actually were: communities that had seemed to be deteriorating and breaking down. Believers discovered how closely knit they were in a community of faith; Americans on the whole discovered how closely knit they were in a community of compassion for their fellow citizens. Thinking they were divided, Americans learned through the fires that they were more or less united across racial and religious lines in their intolerance of hate crime.

In light of such developments, it seemed possible that racism was waning, even as it still bubbled beneath the surface of American life. Incidents such as the Oklahoma City bombing, the Susan Smith case (when authorities unquestioningly accepted the racially charged accusations of a deranged South Carolinian who accused black assailants of taking her children, when in fact she had drowned them herself), the O. J. Simpson trial, and the church burnings forced conscientious American citizens to confront the ongoing signifi-

Fig. 7.4. Sign at Antioch Baptist Church, damaged by fire in 2006 in Bibb County, Ala. 2006. Photo by Hollie Huey, "Centreville (Ala.) Press."

cance of race in modern America. As a disturbing reminder of the nation's racist past, the church burnings convinced many white Americans, lulled into believing that color-blind equity had been achieved in the post–civil rights era, that they could not be passive in the battle against racial hatred. Ignoring the problem, or pretending that racial differences did not divide Americans, was not tenable in light of the church arsons. With regard to racial hatred, as with many other vexing social issues, one was either part of the problem or part of the solution.[25]

Accordingly, one of the most heartening aspects of the fires was the response of tens of thousands of people from all over the nation—including those southern communities in which the arsons had occurred—who contributed time, money, and support to those affected. A July 1996 article in the *Wall Street Journal* discussed how the January 1995 church burnings in Columbia, Tennessee, served to unite rather than divide blacks and whites.

White folks, shamed and outraged by the arsons there, contributed to rebuilding the affected churches. Many thousands more contributed money to help rebuild in Tennessee and elsewhere. If racial hatred destroyed black churches across the South and across the nation, then white labor and money also helped to rebuild those same houses of worship. So obvious an assault on black churches united conservatives and liberals, whites and blacks, Christians and non-Christians alike in moving to condemn those responsible—even as politicians and policymakers (black and white alike) jockeyed to appropriate the image and memory of the civil rights movement in policy discourse and cultural politics. "The alarm raised by reports of what appeared to be a spate of church burnings brought Americans together in their repudiation of racial hatred and in their determination to rebuild the churches and outlaw racism," wrote the editorial board of the *Charleston (S.C.) Post and Courier*. "Men and women of goodwill throughout the nation spoke with one voice in condemning the attacks on churches."[26]

The church arsons instigated a fresh look at the lingering injustices of the civil rights era. Justice played catch-up in the early twenty-first century, when authorities revisited several cold cases from the civil rights era and legal eagles tried to put the nation's ugly racial past squarely behind it. In May 2000, nearly thirty-seven years after what may have been the most heinous attack of the civil rights era, authorities charged two longtime suspects with murder in the 1963 bombing that killed four black girls at Birmingham's Sixteenth Street Baptist Church. Thomas E. Blanton Jr. and Bobby Frank Cherry, both of whom were affiliated with the Ku Klux Klan and both of whom had been considered suspects for decades, turned themselves in after being indicted by a state grand jury. Sixty-two-year-old Blanton was convicted in May 2001; one year later, seventy-one-year-old Cherry was also convicted. Both faced life in prison. In 2003, a federal jury in Jackson, Mississippi, convicted a seventy-two-year-old man in the 1966 slaying of an elderly black sharecropper. Prosecutors in Mississippi won convictions in the Klan killings of civil rights leaders Medgar Evers and Vernon Dahmer, and, in 2005, Edgar Ray Killen was convicted and sentenced for his role in the 1964 deaths of civil rights volunteers James Chaney, Andrew Goodman, and Michael Schwerner. Such prosecutions began to set right not only the wrongful arrests of civil rights workers but also the collusions between law-enforcement officers and the perpetrators of anti-black violence, who enjoyed full immunity, slipped through court on nominal charges, or escaped punishment after sham proceedings. If justice delayed is justice denied, then family members who lost loved ones to racist violence in the 1960s may have found small comfort in the outcome of these newer trials, but the net impact in exorcising the residual ghosts of the civil rights era was invaluable. Without doubt, the prosecutions facilitated community reconciliation.[27]

On the whole, the fires of the 1990s were neither universal acts of racist violence nor events overblown by "race hustlers"; however, they did closely resemble the brazen attacks by white supremacists on black Americans in the 1960s, and whether racially malicious or not, a person could not burn a black church in the South or anywhere else without evoking memories of the violent opposition faced by civil rights workers and other black Americans in decades past. Whether or not the KKK was involved remained unclear, but that aspect of the story was not, as some believed at the time, crucial. In the end, it did not really matter because the net effect was the same. Likewise, how the press handled this news event was not the real story. The real story is what happened to certain citizens across the nation and how the rest of us responded. Perhaps, in a by-product of their actions that the firebugs could never have intended or anticipated, the church arsons and the national reaction to them signaled the beginning of the creation of what Martin Luther King Jr. called the "beloved community." Reverend Dr. Charles Cravey, in contemplating rebuilding efforts at Gay's Hill Baptist Church in Georgia, wrote, "What Satan tried to accomplish through hate, God conquers and rebuilds with love."

> Block by block, board by board, Gay's Hill Baptist Church begins to take shape, with volunteer labor from across America breaking down racial and religious barriers. It is not so much the physical church being rebuilt as the spiritual church. Blacks and whites are working side by side. Martin, your dream has finally come to fruition. It's beginning to work at Gay's Hill and elsewhere across America. . . . The dream IS alive![28]

As HUD secretary Andrew Cuomo told the an oversight hearing on the Federal Loan Guaranty Program in 1997: "[T]he story of church burning in America over the past few years is a story with two bookends, one a bookend of discrimination and anger, the other a bookend of hope and renewal. In between is a story of national faith, devotion and humanity—the best chapters of which are still being written today."[29]

epilogue

Church arson again dominated national headlines in early 2006, when a series of fires scorched six rural churches in a single night in central Alabama. All but one were in Bibb County, south of Birmingham. The sixth church, New Harmony Holiness Baptist in Chilton County, had been under construction when it was destroyed. Ragan Ingram, a spokesperson for the state insurance agency that oversees fire investigations, speculated that the New Harmony fire was accidental as investigators flocked to the other churches to determine whether arson was involved. Ashby Baptist, Rehobeth Baptist, and Pleasant Sabine all burned to the ground in the early morning hours of February 7; Old Union Baptist and Antioch Baptist were damaged but not completely destroyed. Local residents reported seeing an unfamiliar, dark-colored SUV in the vicinity of the churches at daybreak.[1]

"My initial thought was just shock, just unbelief really," said Reverend Robert Murphy, pastor of Pleasant Sabine. "Even when I got there, it was even more like a dream. I didn't want to face the fact that it had happened." Ernie Wallace, a volunteer fireman from nearby Lawley, expressed his sorrow. "It's sad when any church is on fire because the memories of homecomings and singings automatically come to mind," he said. "You just feel helpless when you get there and the roof is already gone."[2]

Governor Bob Riley visited the sites of the arsons the following weekend to see the damage firsthand. Riley met with pastors and congregation

Fig. 8.1. Front steps of Galilee Baptist Church, destroyed by fire in 2006 in Panola, Ala. 2006. Photo by author.

members at each church. "I am outraged that anyone would deliberately set fire to churches," he said. "I want the people of the affected congregations to know that the state will do all that's possible to find those responsible and bring them to justice." Jim Walker, Alabama director of Homeland Security, said, "What strikes us the most is the senseless, needless act of burning down churches. . . . It's hard to imagine a world that is starved for faith, love, and hope and the institutions that nurture those qualities would be the ones that these perpetrators chose to damage."[3]

Four days after the Bibb County fires, four more fires were reported at black Baptist churches in western Alabama, in sparsely populated areas spread out over three counties, about sixty miles west of the earlier fires. Morning Star Baptist, near Boligee, and Dancy Baptist, near Aliceville, were destroyed.

The *New York Times* reported that Galilee Baptist suffered extensive damage while Spring Valley Baptist suffered "only minor damage"; however, the fire at Spring Valley, which endured heavy smoke damage, required not only removal of the church's pews, carpet, drapes, and other furniture but also repainting of the entire building as well as replacement of the building's insulation. A visitor to the church in mid-March would have found Spring Valley completely gutted and empty save two local Mennonite painters—a father-and-son team—methodically repainting the sooty interior.[4]

The arsons in central and western Alabama were markedly similar. In each case, the arsonists deliberately made their way to the sanctuary to start multiple fires. Investigators found similar burn patterns at the churches. Fires were started in the area of the pulpit or on the church organ; the arsonists also burned U.S. and religious flags in the front of the church, as well as any floral arrangements. All of the fires occurred at Baptist churches. All of the churches were isolated, often tucked deep in the woods at the end of dirt roads. Because the churches were so remote, investigators suspected that the arsonists were local residents. "They've been around, they've searched it out, they might have traveled back here as a hunter," ATF Special Agent-in-Charge James Cavanaugh predicted. "Somebody in the area knows probably who these people are and they need to give us a call."[5]

Investigators soon determined that the New Harmony fire in Chilton County was, in fact, accidental; however, another fire at Beaverton Freewill Baptist in northwest Alabama on February 11 brought the number of confirmed arsons in Alabama to ten—all in less than a week. If the first wave of arsons caused concern among some, then the second wave surely shocked the entire nation. National newspapers covered the fires, editorials decried the crimes. The investigation quickly turned into the biggest domestic manhunt since 9/11. Over two hundred investigators—ATF agents, FBI agents, state fire marshals, Justice Department officials, and local law enforcement personnel—sifted through seven hundred leads as they searched for the arsonists.[6]

Authorities speculated about the culprits and their motives. "We do think they have a message," Jim Cavanaugh said. "We would like to hear what they would have to say. . . . We want them to call us. We want to listen. . . . I think there's probably some stressors in their life: family, relationships, work, the economy. The region's been devastated by a hurricane, there's a war in Iraq, there's a lot of terrible things going on." Responding to witnesses' accounts of two men leaving the scene of several of the arsons in a dark-colored SUV, he continued, "We think they're buddies, partners, an inseparable team."[7]

Local churches heightened security measures as church members patrolled their churches at night. Representative Artur Davis (D-Alabama) surveyed the damage at Spring Valley Baptist Church and found many congregants ready to rebuild. "If you think you've intimidated somebody, you haven't intimidated anybody," he said to whoever had committed the crimes. "If you think you've got a lot folks scared in west Alabama, you've also got a lot of folks praying in west Alabama."[8]

On March 8, authorities arrested three suspects, all college students from Birmingham, for burning nine churches in central and western Alabama. Two of the suspects were identified as Benjamin Nathan Moseley and Russell Lee DeBusk Jr., both nineteen-year-old students at Birmingham-Southern College. Matthew Lee Cloyd, a twenty-year-old junior at the University of Alabama at Birmingham, also was arrested. The three were not only jailed on federal charges of conspiracy and arson but also faced state charges. Confronted by authorities, the young men claimed that the arson spree was a "joke" that "got out of hand," according to an affidavit, but this explanation rang hollow for two main reasons. First, most folks failed to see the humor in burning a church, and burning nine of them was distinctly *un*funny. "The lawyers are doing their part, but I don't buy that for a minute," said Sheriff J. L. Isaac of Greene County. "I don't think it was a joke and I don't think it was a prank." Isaac noted that local citizens were terrified by the arsons, and conspiracy to burn down nine houses of worship, as one Birmingham editorialist noted, is no joke. Second, even if one took into consideration the youth of the suspects, there were too many fires, set deliberately and methodically over too large an area, for anyone to consider the spree a boyish prank that spun out of control. "When you conspire to come this distance, that's premeditated," said Sheriff Isaac. Reverend Bob Little seemed to agree, noting, "You don't find Galilee without really finding Galilee."[9]

Tire tracks provided a clue that led investigators to the students. Witnesses had provided descriptions of a Toyota 4Runner SUV at several of the fires, and investigators found tracks at one church from a BF Goodrich All-Terrain tire. Federal agents checked regional tire dealers for records of purchases for that brand of tire on that particular vehicle. Doing so led them to Cloyd's mother.[10]

Searching for racist rednecks, authorities were surprised to find clean-cut,

Fig. 8.2. Charred ruins of Galilee Baptist Church, destroyed by fire in 2006 in Panola, Ala. 2006. Photo by author.

Fig. 8.3. Tire tracks at Spring Valley Baptist Church in Gainesville, Ala. These tracks led to the arrest of three arson suspects. 2006. Photo by author.

upper-middle-class college kids who did not match their initial criminal profiles. Cloyd was a pre-med student, the son of a doctor. DeBusk attended
college on a theater scholarship. Moseley was student council president at
his high school. Investigators were seemingly befuddled by the identities of
the suspects. "This is just so hard to believe," said state fire marshal Richard
Montgomery. "My profile on these suspects is shot all to heck and back."
Alice Martin, U.S. Attorney for the northern district of Alabama, stated on
March 9 that what had happened did not constitute a hate crime. The best
explanation authorities could provide was that alcohol may have fueled the
suspects' wilding. Deputy state fire marshal Ed Paulk said he did not know
if alcohol use was directly involved in the arsons; but, he added, the crimes
would break a well-established pattern if alcohol was not a factor.[11]

On March 10, many Birmingham listeners dialed "Burt & Kurt," a popular radio show that devoted its entire four-hour program to discussing the
fires. Expressing a popular sense of embarrassment and outrage, these callers
creatively described appropriate punishments for the suspects who—perhaps
unwittingly—had resurrected a ghost that most Alabamans believed to have
been excised. A federal judge in Birmingham set bond at $50,000 each for the
three college students. The suspects were granted bail with thirteen stipula-
tions on March 16. The judge determined they were not a flight risk; however,
the suspects—in a seeming act of penance—chose to remain in jail.

Again, Americans were left to make sense of a senseless crime. "When are
people gonna stop this?" wondered Sheriff Isaac. "Why?" Some of the authorities' speculations proved accurate; others did not. As it turned out, the
three young men did not have a message, as Special Agent Cavanaugh had
suggested. If they were disturbed by Hurricane Katrina or the war in Iraq,
they did not identify these calamities as reasons for their behavior. They did
not seem troubled; in fact, they seemed rather to be enjoying themselves. The
three chatted casually about their plans for 2006 on Facebook.com, a net-
working Web site for high school and college students. Newspapers reprinted
a January 9 posting on Moseley's profile from Cloyd:

To my dearest friend Moseley:
The nights have grown long and the interstates of Alabama drunk
driverless, the state troopers bored, the county sheriffs less weary, and
the deer of Bibb County fearless. 2006 is here, it is time to reconvene
the season of evil! Only one problem stands in our way. I got a new cell

phone for Christmas and I no longer have your number, so send it to me and evil shall once again come to pass!

May our girlfriends be concerned about our safety, may our parents be clueless, may our beers be frosty, may our love lives be fruitful, may our weed be as green as the freshly mowed grass![12]

Scrounging for clues as to the suspects' motivation, thousands of people visited the Web site, where many posted messages of outrage (and some posted messages of support).

Alice Martin's proclamation on March 9 that the fires did not constitute a hate crime left many concerned citizens cold. Martin apparently made this statement because there was no racial angle to the story (five of the churches were white; five were black); nor were there any overtly satanic messages left behind by the culprits. However, while it may have comforted some who heard it, her announcement seemed premature, coming one day after the arrests. Christian bloggers wondered: if ten burned churches did not constitute a hate crime, what did? As Reverend Glenn Harris—pastor of Spring Valley Baptist Church—observed, without a full investigation, and without a more complete explanation from the suspects themselves, who could say whether these incidents were hate crimes or not? Martin's statement raised serious questions about how aggressively the government would prosecute the case. Officials seemed willing to accept the defense that these were "kids" who had exercised poor judgment in carrying out a joke or "prank." After this seemingly senseless series of arsons in Alabama that had no apparent racial or religious motivation, perpetrated by suspects who torpedoed all of the experts' profiles of people who committed similar crimes, many Americans were again left scratching their heads, wondering how long such crimes would continue, and how long they would be shrugged off as common property crimes.[13]

The arsonists left their mark. "This church will always be 'pre-fire' and 'post-fire,'" said Reverend Harris of Spring Valley Baptist. "I hope it will be a greater church." He found himself changed in the aftermath of the arsons. "This has made me compassionate to other hurts," he said one month later in the smoke-damaged kitchen of his church. "I ask myself, 'What would Jesus do?' We have no ill will toward the perpetrators. They are forgiven."[14]

The young men pled guilty to federal charges in December 2006. On April

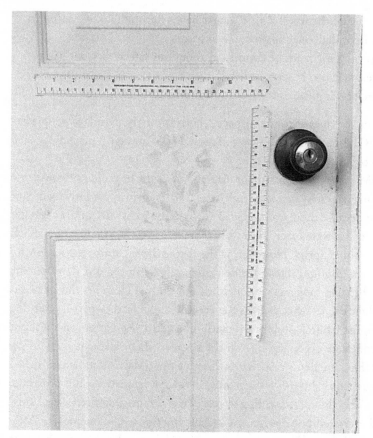

Fig. 8.4. Door at Spring Valley Baptist Church, damaged by fire in 2006 in Gainesville, Ala. Note footprint and measuring tape left by ATF investigators. 2006. Photo by author.

9, 2007, Cloyd and Moseley were sentenced to eight years in prison for conspiracy and arson, five years of probation, and three hundred hours of community service at the burned churches. U.S. District Judge David Proctor also ordered both to pay $3.1 million in restitution. DeBusk, sentenced to seven years and ordered to pay $1.8 million, received a slightly lighter sentence because he was not involved in as many of the fires. Three days later, the three former college students pled guilty to state arson and burglary charges, which netted them each two more years in prison to be served after their federal sentences. Moseley also pled guilty to animal cruelty for shooting a cow during what they described as a night of drunken joy riding. The defendants still faced charges related to the second round of fires in Greene County.[15]

Fig. 8.5. Reverend Glenn Harris, pastor of Spring Valley Baptist Church in Gainesville, Ala. 2006. Photo by author.

The Need for Community

The causes of crime are incredibly complex. It does not correlate to race or—as Moseley, DeBusk, and Cloyd so vividly demonstrate—socioeconomic status. There is no single cause, no single explanation, no single cure. In the few cases that have been solved, the confessions of persons convicted provide little insight; in fact, the criminal evidence from these many cases points to a range of motives—from boredom to racial hatred. As a result, any attempt to explain these arsons ultimately falls short. As Nikki Giovanni observed, there is little reason to ask why because doing so presumes reason in a fundamentally unreasonable act.

On a general level, however, the roots of church arson seem to be entangled in the absence of community in contemporary society. The church arsons speak less of open racial hatred and more of the fragmentation of social disorder and meaningless violence of the 1990s—even as they remind that racism still manifests itself in raw, ugly ways. To reduce the number of such incidents, concerned citizens and their elected officials must look beyond punitive, after-the-fact measures and look toward creating an inhospitable environment for hate crime. To be sure, there exists a need for police, prisons, social workers, and psychologists to deal with social pathology, but reacting to hate crime after it happens is often too little, too late. "It's fine to swat the mosquitoes," writes David Myers, "but better to drain the swamps—by re-envisioning our culture, by challenging the 'principalities and powers' that corrupt families and youth, and by renewing the moral and spiritual roots of character."[16]

Because civility and hate crime are mutually exclusive, civil society in the United States must be invigorated to reduce church arsons. Civility, as Joan McGregor has written, is an ethic for relating to strangers: it requires in some basic sense that we exhibit respect toward people with whom we share space but do not know. It is therefore a matter of respect. Hate crime, conversely, is a matter of *dis*respect. Where hate crime exists, civility does not, and vice versa. Church arson—an anonymous crime perpetrated against faceless strangers—defies civility insofar as it treats other people as if they do not matter.[17]

The philosopher Richard Rorty has hoped that people place "faith in the future possibilities of moral humans, a faith which is hard to distinguish from love for, and hope for, the human community." Rorty has alternately identified "this fuzzy overlap of faith, hope, and love" as "romance," as "social hope," as "solidarity," and as "a religion of democracy." Rorty's love is a love of country based not on race, ethnicity, nationalism, supremacy, or even patriotism, but on mutual respect, shared values, and a shared history and culture (which can be adopted by immigrants through an identification with the nation's past and assimilation of its traditions)—a love not of affinity but of obligation. In such a nation, individual citizens must reciprocate, balancing a sense of entitlement with a sense of duty to one another as human beings. It is essential for active citizenship in a self-governing polity.[18]

Such love sustains the kind of civic responsibility and morality that nine-teenth-century statesmen identified as "republicanism," the political culture of the early republic. Republicanism (with a small *r*) had nothing to do with the modern political party of the same name but everything to do with civic virtue, public morality, and educated citizenry, vested in the communal endeavor of nation-building. With a little effort, a similar kind of political culture might flourish in the early twenty-first century—in fact, one could argue that it must, lest the social fabric rend completely. Families, schools, and communities—"all the factors that go into making the moral infrastruc-ture"—combine "to support moral conduct," as Amitai Etzioni has observed. "In effect," he writes, "they work not merely or even mainly to fight crime, but to sustain civility and values in general. Prevention of crime is a bonus of a moral and civil society."[19]

Americans today tend to confine the ideas of love, home, and family to individual dwellings, but other societies across time have easily blended them with community. While it might be strange to think of the United States as a family, such language captures the spirit of care necessary to build com-munity in the twenty-first century. The evocation of family can be confusing and confused, particularly when evoked by the political right: while nuclear families are a key ingredient in knitting the social fabric that unites us, it seems clear that the fragmentation of today's social order does not necessi-tate a return to the nineteenth century or a resurrection of so-called "family values" from the 1950s, an era rife with its own intolerances, ill-equipped to deal with the pluralist concerns of contemporary life in the United States. Rather, it necessitates a forward-thinking social model of tolerance, accep-tance, understanding, and empathy in which Americans unite across the color line, across the pew, across the ballot box, and across other artificial divisions that undercut community. It is not a conservative agenda. It is not a liberal agenda. It is an American agenda. We must recognize our dependence upon one another—recognize, in fact, that there is no "them," only us. Only then can the problems of racism, interethnic conflict, prejudice, intolerance, and exclusion be addressed and eradicated. As one interviewee observes in Studs Terkel's *American Dreams: Lost and Found* (1980), "We are all in the same canoe."[20]

As Deval Patrick, Joe Biden, and Richard Cohen all intuited, the lack of conspiracy was much more troubling than a KKK-engineered campaign of terror. Old-fashioned, Klan-type racism was much easier to combat than the complicated origins of these newer arsons. Today the problems of the urban poor related to work, education, training, transportation, resources, and privileges—and specifically related to joblessness, the disappearance of unskilled jobs, and the rise of single-parent families—are the same problems of the rural poor. Therefore, in moving to revitalize urban communities, planners and developers must also revitalize rural communities where church arsons proliferated in the 1990s; revitalizing the suburbs where the "geography of nowhere" threatens communal bonds is also a priority. The answer lies, in part, in making an effort to know one's neighbors, in increasing civic participation—in short, in joining one's community. It lies in creating social justice, in making those individuals divorced from their communities feel connected through better opportunities and better social services. It lies also in monitoring sprawl, and recognizing that growth does not always indicate success. Finally, it lies in substantive political programs that have become somewhat clichéd in their rhetoric but no less imperative: because it takes a village to raise a child, we must leave no child behind. Combating hate crime is a function not only of civil society but also the welfare state and the market economy.

Whatever one chooses to call it—a web of social bonds, a communitarian nexus, the commonweal—this notion of community must anchor the ongoing experiment in American democracy. Such notions may be considered naively optimistic, but the well-being of the whole, the collective good, and a devotion to the common are all key in nourishing the body politic. That is, they are crucial in energizing a civil society—or a kind of civic religion, if we are comfortable calling it such—moderated by care and compassion.

If civic virtue is needed to police hate crimes, then civility is needed to prevent them. Those committing church arsons have not signed the social contract by which the rest of us abide, and to suggest that community-building measures alone can eliminate hate crime would be silly. A certain criminal element will always exist, and no degree of community will bring it into the fold. But encouraging the practice of treating strangers as if they matter might go a long way toward reducing the kind of intolerance that compelled Moseley, DeBusk, and Cloyd to torch ten churches. Bringing such young men into the communitarian nexus that unites us as a nation-family *before* they commit such acts should be advanced regardless—not only because it is likely to reduce crime significantly but also because it is a good in itself.

In building community, it is important neither to romanticize a more morally responsible civic past nor to overemphasize the gains made in the post–civil rights era. Because of what one author has called "the dangers of bigotry and Babbitry in small circumferences," we also cannot idealize the lure of small-town life. In the same breath, however, we might acknowledge the difference between living in close proximity and being truly connected to one another—and here community offers hope. Community-building efforts will not eliminate hatred and intolerance, but with greater connectedness come fewer hate crimes. "To ignore the need for community," writes Suzanne Keller, "is to invite its reactionary manifestations in a lockstep mass conformity that feeds on the potential for hatred and destructiveness behind the intricate façade of contemporary society."[21]

In the end, the full story of the fires of the last decade may never be told; but, if the fires lit the way toward a new understanding of community in the United States, then some good clearly came out of these terrible events. The fires showed that race still affected human relations in the 1990s in profound ways—regardless of whether the fires themselves indicated a racist conspiracy, or whether they were even actually racially inspired hate crimes. Just as the arson attacks laid bare a certain meanness in American society that imperiled the civic health of the United States, they also helped to create a new dialogue about race in the United States in the post–civil rights era, when many Americans were congratulating themselves for having overcome racism. If the fires backlit the sins of the past, they also illuminated the challenges to be faced in the new millennium.

Notes

Preface

1. "Arson in the United States," *U.S Fire Administration Topical Fire Research Series* 1, no. 8 (January 2001): 1; National Fire Prevention Association, Fact Sheet on Arson and Church Fires in the USA, www.dps.la.us/sfm/arson/churchfires.htm.

2. For example, see Mills, *The Triumph of Meanness*.

3. Bugeja, *Interpersonal Divide*, 3; see also Kunstler, *The Geography of Nowhere*.

4. Etzioni, *The Spirit of Community*, 190.

Chapter 1. fire

1. "Three Defendants Plead Guilty to Church Burnings in Mississippi," *Baltimore Afro-American*, October 9, 1993; "Three Plead Guilty to Mississippi Church Burning," *Washington Informer*, October 20, 1993; "3 Teenagers Sent to Prison for Burning Black Churches," *New York Times,* December 5, 1993.

2. "Black Church Burnings in the South—Statistical Data," Center for Democratic Renewal, www.hartford-hwp.com/archives/45a/121.html.

3. "List of Black Church Fire Investigations," CNN Interactive June 8, 1996, www.cnn.com/US/9606/08/arson.timeline/index.html; "Across the USA, News from Every State," *USA Today*, February 20, 1995.

4. Ibid; "Crime Report—Portsmouth," *Norfolk Virginian-Pilot*, June 2, 1995, Portsmouth Currents section, final ed.; "Members Work to Rebuild Church after Fire; Greater Mount Zion Tabernacle Wants to Raise $148,000 for Its New Facility," *Norfolk Virginian-Pilot*, June 9, 1995, Portsmouth Currents section, final ed.

5. Reverend Dr. Charles Hicks, interview by author, Portsmouth, Va., August 13, 2005.

6. Bill Frischling, "Blaze That Ravaged Church Looks Like an Arson, Chief Says," *Philadelphia Inquirer*, September 30, 1994; "Fire at a Church Is Ruled an Arson," *Philadelphia Inquirer*, October 2, 1994; "Arson Link Probed in Blaze That Left Church in Ruins," *Philadelphia Inquirer*, February 21, 1995.

7. "Norway Celebrates a Millennium of Christianity despite Fires," *New York Times*, June 4, 1995.

8. Lamy, *Millennium Rage*, 190, 202.

9. Abanes, *American Militias*, 172.

10. James Brooke, "Attacks on U.S. Muslims Surge Even as Their Faith Takes Hold," *New York Times*, August 28, 1995.

11. For more, see Abanes, *American Militias*; and Lamy, *Millennium Rage*.

12. *Forgotten Fires*, produced and directed by Michael Chandler.

13. Michael Janofsky, "True Believers Gather to Honor the White Race," *New York Times*, July 23, 1995.

14. Bob Herbert, "A Church Destroyed by Hate," *New York Times*, May 24, 1996.

15. Deutsch and Fleeman, *Verdict*, 2–4.

16. Ibid, 121.

17. Brian Cabell, "Arson at Black Churches Revives Old Fears," CNN Interactive, January 19, 1996, www.cnn.com/US/9601/church_arson/.

18. Thomas George, "For Reggie White, Racism Is Hardest Foe," *New York Times*, January 11, 1996; see also Bob Ford, "Reggie Just Wants to Play through Terrible Distraction of Church Fire," *Philadelphia Inquirer*, January 12, 1996.

19. Thomas George, "For Reggie White, Racism Is Hardest Foe," *New York Times*, January 11, 1996.

20. Linda Kanamine, "'Unmistakable' Terrorism in Arson at Tenn. Church," *USA Today*, January 12, 1996.

21. George, "For Reggie White, Racism Is Hardest Foe"; "Publicity Is Not a Cure-All," *U.S. News & World Report*, July 1, 1996, 8–9; Dave Anderson, "Away from the Football Field, Reggie Lives the Life He Preaches," *New York Times*, June 30, 1996.

22. Kelly Carter, "Inner Faith Keeps White Positive," *USA Today*, January 9, 1996; Kelly Carter, "Church Fire Isn't a Distraction, Blames Racism for Church Arson," *USA Today*, January 12, 1996; Cabell, "Arson at Black Churches Revives Old Fears."

23. Ronald Smothers, "Black Church Fires Are under U.S. Review," *New York Times*, January 20, 1996; Gary Fields, "Church-Fire Inquiry Grows," *USA Today*, March 1, 1996.

24. Gary Fields and Tom Watson, "Arson at Black Churches Echoes Bigotry of the Past," *USA Today*, February 8, 1996; "U.S. Investigates Fires at Black Churches," *New York Times*, February 9, 1996.

25. Gary Fields and Tom Watson, "In 3 Years, 23 Churches Burned, Rate of Fires Higher Than First Thought," *USA Today*, February 16, 1996; Gary Fields, "Church-Fire Inquiry Grows," *USA Today*, March 1, 1996.

26. Shannon Tangonan, "Gun Blasts Hit Home of Judge in Church-Vandal Cases," *USA Today*, February 26, 1996.

27. Ibid.

28. "State Ban on Cross Burning Let Stand," *New York Times*, February 27, 1996; "Alabama Teen Arrested for Latest Fire at Black Church," CNN Interactive, March 6, 1996, www.cnn.com/US/Newsbriefs/9603/03–06/pm.html.

29. Gary Fields, "Church Fires Prompt Study on Racial Tension," *USA Today*, March 6, 1996; Claudine Kriss, "3 Sentenced for Arsons of Tenn. Black Churches," *USA Today*, March 13, 1996; Gary Fields, "Church Has Been Heart of Black Life," *USA Today*, March 18, 1996; Gary Fields and Tom Watson, "Rebuilt with Love," *USA Today*, March 18, 1996; Gary Fields, "Church Fires May Have No Racial Link," *USA Today*, March 19, 1996; Gary Fields, "Some Blacks 'Leery' of Church Arson Probe," *USA Today*, March 26, 1996; Gary Fields, "Donors Boost Black Church Recovery Funds," *USA Today*, April 1, 1996; "Bank Gives $94,782 to White's Church," *USA Today*, April 4, 1996.

30. Gary Fields, "Church Fires May Have No Racial Link," *USA Today*, March 19, 1996.

31. Gary Fields, "Church Arson Investigators Face Race Probe," *USA Today*, April 3, 1996; Gary Fields, "Roundup Link Offensive to Rights Groups," *USA Today*, April 3, 1996; Paul Leavitt and Gary Fields, "'Roundup' Ties Force Agents Off Arson Probe," *USA Today*, April 5, 1996.

32. "Black Ministers Ask for Arson Inquiry," *New York Times*, April 23, 1996; "Arson Fire Guts a Church," *New York Times*, April 29, 1996; Gary Fields and Richard Price, "Church's Faith Withstands the Fire," *USA Today*, May 6, 1996.

33. The Freemen standoff ended peacefully in June 1996, when the group emerged from their hideout. Federal agents showed restraint, uneager to repeat what had happened in Ruby Ridge and Waco. Abanes, *American Militias*, 38–39.

34. Paul Leavitt and Gary Fields, "Evidence Is Released in Church Arson Probe," *USA Today*, May 1, 1996; "Across the USA, News from Every State," *USA Today*, May 1, 1996.

35. Evelyn Nieves, "A Church Robs a Town of Its Peace," *New York Times*, May 5, 1996.

36. Kevin Sack, "Links Sought in 'Epidemic of Terror,'" *New York Times*, May 21, 1996.

37. Mary Otto, "No Conspiracy Found in Fires at Black Churches," *Philadelphia Inquirer*, May 22, 1996; Eric Schmitt, "Few Links in Church Fires, Panel Is Told," *New York Times*, May 22, 1996; "Congress Discusses Burning of Black Churches," CNN Interactive, May 21, 1996, www.cnn.com/US/9605/21/newbriefs/; Gary Fields, "'Conspiracy of Attitude' Cited in Church Fires," *USA Today*, May 22, 1996; Gary Fields, "'Disparity' Cited in Effort on Arson Probe," *USA Today*, May 22, 1996.

38. Gary Fields, "Another Church in South Falls Victim to Fire," *USA Today*, May 29, 1996.

39. Fields and Watson, "In 3 Years, 23 Churches Burned"; Gary Fields and Richard Price, "Black Church Fires at 30," *USA Today*, June 4, 1996; "List of Black Church Fire

Investigations," CNN Interactive, June 8, 1996, www.cnn.com/US/9606/08/arson.timeline/index.html.

40. "Fire Destroys a Black Church in Alabama," *New York Times*, June 4, 1996; "Investigators Sift through Ashes of Latest Black Church Fire," CNN Interactive, June 4, 1996, www.cnn.com/US/9606/04/church.fires/.

41. Claude Lewis, "Church Burnings Don't Intimidate, They Spark Revolutions," *Philadelphia Inquirer*, June 5, 1996; Bernice Powell Jackson, "The Shame Continues," *New York Beacon*, June 5, 1996.

42. Wilson Kendall, "Another Black Church Burns as Southern Terror Continues," *Philadelphia Tribune*, June 7, 1996.

Chapter 2. fear

1. "Vanderbilt University Professor Links Church Burnings to '60s," Vanderbilt News Online News Releases, June 13, 1996, www.vanderbilt.edu/News/news/jun96/nr2.html.

2. Altschiller, *Hate Crimes*, 53–86.

3. Newton and Newton, *The Ku Klux Klan*; Reginold Bundy, "Trail of Ashes," *Tri-State Defender*, January 24, 1996.

4. Bundy, "Trail of Ashes."

5. Gary Fields and Tom Watson, "Rebuilt with Love: Torched Black Church Gets Help from White Neighbors, 'Decent Folks' Don't Accept Arsons, Hatred," *USA Today*, March 18, 1996.

6. Woodson, *The History of the Negro Church*; Frazier, *The Negro Church in America*, 45–46.

7. Lincoln, quoted in Jim Campbell, "The Burning of Black Churches Has a Long History in America," *Philadelphia Inquirer*, June 19, 1996.

8. Gary Fields, "Church Has Been Part of Black Life," *USA Today*, March 18, 1996.

9. "FBI Not Biased Official Says," *New Pittsburgh Courier*, November 24, 1962; Bill Peterson, "Voting Rights Debate Opens with Poignant Look Back," *Washington Post*, May 7, 1981.

10. "United Methodists Recall 1964 Church Burning," United Methodist News Service, November 14, 2001, umns.org/01/nov/533.htm.

11. *Forgotten Fires*, directed and produced by Michael Chandler.

12. Ibid.

13. Ibid.

14. Ibid.

15. Ibid.

16. Vern E. Smith and Marc Peyser with Daniel Klaidman, "Terror in the Night Down South," *Newsweek*, June 3, 1996, 34; Larry Copeland, "Church Burnings in South Leaving Blacks Bewildered," *Philadelphia Inquirer*, June 10, 1996.

17. Rick Bragg, "Arrest in Church Fire Does Little to Dispel Parishioners' Pain," *New York Times*, June 12, 1996; "Arson Strikes Black Church, 30th in 18 Months," *New York Times*, June 8, 1996.

18. Ronald Smothers, "Church Sues Extremist Group over Fire," *New York Times*, June 8, 1996.

19. Bob Twigg, "NAACP's Leader Calls for Show of Unity," *USA Today*, June 10, 1996; "Inquiry Is Harassing Parishioners, Pastors of Burned Churches Say," *New York Times*, June 10, 1996; Gary Fields, "Frustration over Church Fires; Investigators Struggling for Trust, Answers," *USA Today*, June 10, 1996.

20. Alison Mitchell, "Clinton Calls on the Nation to Defy 'Forces of Hatred,'" *New York Times*, June 11, 1996.

21. Phil Long, "Church Fires Spawned Host of Copycats," *Miami Herald*, December 20, 1993; Leon Tucker, "Civic Leaders, Clergy Join to Deter Fires," *Miami Herald*, June 21, 1996; Tom Morganthou with Ginny Carroll, Daniel Klaidman, Mark Miller, and Martha Brant, "Fires in the Night," *Newsweek*, June 24, 1996, 28; "Publicity Is Not a Cure-All," *U.S. News & World Report*, July 1, 1996, 8–9. Investigators believed that three attacks on two predominantly white churches and one black church in August 1996 may have been the work of a copycat; see "3 Church Attacks," *Miami Herald*, August 9, 1996.

22. "Men Questioned in Fire at Black Texas Church," CNN Interactive, June 10, 1996, www.cnn.com/US/9606/10/church.fire/index.html; "Black Teen Held in Texas Church Fire," *Washington Post*, July 21, 1996; "Church Arson Charges," *Washington Post*, August 6, 1996.

23. Stephen Labaton, "Suspects Are Held in 2 Fires at Black Churches in the South," *New York Times*, June 11, 1996.

24. Mark Miller and Marc Peyser, "We Live in Daily Fear," *Newsweek*, September 2, 1996, 52.

25. A. M. Rosenthal, "On My Mind: Color Them White," *New York Times*, June 11, 1996.

26. "Hunt Them Down!" *Miami Herald*, June 12, 1996.

27. Leonard Pitts Jr., "Burning Questions, Arsonists Are Preying on Black Churches," *Miami Herald*, June 12, 1996.

28. Ibid.

29. Ibid.; "Fire This Time," *Philadelphia Inquirer*, June 13, 1996.

30. "Church Burnings," *Baltimore Afro-American*, June 15, 1996; Dorothy Gilliam, "Scorching the Soul of a Community," *Washington Post*, June 15, 1996.

31. "Suspicious Fire Destroys Black Oklahoma Church," CNN Interactive, June 14, 1996, www.cnn.com/US/9606/13/church.fire/; "Suspect Arrested in Oklahoma Church Fire," CNN Interactive, www.cnn.com/US/9606/15/ok.arson.arrest/index.html; "White Man Arrested in Arson at a Church," *New York Times*, June 15, 1996; "U.S. News Briefs: Mother of Arson Suspect Says Son Mentally Handicapped," CNN Interactive, June 16, 1996, www.cnn.com/US/9606/16/newsbriefs/index.html.

32. "South's Black Churches Placed on 'Endangered' List," CNN Interactive, June 18, 1996, www.cnn.com/US/9606/18/endangered.

Chapter 3. faith

1. Joseph E. Agne, "The Church's Response to Hate Group Violence," *New World Outlook*, March-April 1996, gbgm-umc.org/advance/Church-Burnings/hategrup.html; "Statement on Church Burnings and Plan's for Nationwide Response," NCBI Response

to Church Burnings, www.kornet.org/ncbi/churches.htm. Not long after James Agne presented the United Methodist Church's plan to address the "climate of hate" in America through the GBGM's ten-point program, the United Methodist Council of Bishops affirmed the church's opposition to homosexuality and the ordination of gay ministers. The council acknowledged that the nation's 8.5 million Methodists (the second-largest Protestant denomination in the United States) were deeply divided, a split evident at the denomination's General Conference in Denver. The bishops declared that homosexuality was incompatible with scriptural teaching and that the council was committed to church laws banning gay ordinations. Paul Leavitt, "Methodist Bishops Affirm Anti-Gay Policy," *USA Today*, April 24, 1996.

2. "Black Ministers Ask for Arson Inquiry," *New York Times*, April 23, 1996.

3. Joretta Purdue, "Lowery, NCC Express Concerns Related to Investigations of Black Church Burnings," GBGM New Archives, May 22, 1996, gbgm-umc.org/mission/news/blchburn.html; "Publicity Is Not a Cure-All," *U.S. News & World Report*, July 1, 1996, 8–9.

4. Allison Askins, "South Carolina United Methodists Denounce Church Burnings, Establish Recovery Fund to Help Congregations," GBGM News Archives, June 6, 1996, gbgm-umc.org/advance/Church-Burnings/fire-sc.html.

5. "Clergy Angry, Frustrated over Church Fires," CNN Interactive, June 10, 1996, www.cnn.com/US/9606/10/texas.fire2/index2.html; "ADL Acts in Response to Black Church Arsons," ADL press release, June 11, 1996, www.adl.org/presrele/CvlRt_32/2757_32.asp; Dick Polman, "Black Ministers Pressure U.S. Officials on Burnings," *Philadelphia Inquirer*, June 11, 1996; Mary Otto, "Black Pastors Appeal to U.S.: Stop the Fires," *Miami Herald*, June 11, 1996.

6. Joretta Purdue, "United Methodists Respond Actively to Burning of African-American Churches," United Methodist News Service, June 12, 1996, gbgm-umc.org/advance/Church- /Burnings/fire-umc.html; Linda Green, "Oklahoma United Methodists Respond to Fire at Baptist Church," United Methodist News Service, June 13, 1996, gbgm-umc.org/advance/Church-Burnings/fire-ok.html.

7. "The Churches Are Burning!! The Churches Are Burning!!" Christian Updates—New World Order, June 14, 1996, www.cuttingedge.org/news/n1013.html.

8. William R. Macklin, "Amid Ashes, Divide among Black, White Pastors," *Philadelphia Inquirer*, June 16, 1996; Angie Cannon, "Christian Coalition Chief Calls for Reconciliation with Blacks," *Miami Herald*, June 17, 1996; "Mission Board to Assist Burned Churches; Lowery, Christian Coalition Differ in Media," United Methodist News Service, June 18, 1996, gbgm-umc.org/advance/Church-Burnings/fire-nug.html; Kevin Sack, "A Penitent Christian Coalition Offers Aid to Burned Churches," *New York Times*, June 19, 1996.

9. "Investigators Checking Two More Church Fires," CNN Interactive, June 17, 1996, www.cnn.com/US/9606/17/nc.ga.fires/index.html; Kevin Sack, "4 More Southern Churches Burn; Causes Are Not Yet Known," *New York Times*, June 18, 1996; "Two More Black Churches Destroyed by Fire," CNN Interactive, June 18, 1996, www.cnn.com/US/9606/18/church.fires.update/index.html; Ronald Smothers, "2 More Black Churches Burn, This Time in Rural Mississippi and Investigators Flood In," *New York*

Times, June 19, 1996; "Fire at Black Church in Maryland Ruled Accidental," CNN Interactive, June 19, 1996, www.cnn.com/US/9606/19/maryland.church/.

10. "Church Fire in Oregon Ruled Arson," CNN Interactive, June 20, 1996, www.cnn.com/US/9606/20/oregon.fire/index.html. Another source refers to this church as Immanuel Christian Fellowship; see "Black Church Burns in Oregon," *New York Times*, June 21, 1996. Robyn Meredith, "2 Black Men Are Arrested in N. Carolina Church Fire," *New York Times*, June 20, 1996; Ronald Smothers, "Burning of Black Churches Tries the Souls of Southern Towns," *New York Times*, June 23, 1996.

11. Colbert King, "Separate Sundays," *Washington Post*, June 22, 1996; "This Isn't Brotherhood," *New York Times*, June 29, 1996; "Put Out the Ethnic Flames, Here and in Bosnia; Irrelevance in Boston," *New York Times*, June 26, 1996; Gustav Niebuhr, "Unholy Fires on Hallowed Ground," *New York Times*, June 23, 1996.

12. "Seeking Out an Answer in the Ashes," *New York Times*, June 23, 1996; Bob Herbert, "Burning Their Bridges," *New York Times*, June 21, 1996; Jon Meacham and Vern E. Smith with Martha Brandt, Mark Miller, Howard Fineman, and Daniel Klaidman, "Southern Discomfort," *Newsweek*, June 24, 1996, 32.

13. "Church Burnings Local Problem," *Charleston (S.C.) Post and Courier*, June 30, 1996.

14. "Southeast Black Methodists Call on Christian Community to Help Stop Church Burnings," United Methodist News Service, June 18, 1996, gbgm-umc.org/advance/Church-Burnings/fire-se.html; "Mission Board to Assist Burned Churches; Lowery, Christian Coalition Differ in Media," United Methodist News Service, June 18, 1996, gbgm-umc.org/advance/Church-Burnings/fire-nug.html; "Leaders Continue to Speak out against Church Burnings," United Methodist News Service, June 20, 1996, gbgm-umc.org/advance/Church-Burnings/fire-ch.html.

15. "On the Burning of Black Churches," AEU Resolution, June 1996, www.ethicalculture.org/neac/aeuresolutions/1996–02.html; Athelia Knight, "Young Talks on Burnings," *Washington Post*, June 22, 1996.

16. Knight, "Young Talks on Burnings."

17. John Heilprin, "Coretta Scott King Says Church Arson Strikes at Everyone," *Charleston (S.C.) Post and Courier*, June 25, 1996, Avery Research Center Vertical File.

18. Frank Bruni, "O'Connor Reaches out after Fires," *New York Times*, July 1, 1996.

19. "Arson Is Suspected at Another Church," *New York Times*, July 1, 1996; "Motive for Fire Unclear," *Charleston (S.C.) Post and Courier*, July 2, 1996.

20. "Amid Memories of Holocaust, Church Burnings Are Denounced," *New York Times*, July 2, 1996; Ajowa Ifateyo, "Church Fires Prompt Broward Symposium," *Miami Herald*, July 4, 1996; Corey Dade, "Church Takes Steps against Arson," *Miami Herald*, July 6, 1996; David O'Reilly, "Witness," *Philadelphia Inquirer*, July 18, 1996.

21. Vanessa Gallman, "After Years of Turmoil, NAACP Works to Rebuild," *Miami Herald*, July 6, 1996; "Church Fire in Northwest," *New York Times*, July 8, 1996.

22. "Texas Man Charged in Church Burning," *New York Times*, July 13, 1996; Terry Pristin, "Church Damaged by Fire," *New York Times*, July 17, 1996.

23. Tyler Bridges, "Repairman Is Accused of Arson at Church," *Miami Herald*, July 19, 1996.

24. Fox Butterfield, "Old Fears and New Hope: Tale of Burned Black Church Goes Far beyond Arson," *New York Times*, July 21, 1996.

25. Butterfield, "Old Fears and New Hope"; see also Johnson, *Standing on Holy Ground*.

26. Salim Muwakkil, "Burning Hate," *In These Times*, July 8, 1996, 14–16.

Chapter 4. doubt

1. Phil Long and Martin Merzer, "Church Arson: Cause May Not Be Black and White," *New York Times* Information Bank Abstract, June 15, 1996.

2. Jack White, "First the Flame, Then the Blame: As Black Churches Go on Burning, Ministers and Members Get the Third Degree," *Time*, June 17, 1996, 35.

3. William Booth, "In Church Fires, a Pattern but No Conspiracy," *Washington Post*, June 19, 1996; "Separate Acts of Hate May Spark Church Fires," *Charleston (S.C.) Post and Courier*, June 23, 1996.

4. "Review and Outlook: Arkansas Burning?" *Wall Street Journal*, June 21, 1996; see also Landsberg, *Prosthetic Memory*.

5. Robyn Meredith, "Investigators of Church Fires Face Daunting Task," *New York Times*, June 22, 1996.

6. "Racism behind Few Fires," *Charleston (S.C.) Post and Courier*, July 7, 1996.

7. Michael Fumento, "A Church Arson Epidemic? It's Smoke and Mirrors," *Wall Street Journal*, July 8, 1996.

8. Ibid; for a rebuttal, see "Someone's Torching the Churches," *Wall Street Journal*, August 2, 1996.

9. Irvine F. Belser Jr., letter to the editor, *Charleston, (S.C.) Post and Courier*, July 10, 1996, Avery Research Center Vertical File; Steve Macko, "Statistics Paint Different Picture of Southern Church Fires," EmergencyNet News Service, July 12, 1996), www.emergency.com/arsnstat.htm.

10. William L. Pierce, "Watching the News," *National Vanguard* (August-September 1996), www.natvan.com/national-vanguard/116/news.html.

11. Ibid.

12. Chimbuko Tembo, "The Outrage, Terror, and Talk of Fire," *Cincinnati Call and Post*, July 18, 1996.

13. Ron Daniels, "Beware the Wolf in Sheep's Clothing," *Michigan Citizen*, July 27, 1996.

14. Ibid.

15. Ellen Hyatt, "Church Burnings: Where There Is Smoke There Is Fire—But Wait a Minute," *Tri-State Defender*, July 31, 1996.

16. Dorothy Leavell, "A 'State of Non-Spirituality' Claims the Souls of Americans," *Philadelphia Tribune*, August 2, 1996; Angela Wilson, "Black Man Pleads Guilty to Church Burning," *Portland Skanner*, August 8, 1996.

17. "Dillon Church Burns to Ground," *Charleston, (S.C.) Post and Courier*, August 2, 1996.

18. "Klan Group Wants Suit Thrown Out," *Charleston (S.C.) Post and Courier*, Au-

gust 9, 1996; "Two Plead Guilty in Fires at Black Churches," *Washington Post*, August 15, 1996; Eric Frazier, "Ex-Klansmen Confess in 2 Church Blazes," *Charleston (S.C.) Post and Courier*, August 15, 1996; "Reno Praises Pleas in Church Arsons," *Charleston (S.C.) Post and Courier*, August 16, 1996; Eric Frazier, "Klan Denies Ordering Two Arsons," *Charleston (S.C.) Post and Courier*, August 16, 1996; "Church Arson: Victory for Justice," *Charleston (S.C.) Post and Courier*, August 17, 1996; Eric Frazier, "Judge Denies Bail for Ex-Klansmen," *Charleston (S.C.) Post and Courier*, August 21, 1996; see also *Forgotten Fires*, directed and produced by Michael Chandler.

19. Jason DeParle, "The Christian Right Confesses Sins of Racism," *New York Times*, August 4, 1996.

20. Cinque Henderson, "Twice Burned," *New Republic*, August 5, 1996, 9.

21. Monica Langley, "Black Church Arsons Win Donor Millions—Now, How to Spend It?" *Wall Street Journal*, August 9, 1996.

22. "National Council of Churches Responds to Conservative Think Tank's Charges," United Methodist News Service, August 14, 1996, gbgm.umc.org/advance/Church-Burnings/firenccc.html.

23. Ibid.

24. "Presbyterians Continue to Aid Burned Churches despite Controversy," Worldwide Faith News, August 22, 1996, www.wfn.org/1996/08/msg00168.html.

25. Lawrie Mifflin, "TV Notes: Examining Church Burning," *New York Times*, August 28, 1996; "'7th Heaven': Aftermath of a Church Burning," *Oakland Post*, October 6, 1996.

26. "Penalties against Vandalism of Religious Property Toughened," *New York Beacon*, August 28, 1996; "Wilson Signs Church Burning Bill," *Sacramento Observer*, September 18, 1996; Geoff Seal, "No Suspects in Church Fire," *Sacramento Observer*, September 18, 1996.

27. G. Quinton Brathwaite, "The Fires This Time," *Reunion*, August 31, 1996, 6; "Conspiracy behind Arson at Black Churches," *Workers World*, August 29, 1996, www.workers/org/ww/churches.html.

28. Jared Taylor, "Burning with Self-Righteousness," *American Renaissance*, August 1996, www.amren.com/church.htm; Wesley Pruden, "Setting Fire on Facts in Pursuit of Justice," *Washington Times*, June 18, 1996, www.constitution.org/piml/96061904.txt; Patricia Neal, "Hypocrisy in Action: Clinton and the Church Burnings," www.constitution.org/piml/96061904.txt.

29. John Elvin, "Burned Out and Washed Up," *Insight*, September 2, 1996, 16; Pierre Thomas and Michael Fletcher, "Arrests in Black Church Fires Racially Mixed," *Washington Post*, September 14, 1996; Kelly Heyboer, "The 'Epidemic' of Black Church Fires," *American Journalism Review*, September 1996, 10–11; Michael Fumento, "Politics and Church Burnings," *Commentary*, October 1996.

30. "March to Protest Black Church Burnings," *Albion Monitor*, October 7, 1996, www.monitor.net/monitor/free/fireprotest.html; "Man Gets 5 Years for Burning Black Church," *New York Times*, October 9, 1996.

31. Michael Fletcher, "Church Fires Said to Reflect Racial Tension Problem Deep-Rooted, Rights Agency Asserts," *Washington Post*, October 10, 1996; Steve Piacente,

"Church Fire Inquiry Unearths Rise in Tensions," *Charleston (S.C.) Post and Courier*, October 10, 1996.

32. Anthony Walton, "Why Race Is Still a Burning Issue," *U.S. Catholic*, October 1996, www.uscatholic.org/1996/10/cov9610.htm; Peter Steinfels, "Beliefs," *New York Times*, October 19, 1996.

Chapter 5. law

1. Ronald Smothers, "Black Church Fires Are under U.S. Review," *New York Times*, January 20, 1996; "U.S. Investigates Fires at Black Churches," *New York Times*, February 9, 1996; Gary Fields, "Church Has Been Heart of Black Life," *USA Today*, March 18, 1996; "Black Ministers Ask for Arson Inquiry," *New York Times*, April 23, 1996; Kevin Sack, "Links Sought in an 'Epidemic of Terror,'" *New York Times*, May 21, 1996.

2. Eric Schmitt, "Few Links in Church Fires, Panel Is Told," *New York Times*, May 22, 1996; Mary Otto, "No Conspiracy Found in Fires at Black Churches," *Philadelphia Inquirer*, May 22, 1996; "An 'Epidemic of Terror,'" *New York Times*, May 24, 1996; Bob Herbert, "A Church Destroyed by Hate," *New York Times*, May 24, 1996.

3. U.S. Congress, House, Committee on the Judiciary, *Church Fires in the Southeast: Hearing before the Committee of the Judiciary*, 104th Cong., 2nd sess., May 21, 1996, 2–8.

4. Ibid.

5. "Arson Strikes Black Church, 30th in 18 Months," *New York Times*, June 8, 1996; Radio Address by the President to the Nation, Oval Office, June 8, 1996; Jill Dougherty, "Clinton Sounds Call to Stop Church Burnings," CNN Interactive, June 8, 1996, www.cnn.com/US/9606/08/clinton.radio.cnn/.

6. "Reno Meets with Ministers Worried about Church Fires," CNN Interactive, June 9, 1996, www.cnn.com/US/9606/09/church.fires/index.html; "Jackson Criticizes Clinton's Speech to Black People," *Chicago Weekend*, June 9, 1996, 2; "Clinton Takes Good Steps to Halt Black Church Fires," *Philadelphia Tribune*, June 11, 1996; Geoff Seal, "Anger over Church Bombings, Local Pastors Share Reactions," *Sacramento Observer*, June 12, 1996; Alison Mitchell, "Clinton Calls on Nation to Defy 'Forces of Hatred,'" *New York Times*, June 11, 1996.

7. Gary Fields, "Church Fire Probe Intensified," *USA Today*, June 10, 1996; Anthony Collings, "Clinton to Visit Site of Church Fire," CNN Interactive, June 10, 1996, www.cnn.com/US/9606/10/church.fire.pm/.

8. Phil Long, "Florida Shares Files in Probe of Church Fires," *Miami Herald*, June 13, 1996; Alison Mitchell, "In Town Hit by Church Arson, Clinton Recalls South's Past," *New York Times*, June 13, 1996.

9. William Safire, "Eloquence Not Dead," *New York Times*, June 13, 1996; "Churches in Flames," *New York Times*, June 16, 1996; Ron Walters, "Black Churches Burning," *Washington Informer*, June 19, 1996; Rosa Reed, "Church Fires Burn at Soul of Black America," *Miami Times*, June 20, 1996; James K. Glassman, "Hiding behind the Smoke," *Washington Post*, June 18, 1996.

10. Todd Purdum, "Clinton and Southern Governors Confer on Efforts to Deter Burning of Black Churches," *New York Times*, June 20, 1996; "Rare Bipartisanship on

Arson," *New York Times*, June 21, 1996; Allison Jones, "Efforts Mount to End Terrorism Against Black Churches," *Michigan Citizen*, June 22, 1996.

11. Cathy Connors, "Church Burnings Generate Action from All Quarters to Rebuild," *New York Amsterdam News*, June 22, 1996, 4; Carl Mollins, "Flames of Racial Tension," *Maclean's*, June 24, 1996, 27.

12. U.S. Congress, Senate, Committee on the Judiciary, *Church Burnings: Hearing before the Committee of the Judiciary*, 104th Cong., 2nd sess., 27 June 1996, 1–5.

13. Ibid, 6–12.

14. Ibid, 55.

15. "Congress Votes to Toughen Penalties for Church Arson," *Wall Street Journal*, June 28, 1996; "Clinton Designates $6 Million to Fight Church Burnings," CNN Interactive, July 2, 1996, www.cnn.com/US/9607/02/church.fires/; Steven Holmes, "Clinton Seeks Money to Halt Church Fires," *New York Times*, July 3, 1996; Mary Otto, "Clinton Plans to Send $6 Million to 12 States Struck by Church Fires," *Philadelphia Inquirer*, July 3, 1996).

16. "KKK Linked to Church Arson," Office of Congressman John Conyers Jr., press release, July 9, 1996, www.house.gov/judiciary_democrats/dpr40047.htm; "Church Arson Bill's Sponsor Pushing Vote," *Journal of Commerce*, August 2, 1996; "Church Fires Show Racism, a Panel Says," *New York Times*, October 10, 1996; Paul Macey, "Racial Tension Remains Rife in Southern States," *Voice*, October 22, 1996, .

17. "A Tough Fine for ATF," *Washington Post*, July 11, 1996; Jan Thorpe and Thomas Whittle, "A Fire on the Cross," *Freedom* 29 no. 1 (1996): 4–9.

18. Cinque Henderson, "Twice Burned," *New Republic*, August 5, 1996, 9.

19. Ibid.

20. Dennis Bernstein and Ron Nixon, "Black Churches under Fire, Activists Rise to the Call," *Third Force*, October 10, 1996, 18; "AFRO Endorsement: Presidential Race," *Washington Afro-American*, November 11, 1996; John Eggleston Jr., "Black Church Burnings," *Ebony*, November 1996, 12; Todd Burroughs, "Anti-Racism Conference Reveals Racial Divisions in S. Carolina," *New Pittsburgh Courier*, November 11, 1996.

21. Julian Shipp, "Presbyterians Continue to Aid Burned Black Churches despite Controversy," Presbyterian News Service, August 30, 1996, www.pcusa.org/pcnews/oldnews/1996/96302.htm.

22. "More Burned Churches Receive Rebuilding Funds," United Methodist News Service, October 22, 1996, gbgm-umc.org/advance/Church-Burnings/firefund.html.

23. Michael Dabney, "Deval Patrick Resigns from U.S. Attorney General's Office," *Philadelphia Tribune*, November 19, 1996.

24. Michael Fumento, "*USA Today's* Arson Artistry," *American Spectator*, December 1996, 28–33.

25. National Church Arson Task Force, *Interim Report for the President*, January 1997.

26. David Gonzalez, "Fire Leaves Faith Unscathed," *New York Times*, January 22, 1997.

27. "4 Indicted in Church Fire," *New York Times*, January 24, 1997.

28. "Fund Set up to Rebuild Black Churches," *New York Times*, January 28, 1997.

29. Robert Thomas Sr., "Mac Jones, 47, Who Aided Burned Churches," *New York Times*, March 10, 1997; "17 More Congregations Receive NCC Burned Churches Grants," United Methodist News Service, May 28, 1997, gbgm-umc.org/advance/Church-Burnings/fnews.html; "United Methodist Pastor Contributes to NCC Book on Burned Churches," United Methodist News Service, June 4, 1997, gbgm-umc.org/advance/Church-Burnings/fnews1.html; Statement of Patricia Glenn, national coordinator of the Church Burning Response Team, Community Relations Service, U.S. Department of Justice, before the House Judiciary Committee, March 19, 1997, www.house.gov/judiciary/198.htm; "NCC Accounts for Burned Churches Fund Disbursements at National Convention," United Methodist News Service, June 11, 1997, gbgm-umc.org/advance/Church-Burnings/fnews2.html.

30. "Teenager Pleads Guilty to 1 Count of Arson," *New York Times*, March 25, 1997; Carri Geer, "Man's Arson Law First under New Law," *Las Vegas Review-Journal*, March 27, 1997; "Memorial and Procession Recall Burned Churches," *New York Times*, April 13, 1997.

31. "New Law on Church Arson Leads to 2 Convictions," *New York Times*, May 5, 1997; "Feds Must Update Status of Church Burnings," *New Pittsburgh Courier*, May 10, 1997; "Feds Must Update Status of Church Burnings," *Michigan Chronicle*, May 27, 1997; "Black Church Damaged by Arson Fire in Georgia," *New York Times*, May 8, 1997; "Glassboro Church Destroyed by Arson," *Philadelphia Inquirer*, May 31, 1997; Andy Newman, "Arson Bill to Become Law," *New York Times*, June 2, 1997; Noel Holton and Patricia Smith, "In Glassboro, Hearts Unscathed by Arsons," *Philadelphia Inquirer*, June 8, 1997.

32. "Panel Says Churches Are Still Targets," *New York Times*, June 9, 1997; Peter Slevin and Angie Cannon, "Church Arsons Were Not a Racist Conspiracy, Panel Concludes," *Philadelphia Inquirer*, June 9, 1997; "Rising from the Ashes," *Miami Herald*, June 10, 1997; Michael Fumento, "Who's Fanning the Flames of Racism?" *Wall Street Journal*, June 16, 1997; Robin Leary, "Leaders Cautious about Clinton's Race Plan," *Philadelphia Tribune*, June 17, 1997.

33. Mireya Navarro, "Aftermath of Fire Jolts Denomination," *New York Times*, July 10, 1997; Mireya Navarro and Gustav Niebuhr, "A Baptist Church Scrutinizes Its Leader's Lavish Life Style," *New York Times*, July 29, 1997.

34. Hjelm, *Out of the Ashes*, 37.

35. Brenda Wilkinson, "United Methodists Attend Church Burning Convocation," United Methodist News Service, undated, gbgm-umc.org/advance/Church-Burnings/fnews4.html; Mary Frances Berry, "Embers of Anger in the South," *New York Times*, July 17, 1997.

36. Conrad Goeringer, "The Great and Late Church Arson Conspiracy Hoax," *American Atheist* 35, no. 4 (Autumn 1997): 8–16.

37. Richard Sine, "Arson Is Feared in Blaze at Church," *Philadelphia Inquirer*, November 17, 1997; Lisa Sandberg, "Church Fire Arson, Officials Say," *Philadelphia Inquirer*, November 18, 1997; Thomas Gibbons Jr., "Arson Not Likely in Church Fire," *Philadelphia Inquirer*, November 18, 1997; "Arson Hits Third Church in Rural

Pennsylvania," *New York Times*, January 29, 1998; Rena Singer, "Churches Fight Arson Fires with Vigilant Faith," *Philadelphia Inquirer*, March 22, 1998; Lisa Sandberg, "From a Pulpit of Ashes, a Message of Resurrection," *Philadelphia Inquirer*, April 11, 1998; Richard Sabatini, "Church Fire Found to Be Arson," *Philadelphia Inquirer*, May 16, 1998.

Chapter 6. strength

1. Peter Applebome, "Nightmare Is Remade a 'Miracle,'" *New York Times*, January 3, 1994.
2. Ibid.
3. John Carlin, "Why Mississippi Is No Longer Burning," *Independent*, October 15, 1995, .
4. Eric Harrison, "Tension Has Been Rising as Burning Black Churches Light up the Night Sky Again," *Guardian* (London), January 23, 1996.
5. Gary Fields, "Donors Boost Black Church Recovery Funds," *USA Today*, April 1, 1996; "Bank Gives $94,782 to White's Church," *USA Today*, April 4, 1996.
6. "White Gives Thanks," *New York Times*, March 1, 1996; "Bank Gives $94,782 to White's Church"; Johnette Howard, "Up from the Ashes," *Sports Illustrated*, September 2, 1996, 140–46; "Remarks by Packers' White Draw Criticism in Wisconsin," *New York Times*, March 26, 1998.
7. "Across the USA: News from Every State," *USA Today*, May 3, 1996; Elizabeth Farnsworth, "Resurrection," PBS Online *Newshour*, June 12, 1996, www.pbs.org/newshour/bb/race_relations/church_burnings_6–12.html.
8. David Gonzalez, "About New York: Joining Hands to Rebuild Church Ruins," *New York Times*, June 19, 1996; Peter Nicholas, "$2.7 Million for Burned Churches," *Philadelphia Inquirer*, June 21, 1996; "Faith to Build On," *Philadelphia Inquirer*, June 23, 1996.
9. Margo Beller, "Church Insurers Feel Heat of Arsons," *Journal of Commerce*, June 21, 1996; Stephanie Esters, "Insurers Help to Fight Church Fires," *National Underwriter*, June 24, 1996, 1+; Steven Brostoff, "Insurer Groups, White House Link Up in Church-Fire Battle," *National Underwriter*, July 15, 1996, 1+.
10. Emily Yellin, "Burning of Black Churches Tries the Souls of Southern Towns: Tennessee; For One Congregation, Trying to Regain a Sense of Confidence," *New York Times*, June 23, 1996.
11. Ronald Smothers, "Burning of Black Churches Tries the Souls of Southern Towns," *New York Times*, June 23, 1996; Ed Henry, "A Man with a Mission," *Kiplinger's Personal Finance Magazine* 50 (October 1996): 128.
12. Reverend Dr. Charles Hicks, interview by author, Portsmouth, Virginia, August 13, 2005.
13. Ibid.; Diane Tennant, "Volunteers Raise Burned Church, Nationwide Organizations Lend Money, People to Work a Miracle," *Norfolk Virginian-Pilot*, January 15, 1997; "Rebuilding Burned Churches," *Christian Century* 114 (April 9, 1997): 357–58.
14. "Rebuilding Burned Churches."

15. Hicks interview; Janie Bryant, "Loan Plan Helps Portsmouth Church," *Norfolk Virginian-Pilot*, June 11, 1997.

16. Bryant, "Loan Plan Helps Portsmouth Church."

17. Hicks interview; "News and Notes," *Norfolk Virginian-Pilot*, July 12, 1997; "After the Fire, Rebuilt Church," *Norfolk Virginian-Pilot*, October 3, 1997; "Whatever Happened to . . . the Portsmouth Church Destroyed by Arson?" *Norfolk Virginian-Pilot*, March 23, 1998.

18. "Two Black Churches Set on Fire, Brings Total to 32," *Jet*, June 24, 1996, 54.

19. "Local Pastors to Help to Rebuild Fire Bombed Churches," *Cleveland Call and Post*, June 27, 1996; Michael Gelbwasser, "Local Jews Aid Black Churches," *Jewish Advocate*, June 27, 1996, ; Norma Quarles, "Relief Organization Sends Prefabs to Replace Burned out Black Churches," CNN Interactive, June 27, 1996, www.cnn.com/US/9606/27/spiritual.sendoff/index.html; see also Christopher Weems, "High-Level and Grassroots Action Resulting from More Black Churches Being Burned to the Ground," *Atlanta Inquirer*, June 29, 1996.

20. "Church Is Reborn After Burning," *New York Times*, June 28, 1996; "Fund Drive Planned for Burned Churches," *Miami Herald*, June 28, 1996.

21. Ronald Smothers, "After Fires, Some Black Churches Face Insurance Troubles," *New York Times*, July 3, 1996.

22. Smothers, "After Fires"; Stephanie D. Esters, "Reports of Church Policy Cancellations Probed," *National Underwriter* 100 (July 8, 1996): 3.

23. Toby Axelrod, "Bigotry Watch: With a Mission of Defense, Interfaith Coalition Arises from the Ashes of Southern Churches," *Jewish Week*, July 5, 1996, 6. One Internet blogger would later compare black church arsons in the United States to the torching of Serbian Orthodox churches by Albanian Muslims in Kosovo; see Mary Mostert, "When Is It OK for Majorities to Kill?" Original Sources, May 1, 2000, www.balkanpeace.org/hed/archive/may00/hed84.shtml.

24. Christina Cheakalos, "Teens Build Cultural Bridges by Rebuilding Black Churches," *Atlanta Journal/Constitution*, July 5, 1996.

25. "Insurance Industry to Offer Aid to Black Churches Hit by Arson," *New York Times*, July 13, 1996; Brostoff, "Insurer Groups, White House Link up in Church-Fire Battle"; Luix Virgil Overbea, "Gospel Groups, WILD Raise Funds for Southern Churches," *Bay State Banner*, July 18, 1996; "Nine Black Churches Get Grants to Rebuild," *Charleston (S.C.) Post and Courier*, July 24, 1996; "Fires and Fund Raising," *Christian Century* 113 (August 28–September 4, 1996): 806–7.

26. "Korean Merchants Support Black Church Burning Efforts and MLK Nonviolence Academy," *New York Beacon*, August 7, 1996; "Partnership Formed to Rebuild Burned Churches Includes NCC, HUD, and Black Church Consortium," Disciples News Service, September 23, 1996, www.disciples.org/dns/releases96/96b80.htm.

27. Dennis Bernstein and Ron Nixon, "Black Churches under Fire, Activists Rise to the Call," *Third Force*, October 31, 1996, 18.

28. John Greenya, "Fired up about Church Burnings," *Washington Lawyer*, November 1996, 20–27.

29. Ted Olsen, "Rising from the Ashes: Congregations Rebuild After Satanist Arsons," *Christianity Today*, November 17, 1997, 90.

30. Matt Andrews, "The Flames of Religious Hatred," *Midwest Today*, Summer 1996, www.midtod.com/9608/faith9608.phtml; see also Matt Slagle, "Arsons Targeting Churches Surge," *South Bend Tribune*, November 27, 1998, www.southbendtribune.com/98/nov/112798/local_ar/134192.htm.

31. "Davis Chapel Receives Funds from National Council of Churches to Assist in Rebuilding Church," GBGM News, www.gbgm-umc.org/advance/Church-Burnings/davischa.html.

32. Christie House, "Rebuilding Burned Churches," *New World Outlook*, January–February 1998, gbgm-umc.org/now/98jf/burned1.html.

33. "Three Alabama Youths Convicted of Church Burning," The Southern Catalyst Network Weekly Action Report, November 4, 1997, www.tulane.edu/~so-inst/catalyst/war2.html.

34. "North Carolina Churches Hit in Outbreak of Fires," *New York Times*, February 16, 1998; "NC Church Fires May Be Connected," Associated Press, February 17, 1998, www.quaker.org/qwi/burning/news/news982.html; "4 Teenagers Arrested in Texas Church Fires," *New York Times*, March 8, 1998.

35. Sandra Peters, "Ministry in the Midst of Hate and Violence: The Press Has Lost Interest, The Nation Has Lost Interest, The Church Arsonists Have Not," GBGM press release, January 1998, gbgm-umc.org/advance/Church-Burnings/arson.html.

36. Lynna Goch, "Arson Dims as Burning Issue," *Best's Review*, March 1998, 111; Robert Press, "Church Arsons Continue—Concern Oddly Low," *Christian Science Monitor* Online, January 26, 1999, www.csmweb2.emcweb.com/durable/1999/01/26/p11s1.htm.

37. "Indiana Man Charged with Burning Churches," *Christian Century* 116, no. 8 (March 10, 1999): 273; "Indiana Man Indicted in Church Fires," *Christian Century* 116, no. 15 (May 12, 1999): 529–30; Angie Cannon and Chitra Ragavan, "Another Look at the Church Fire Epidemic," *U.S. News & World Report* 127, no. 20 (November 22, 1999): 26.

38. Earl Howard, interview by author, Amazing Grace Baptist Church, Crandall, Ga., July 19, 2005.

39. Earl Shoemaker, interview by author, Amazing Grace Baptist Church, Crandall, Ga., July 19, 2005.

40. Ibid.

41. Howard interview, July 19, 2005.

42. Shoemaker interview, July 19, 2005.

43. Howard interview, July 19, 2005.

44. "Church Arson Cases Continue in 'High Numbers,'" United Methodist News Service, April 5, 1999, gbgm-umc.org/advance/Church-Burnings/arsonhigh.html Lisa Greene, "St. John Church Rises Again," *State*, August 16, 1999, B1, Avery Research Center Vertical File, Charleston, S.C. For more on the St. John ordeal, see Johnson, *Standing on Holy Ground*.

Chapter 7. hope

1. See Mello, *The United States versus Theodore John Kaczynski*.

2. Eric Frazier, "Burnings Bring Call for Unity," *Charleston (S.C.) Post and Courier*, June 30, 1996, Avery Research Center Vertical File; Richard Cohen, "Torch of Hate," *Washington Post*, June 20, 1996.

3. Cohen, "Torch of Hate"; Gustav Niebuhr, "Unholy Fires on Hallowed Ground," *New York Times*, June 23, 1996; Jon Meacham and Vern E. Smith with Martha Brandt, Mark Miller, Howard Fineman, and Daniel Klaidman, "Southern Discomfort," *Newsweek*, June 24, 1996, 32.

4. Nikki Giovanni, "Don't Worry, There's No Racial Hatred Here," *New York Times*, July 11, 1996.

5. "Hate Crimes," FBI Civil Rights Program, www.fbi.gov/hq/cid/civilrights/hate.htm.

6. Toni Morrison, "Clinton as the First Black President," ontology.buffalo.edu/smith/clinton/morrison.html; Marc Morano, "Clinton Honored as 'First Black President' at Black Caucus Dinner," CNS News, October 1, 2001, www.cnsnews/com/ViewPrint.asp?Page=\Nation\archive\200110/NAT20011001e.html.

7. James Wright, "Pastors of Burned Churches Seek Help," *Washington Afro-American*, June 15, 1996.

8. Michelle Phipps, "Black Churches Continue to Burn across the Country," *Washington Afro-American*, June 22, 2001.

9. "Hate Crime Reports up in Wake of Terrorist Attacks," CNN News, September 17, 2001, cnn.com/2001/US/09/16/gen.hate.crimes/; "Gunman Attacks Memphis Mosque," About Islam, June 21, 2000, islam.about.com/library/weekly/aa062100a.htm; James Brooke, "Attacks on U.S. Muslims Surge Even as Their Faith Takes Hold," *New York Times*, August 28, 1995.

10. "Hate Crime Reports up in Wake of Terrorist Attacks."

11. John J. Miller and Ramesh Ponnuru, "The Hateful American: A New Church-Burning Hoax," *National Review* Online, September 20, 2001, www.nationalreview.com/daily/nrprint092001.html.

12. "Was the Church Arson Story Legit?" *Religion in the News* 2, no. 2 (Summer 1999), Leonard E. Greenberg Center for the Study of Religion in Public Life, Trinity College, www.trincoll.edu/depts/csrpl/RINVol2No2/arson.htm.

13. Mark Fitzgerald, "Did Newspapers Douse Fire Story?" *Editor and Publisher Magazine*, September 28, 1996, 14; Joe Holley, "Who Was Burning the Black Churches?" *Columbia Journalism Review*, September-October 1996, 26–33; Michael Fumento, "USA Today's Arson Artistry," *American Spectator*, December 1996, 28–33; Michael Fumento, "USA Today Collects Kudos for Debunking Its Own Myth," *Washington Times*, January 7, 1997, www.fumento.com/kudos.html; Michael Fumento, "Politics and Church Burnings," *Commentary*, October 1996, www.fumento.com/church.html.

14. Kelly Heyboer, "The 'Epidemic' of Black Church Fires," *American Journalism Review*, September 1996, 10–11; Fitzgerald, "Did Newspapers Douse Fire Story?"

15. "Firestorm: A Review of the 1996 Church Fire Scare," *Free Republic*, www.freere-public.com/focus/f-news/691591/posts.

16. Bill Broadway, "Arson at Churches an Ongoing Problem," *Washington Post*, November 9, 2002.

17. Fumento, "Politics and Church Burnings."

18. Herb Frazier, "Greeleyville Church May Join Suit against Klan," *Charleston (S.C.) Post and Courier*, July 15, 1996, Avery Research Center Vertical File.

19. Joseph Broadus, "Church Burnings Come as No Surprise to the Faithful," *Atlanta Inquirer*, October 26, 1996; "After Arson, Faith Triumphs for MS Church," Disaster News Network, March 9, 2001, www.disasternews.net/disasters/3-9-01_ms-faithtri-umphs.html.

20. Fitzgerald, "Did Newspapers Douse Fire Story?"; John Elvin, "Fanning the Flames: Is the Outbreak of Church Burning a National Crisis or Media Conflagration?" *Insight on the News*, September 1996, 18.

21. Hemphill, *The Ballad of Little River*; Richard Bernstein, "Facing Life with a Six-Pack in the Rural South," *New York Times*, May 8, 2000.

22. Riesman, *The Lonely Crowd*; Galbraith, *The Affluent Society*; Putnam, *Bowling Alone*. Jean Bethke Elshtain has defined community as "commitments and ties that locate the citizen in bonds of trust, reciprocity, mutuality, competence for the task at hand"; see Elshtain in Dionne, *Community Works*, 25; see also Selznick, *The Communitarian Persuasion*, 17.

23. Bellah et al., *The Good Society*, 9.

24. For an insightful look at post–9/11 America, see Maharidge, *Homeland*.

25. Herring, Keith, and Horton, eds., *Skin-Deep*, 2; see also Brown et al., *Whitewashing*; and Doane and Bonilla-Silva, *White Out*.

26. Dennis Farney, "In a Tennessee Town, Church Burning Brings Unexpected Results," *Wall Street Journal*, July 15, 1996; "Church Arson: Victory for Justice," *Charleston (S.C.) Post and Courier*, August 17, 1996.

27. Margaret Burnham, "Justice Plays Catch-Up," *Boston Globe*, April 27, 2007, Avery Research Center Vertical File; "1963 Birmingham Church Bombing: Guilty on All Counts," *Atlanta Journal and Constitution*, May 2, 2001; Jay Reeves, "Church Bomb Suspect Guilty," *Chicago Sun Times*, May 23, 2002.

28. "Building Communities of Hope," *New World Outlook*, January-February 1998, gbgm-umc.org/now/98jf/burned4.html.

29. Prepared Testimony of Andrew Cuomo, Senate Banking, Housing, and Urban Affairs Committee, Subcommittee on Financial Institutions and Regulatory Relief, Oversight Hearing on the Federal Loan Guaranty Program, July 17, 1997.

epilogue

1. "Fires Damage Six Alabama Churches," *New York Times*, February 3, 2006.

2. Hollie Huey, "Arsonists Torch Five Baptist Churches," *Centreville (Ala.) Press*, February 8, 2006.

3. Ibid.

4. John O'Neil, "4 More Fires Reported at Churches in Alabama," *New York Times*, February 7, 2006. This outbreak of fires in western Alabama occurred near Boligee, where three black churches had been set ablaze in December 1995 and January 1996. The fires at Mt. Zion Baptist, Little Zion Baptist, and Mt. Zoar Baptist in 1995 and 1996 were never solved.

5. David Mattingly, "Church Blazes 'No. 1 Priority' for Federal Agency," CNN Online, February 8, 2006, cnn.com.worldnews.

6. "Tenth Alabama Church Fire Ruled Arson," CNN Online, February 12, 2006, cnn.worldnews.

7. Ibid.

8. Reverend Bob Little, quoted in Kathy Lohr, "Suspects Sought in Alabama Church Burnings," NPR *Weekend Edition*, February 12, 2006, www.npr.org/templates/story/story.php?storyId=5202566.

9. Rick Lyman, "3 Students Held in Church Fires Set in Alabama," *New York Times*, March 9, 2006, www.nytimes.com/2006/03/09/national/09arson.html; Robert DeWitt, "Suspects Could Face State Charges," *Tuscaloosa News*, March 11, 2006; J. L. Isaac, interview by author, March 10, 2006, Greene County Courthouse, Livingston, Ala.; John Archibald, "Funny Guy Isn't So Funny Now," *Birmingham News*, March 9, 2006; Rev. Little, quoted in Lohr, "Suspects Sought in Alabama Church Burnings."

10. "Students Say Church Arsons Meant as a 'Joke,'" MSNBC.com, March 8, 2006, www.msnbc.com/id/11726024/print/1/displaymode/1098/.

11. "3 College Students Arrested in Alabama Church Arsons," *USA Today* Online, March 9, 2006, www.usatoday.com/news/nation/2006-03-08-church-fires_x.htm.

12. "Facebook Visitors Show Support and Anger for Suspects," *Tuscaloosa News*, March 10, 2006.

13. Rev. Glenn Harris, interview by author, March 11, 2006, Spring Valley Baptist Church, Gainesville, Ala.

14. Ibid.

15. "Church Arsonists Sentenced," WAFF 48 News, Birmingham, Ala., April 9, 2007; Jay Reeves, "More Guilty Pleas in Alabama Church Fires," *Houston Chronicle*, April 12, 2007, www.chron.com/disp/story.mpl/ap/nation/4709652.html.

16. Myers, *The American Paradox*, 125.

17. Joan McGregor, "Civility, Civic Virtue, and Citizenship," in Sistare, *Civility and its Discontents*, 26.

18. Rorty, quoted in Bofetti, "How Richard Rorty Found Religion."

19. Etzioni, *The Spirit of Community*, 191.

20. Ramona Bennett, quoted in Terkel, *American Dreams*, 178.

21. Keller, *Community*, xiii.

Selected Bibliography

Abanes, Richard. *American Militias: Rebellion, Racism, and Religion*. Downers Grover, Ill.: InterVarsity Press, 1996.

Altschiller, Donald. *Hate Crimes: A Reference Handbook*. Oxford: ABC-Clio, 1999.

Andrews, Matt. "The Flames of Religious Hatred." *Midwest Today* (Summer 1996), www.mid-tod.com/9608/faith9608.phtml.

"Arson in the United States." *U.S Fire Administration Topical Fire Research Series* 1, no. 8 (January 2001): 1.

Bellah, Robert, Richard Madsen, William Sullivan, Ann Swidler, and Steven Tipton. *The Good Society*. New York: Knopf, 1991.

Bofetti, Jason. "How Richard Rorty Found Religion." *First Things* 143 (May 2004): 24–30.

Brostoff, Steven. "Insurer Groups, White House Link Up in Church-Fire Battle." *National Underwriter* 100 (July 15, 1996): 1+.

Brown, Michael K., Martin Carnoy, Elliot Currie, Troy Duster, and David B. Oppenheimer. *Whitewashing: The Myth of a Color-Blind Society*. Berkeley and Los Angeles: University of California Press, 2003.

Bugeja, Michael. *Interpersonal Divide: The Search for Community in a Technological Age*. Oxford: Oxford University Press, 2005.

Cannon, Angie, and Chitra Ragavan. "Another Look at the Church Fire Epidemic." *U.S. News & World Report* 127, no. 20 (November 22, 1999): 26.

"Church Arson Bill's Sponsor Pushing Vote." *Journal of Commerce* (August 2, 1996): A8.

Deutsch, Linda, and Michael Fleeman. *Verdict: The Chronicle of the O. J. Simpson Trial*. Kansas City: Andrews and McMeel, 1995.

Dionne, E.L., Jr., ed. *Community Works: The Revival of Civil Society in America*. Washington, D.C.: Brookings Institution Press, 1998.

Doane, Ashley W., and Eduardo Bonilla-Silva, eds. *White Out: The Continuing Significance of Racism*. New York: Routledge, 2003.

Elvin, John. "Burned Out and Wa-shed Up." *Insight*, September 2, 1996, 16.

————. "Fanning the Flames: Is the Outbreak of Church Burning a National Crisis or Media Conflagration?" *Insight on the News*, September 1996, 18.

Esters, Stephanie. "Insurers Help to Fight Church Fires." *National Underwriter*, June 24, 1996, 1+.

————. "Reports of Church Policy Cancellations Probed." *National Underwriter* 100 (July 8, 1996): 3.

Etzioni, Amitai. *The Spirit of Community: The Reinvention of American Society*. New York: Touchstone, 1993.

"Fires and Fund Raising." *Christian Century* 113 (August 28–September 4, 1996): 806–7.

"Firestorm: A Review of the 1996 Church Fire Scare," Free Republic, www.freerepublic.com/focus/f-news/691591/posts.

Fitzgerald, Mark. "Did Newspapers Douse Fire Story?" *Editor and Publisher Magazine*, September 28, 1996, 14.

Forgotten Fires. Produced and directed by Michael Chandler. 57 min. California Newsreel, 1999. Videocassette.

Frazier, E. Franklin. *The Negro Church in America*. New York: Schocken, 1966.

Fumento, Michael. "Politics and Church Burnings." *Commentary*, October 1996, www.fumento.com/church.html.

————. "*USA Today*'s Arson Artistry." *American Spectator*, December 1996, 28–33.

Galbraith, John Kenneth. *The Affluent Society*. Boston: Houghton Mifflin, 1958.

Goch, Lynna. "Arson Dims as Burning Issue." *Best's Review*, March 1998, 111.

Goeringer, Conrad. "The Great and Late Church Arson Conspiracy Hoax." *American Atheist* 35, no. 4 (Autumn 1997): 8–16.

Greenya, John. "Fired Up about Church Burnings." *Washington Lawyer*, November 1996, 20–27.

Harris, Reverend Glenn. Interview by author. March 11, 2006. Spring Valley Baptist Church, Gainesville, Ala.

Hemphill, Paul. *The Ballad of Little River: A Tale of Race and Restless Youth in the Rural South*. Tuscaloosa: University of Alabama Press, 2001.

Henderson, Cinque. "Twice Burned." *New Republic*, August 5, 1996, 9.

Henry, Ed. "A Man with a Mission." *Kiplinger's Personal Finance Magazine* 50 (October 1996): 128.

Herring, Cedric, Verna Keith, and Hayward Derrick Horton, eds. *Skin-Deep: How Race and Complexion Matter in the Color-Blind Era*. Urbana: University of Illinois Press, 2003.

Heyboer, Kelly. "The 'Epidemic' of Black Church Fires." *American Journalism Review*, September 1996, 10–11.

Hicks, Reverend Dr. Charles. Interview by author. August 13, 2005. Greater Mount Zion Tabernacle Church of God in Christ, Portsmouth, Va.

Hjelm, Norman A., ed. *Out of the Ashes: Burned Churches and the Community of Faith*. Nashville: Thomas Nelson, 1997.

Holley, Joe. "Who Was Burning the Black Churches?" *Columbia Journalism Review*, September/October 1996, 26–33.

House, Christie. "Rebuilding Burned Churches." *New World Outlook*, January-February 1998, gbgm-umc.org/now/98jf/burned1.html.

Howard, Reverend Earl. Interview by author. July 19, 2005. Amazing Grace Baptist Church, Crandall, Ga.

Howard, Johnette. "Up from the Ashes." *Sports Illustrated*, September 2, 1996, 140–46.

"Indiana Man Charged with Burning Churches." *Christian Century* 116, no. 8 (March 10, 1999): 273.

"Indiana Man Indicted in Church Fires." *Christian Century* 116, no. 15 (May 12, 1999): 52–30.

Isaac, J. L. Interview by author. March 10, 2006. Greene County Courthouse, Livingston, Ala.

Johnson, Sandra E. *Standing on Holy Ground: A Triumph over Hate Crime in the Deep South*. New York: St. Martin's Press, 2002.

Keller, Suzanne. *Community: Pursuing the Dream, Living the Reality*. Princeton: Princeton University Press, 2003.

Kunstler, James Howard. *The Geography of Nowhere: The Rise and Decline of America's Man-Made Landscape*. Reprint, New York: Free Press, 1994.

Lamy, Phillip. *Millennium Rage: Survivalists, White Supremacists, and the Doomsday Prophecy*. New York: Plenum Press, 1996.

Landsberg, Alison. *Prosthetic Memory: The Transformation of American Remembrance in the Age of Mass Culture*. New York: Columbia University Press, 2004.

Maharidge, Dale. *Homeland*. New York: Seven Stories Press, 2004.

Meacham, Jon, and Vern E. Smith with Martha Brandt, Mark Miller, Howard Fineman, and Daniel Klaidman. "Southern Discomfort." *Newsweek*, June 24, 1996, 32.

Mello, Michael. *The United States versus Theodore John Kaczynski: Ethics, Power, and the Invention of the Unabomber*. New York: Context Books, 1999.

Miller, John J., and Ramesh Ponnuru. "The Hateful American: A New Church-Burning Hoax." *National Review* Online, September 20, 2001, www.nationalreview.com/daily/nrprint092001.html.

Miller, Mark, and Marc Peyser. "'We Live in Daily Fear.'" *Newsweek*, September 2, 1996, 52.

Mills, Nicolaus. *The Triumph of Meanness: America's War against Its Better Self*. New York: Houghton Mifflin, 1997.

Mollins, Carl. "Flames of Racial Tension." *Maclean's*, June 24, 1996, 27.

Muwakkil, Salim. "Burning Hate." *In These Times*, July 8, 1996, 14–16.

Myers, David G. *The American Paradox: Spiritual Hunger in an Age of Plenty*. New Haven: Yale University Press, 2000.

National Church Arson Task Force. Interim Report for the President, January 1997.

———. Second Year Report for the President, October 1998.

Newton, Michael, and Judy Newton. *The Ku Klux Klan: An Encyclopedia*. New York: Garland Science, 1990.

O'Foran, Shelly. *Little Zion: A Church Baptized by Fire*. Chapel Hill: University of North Carolina Press, 2006.

Olsen, Ted. "Rising from the Ashes: Congregations Rebuild after Satanist Arsons." *Christianity Today*, November 17, 1997, 90.

"Publicity Is Not a Cure-All." *U.S. News & World Report*, July 1, 1996, 8–9.

Putnam, Robert D. *Bowling Alone: The Collapse and Revival of American Community*. New York: Simon and Schuster, 2000.

"Rebuilding Burned Churches." *Christian Century* 114 (April 9, 1997): 357–58.

Riesman, David. *The Lonely Crowd*. New Haven: Yale University Press, 1950.

Selznick, Philip. *The Communitarian Persuasion*. Baltimore: John Hopkins University Press, 2002.

Shoemaker, Earl. Interview by author. July 19, 2005. Amazing Grace Baptist Church, Crandall, Ga.

Sistare, Christine T., ed. *Civility and its Discontents: Essays on Civic Virtue, Toleration, and Cultural Fragmentation*. Lawrence: University Press of Kansas, 2004.

Smith, Vern E., and Marc Peyser with Daniel Klaidman. "Terror in the Night down South." *Newsweek*, June 3, 1996, 34.

Terkel, Studs. *American Dreams: Lost and Found*. New York: New Press, 1980.

Thorpe, Jan, and Thomas Whittle. "A Fire on the Cross." *Freedom* 29, no. 1 (1996): 4–9.

"Two Black Churches Set on Fire, Brings Total to 32." *Jet*, June 24, 1996, 54.

U.S. Congress. House. Committee on the Judiciary. *Church Fires in the Southeast: Hearing before the Committee of the Judiciary*. 104th Cong., 2nd sess., May 21 1996.

———. Senate. Committee on the Judiciary. *Church Burnings: Hearing before the Committee of the Judiciary*. 104th Cong., 2nd sess., 27 June 1996.

———. Senate. Prepared Testimony of Andrew Cuomo before the Committee on Banking, Housing, and Urban Affairs. Subcommittee on Financial Institutions and Regulatory Relief. *Oversight Hearing on the Federal Loan Guaranty Program*. 105th Cong., 2nd sess., 17 July 1997.

"Was the Church Arson Story Legit?" *Religion in the News* 2, no. 2 (Summer 1999), Leonard E. Greenberg Center for the Study of Religion in Public Life, Trinity College, www.trincoll.edu/depts/csrpl/RINVol2No2/arson.htm.

White, Jack. "First the Flame, Then the Blame: As Black Churches Go on Burning, Ministers and Members Get the Third Degree." *Time*, June 17, 1996, 35.

Woodson, Carter G. *The History of the Negro Church*. 3rd ed. Washington, D.C.: Associated, 1972.

Index

Christopher B. Strain, professor of history and American studies at the Wilkes Honors College of Florida Atlantic University, is the author of *Pure Fire: Self-Defense as Activism in the Civil Rights Era.*

Southern Dissent

EDITED BY STANLEY HARROLD AND RANDALL M. MILLER

The Other South: Southern Dissenters in the Nineteenth Century, by Carl N. Degler, with a new preface (2000)

Crowds and Soldiers in Revolutionary North Carolina: The Culture of Violence in Riot and War, by Wayne E. Lee (2001)

"Lord, We're Just Trying to Save Your Water": Environmental Activism and Dissent in the Appalachian South, by Suzanne Marshall (2002)

The Changing South of Gene Patterson: Journalism and Civil Rights, 1960–1968, edited by Roy Peter Clark and Raymond Arsenault (2002; first paperback edition, 2020)

Gendered Freedoms: Race, Rights, and the Politics of Household in the Delta, 1861–1875, by Nancy D. Bercaw (2003)

Civil War on Race Street: The Civil Rights Movement in Cambridge, Maryland, by Peter B. Levy (2003)

South of the South: Jewish Activists and the Civil Rights Movement in Miami, 1945–1960, by Raymond A. Mohl, with contributions by Matilda "Bobbi" Graff and Shirley M. Zoloth (2004)

Throwing Off the Cloak of Privilege: White Southern Women Activists in the Civil Rights Era, edited by Gail S. Murray (2004)

The Atlanta Riot: Race, Class, and Violence in a New South City, by Gregory Mixon (2004)

Slavery and the Peculiar Solution: A History of the American Colonization Society, by Eric Burin (2005; first paperback edition, 2008)

"I Tremble for My Country": Thomas Jefferson and the Virginia Gentry, by Ronald L. Hatzenbuehler (2006; first paperback edition, 2009)

From Saint-Domingue to New Orleans: Migration and Influences, by Nathalie Dessens (2007)

Higher Education and the Civil Rights Movement: White Supremacy, Black Southerners, and College Campuses, edited by Peter Wallenstein (2008)

Burning Faith: Church Arson in the American South, by Christopher B. Strain (2008; first paperback edition, 2020)

Black Power in Dixie: A Political History of African Americans in Atlanta, by Alton Hornsby Jr. (2009; first paperback edition, 2016)

Looking South: Race, Gender, and the Transformation of Labor from Reconstruction to Globalization, by Mary E. Frederickson (2011; first paperback edition, 2012)

Southern Character: Essays in Honor of Bertram Wyatt-Brown, edited by Lisa Tendrich Frank and Daniel Kilbride (2011)

The Challenge of Blackness: The Institute of the Black World and Political Activism in the 1970s, by Derrick E. White (2011; first paperback edition, 2012)

Quakers Living in the Lion's Mouth: The Society of Friends in Northern Virginia, 1730–1865, by A. Glenn Crothers (2012; first paperback edition, 2013)

Unequal Freedoms: Ethnicity, Race, and White Supremacy in Civil War–Era Charleston, by Jeff Strickland (2015)

Show Thyself a Man: Georgia State Troops, Colored, 1865–1905, by Gregory Mixon (2016)

The Denmark Vesey Affair: A Documentary History, edited by Douglas R. Egerton and Robert L. Paquette (2017)

New Directions in the Study of African American Recolonization, edited by Beverly C. Tomek and Matthew J. Hetrick (2017)

Everybody's Problem: The War on Poverty in Eastern North Carolina, by Karen M. Hawkins (2017)

The Seedtime, the Work, and the Harvest: New Perspectives on the Black Freedom Struggle in America, edited by Jeffrey L. Littlejohn, Reginald K. Ellis, and Peter B. Levy (2018; first paperback edition, 2019)

Fugitive Slaves and Spaces of Freedom in North America, edited by Damian Alan Pargas (2018; first paperback edition, 2020)

Latino Orlando: Suburban Transformation and Racial Conflict, by Simone Delerme (2020)